Austin Kimberley, Tasman 1970-73 Autobook

By Kenneth Ball

Graduate, Institution of Mechanical Engineers
Associate Member, Guild of Motoring Writers
and the Autopress Team of Technical Writers.

Austin Kimberley 1970-73
Austin Tasman 1970-73

Autobooks

Autopress Ltd. Golden Lane Brighton BN1 2QJ England

The AUTOBOOK series of Workshop Manuals is the largest in the world and covers the majority of British and Continental motor cars, as well as all major Japanese and Australian models. For a full list see the back of this manual.

CONTENTS

ISBN 0 85147 414 4

First Edition 1973

706

Printed and bound in Brighton England for Autopress Ltd by G Beard & Son Ltd A

ACKNOWLEDGEMENT

My thanks are due to British Leyland Motor Corporation for their unstinted co-operation and also for supply data and illustrations.

I am also grateful to a considerable number of owners who have discussed their cars at length and many of whose suggestions have been included in this manual.

Kenneth Ball
Graduate, Institution of Mechanical Engineers
Associate Member, Guild of Motoring Writers
Ditchling Sussex England.

INTRODUCTION

This do-it-yourself Workshop Manual has been specially written for the owner who wishes to maintain his car in first class condition and to carry out his own servicing and repairs. Considerable savings on garage charges can be made, and one can drive in safety and confidence knowing the work has been done properly.

Comprehensive step-by-step instructions and illustrations are given on all dismantling, overhauling and assembling operations. Certain assemblies require the use of expensive special tools, the purchase of which would be unjustified. In these cases information is included but the reader is recommended to hand the unit to the agent for attention.

Throughout the Manual hints and tips are included which will be found invaluable, and there is an easy to follow fault diagnosis at the end of each chapter.

Whilst every care has been taken to ensure correctness of information it is obviously not possible to guarantee complete freedom from errors or to accept liability arising from such errors or omissions.

Instructions may refer to the righthand or lefthand sides of the vehicle or the components. These are the same as the righthand or lefthand of an observer standing behind the car and looking forward.

CHAPTER 1

THE ENGINE

1 :1 Description

The 2200 power unit incorporates a six-cylinder engine which is based on the four-cylinder version originally designed for the BLMC Maxi and Nomad. That the new engine incorporates most of the Maxi and Nomad features can be understood by a study of the following sections. **FIG 1 :1** shows how the transverse engine is mounted in the engine frame, the length of the engine making it necessary to eliminate the belt-driven fan and side-mounted radiator.

Total capacity is 2227 cc for both models, but the power output from the Tasman is down slightly to that of the Kimberley; being 102 and 115 bhp at 5500 rev/min respectively. Torque figures are approximately the same for both models, in their respective order, 116 and 118 lb ft (16 and 16.3 kgm) at 3500 rev/min. The compression ratio from both models is 8.6:1. Further details are given in the Technical Data at the end of the manual.

At the water-pump end, the seven-bearing crankshaft carries a sprocket for the camshaft timing chain and a skew gear that drives a shaft for the oil pump and distributor. The connecting rods are split horizontally and have renewable bearing liners. The solid-skirt pistons have two compression rings and one segmental oil control ring each. The gudgeon pin is a press fit in the small-end of the connecting rod.

The timing chain is automatically tensioned and drives an overhead camshaft that runs in an aluminium carrier secured to the detachable cylinder head. The cams operate bucket tappets that slide in bores in the carrier. These tappets enclose the top ends of the valve stems and springs and valve clearances are adjusted by shims.

The crankshaft pulley drives a single belt to operate the alternator and water pump. The oil pump circulates oil through a full-flow filter with a renewable element. The oil relief valve is non-adjustable. An exploded view of the components of the engine is shown in **FIG 1 :2**.

1 :2 Overhauling methods and information

Owners who are not trained mechanics will find much useful information in 'Hints on Maintenance and Overhaul' at the end of this manual. This will ensure that work is carried out efficiently and with maximum safety.

Reference to the righthand and lefthand of the car will be those seen from the rear when looking forward. No. 1 cylinder and No. 1 valve are at the water pump end of the engine. When the engine is removed, the water pump end will be called the front.

Special tools are needed for some operations and most of these will be included in the texts with the makers part numbers.

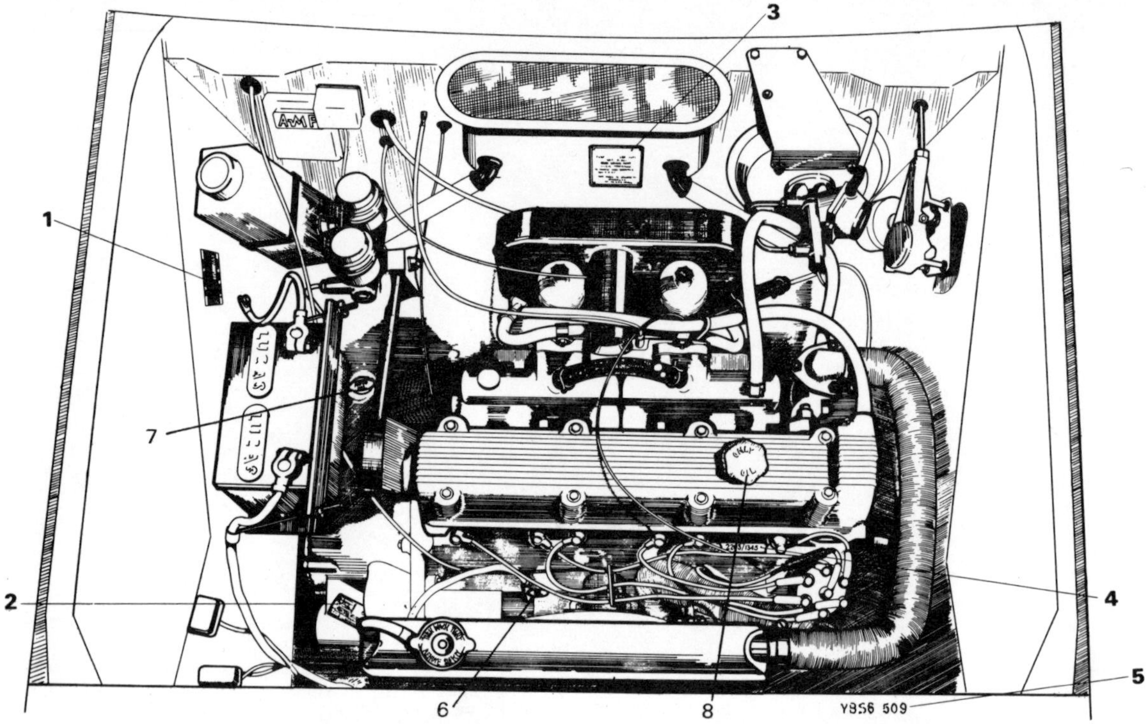

FIG 1:1 Engine and vehicle serial numbers and dipstick locations

Key to Fig 1:1 1 Paint identification (for spraying repaired panels) 2 Automatic transmission number (for service parts or unit exchange) 3 Compliance plate (vehicle serial number, date of manufacture, seating capacity and number of Australian design rules incorporated) 4 Engine number (for service parts of unit exchange) 5 Car serial number (must be quoted also for service parts) 6 Engine oil dipstick 7 Automatic transmission dipstick 8 Oil filter cap

Key to Fig 1:2 1 Cylinder block 2 Mainbearing cap (Nos. 1 and 2) 3 Mainbearing cap dowel 4 Main bearing cap bolt (short) 5 Mainbearing shells 6 Crankshaft thrust washers 7 Crankshaft 8 Connecting rod 9 Connecting rod cap 10 Connecting rod cap bolt 11 Big-end bearing shells 12 Gudgeon pin 13 Piston 14 Piston rings 15 Distributor shaft drive gear 16 Crankshaft sprocket 17 Oil thrower 18 Crankshaft pulley oil seal 19 Crankshaft pulley and damper 20 Crankshaft pulley bolt 21 Crankshaft pulley lock washer 22 Key for distributor drive gear and sprocket 23 Distributor and fuel pump drive shaft 24 Oil pump body 25 Oil pump shaft assembly 26 Oil pump rotor 27 Oil pump base 28 Oil pump drive shaft 29 Cylinder head 30 Cylinder head gasket 31 Cylinder head bolt 32 Camshaft carrier 33 Camshaft carrier dowel 34 Camshaft carrier bolt 35 Camshaft cover gasket 36 Camshaft cover 37 Camshaft cover screw 38 Camshaft cover screw O-ring 39 Oil filter cap 40 Camshaft 41 Camshaft locating plate 42 Camshaft locating plate screw 43 Lockwasher 44 Camshaft sprocket 45 Camshaft sprocket bolt 46 Camshaft sprocket dowel 47 Timing chain 48 Timing chain tensioner assembly 49 Timing chain guides 50 Guide adjuster 51 Inlet valve 52 Inlet valve spring seat and seal 53 Inlet valve spring 54 Exhaust valve 55 Exhaust valve spring 56 Valve cotters 57 Valve spring cups 58 Tappets 59 Tappet adjusting shims 60 Water pump 61 Water pump gasket 62 Engine plate 63 Engine plate gasket 64 Welch plugs 65 Thermostat 66 Thermostat housing 67 Thermostat housing gasket 68 Thermostat housing bolt 69 Water outlet elbow 70 Water outlet elbow gasket 71 Thermostat housing adaptor 72 Manifold gasket (Kimberley) 73 Water pump pulley 74 Manifold assembly (Kimberley—front) 75 Manifold assembly (Kimberley—rear) 76 Alternator drive belt 77 Manifold assembly (Tasman) 78 Manifold gasket (Tasman) 79 Manifold bolt 80 Manifold stud 81 Oil dipstick 82 Oil dipstick tube 83 Sparking plug 84 Timing chain guide bolt 85 Crankshaft dowel—small 86 Crankshaft dowel—large 87 Crankshaft oil seal (Automatic) 88 Crankshaft (Automatic) 89 Oil pump assembly (Automatic) 90 Oil pick up tube 91 O-ring—strainer to pick up tube 92 Oil pick up strainer 93 Oil pick up (Manual models) 94 Oil pump bolt (short) 95 Oil pump gasket 96 Oil pump strainer gauze 97 Oil pump bolt (long) 98 Oil pump bolt 99 Adaptor—oil pump drive shaft to oil pump 100 Timing chain guide adjuster nut 101 Water pump impeller 102 Water pump seal assembly 103 Water pump spindle and bearing assembly 104 Water pump body 105 Water pump pulley hub 106 Water pump bolt 107 Timing chain guide fixing bolt 108 Oil dipstick tube bolt 109 Water outlet elbow bolt 110 Manifold balance pipe clip 111 Manifold balance pipe 112 Manifold balance pipe spring 113 Manifold stud nut 114 Main bearing cap (Nos. 3 to 7) 115 Main bearing bolt (long) 116 Adaptor plate (Automatic) 117 By-pass hose clip 118 By-pass hose 119 Engine plate bolt 120 Water pump pulley bolt 121 Cylinder head locating dowel

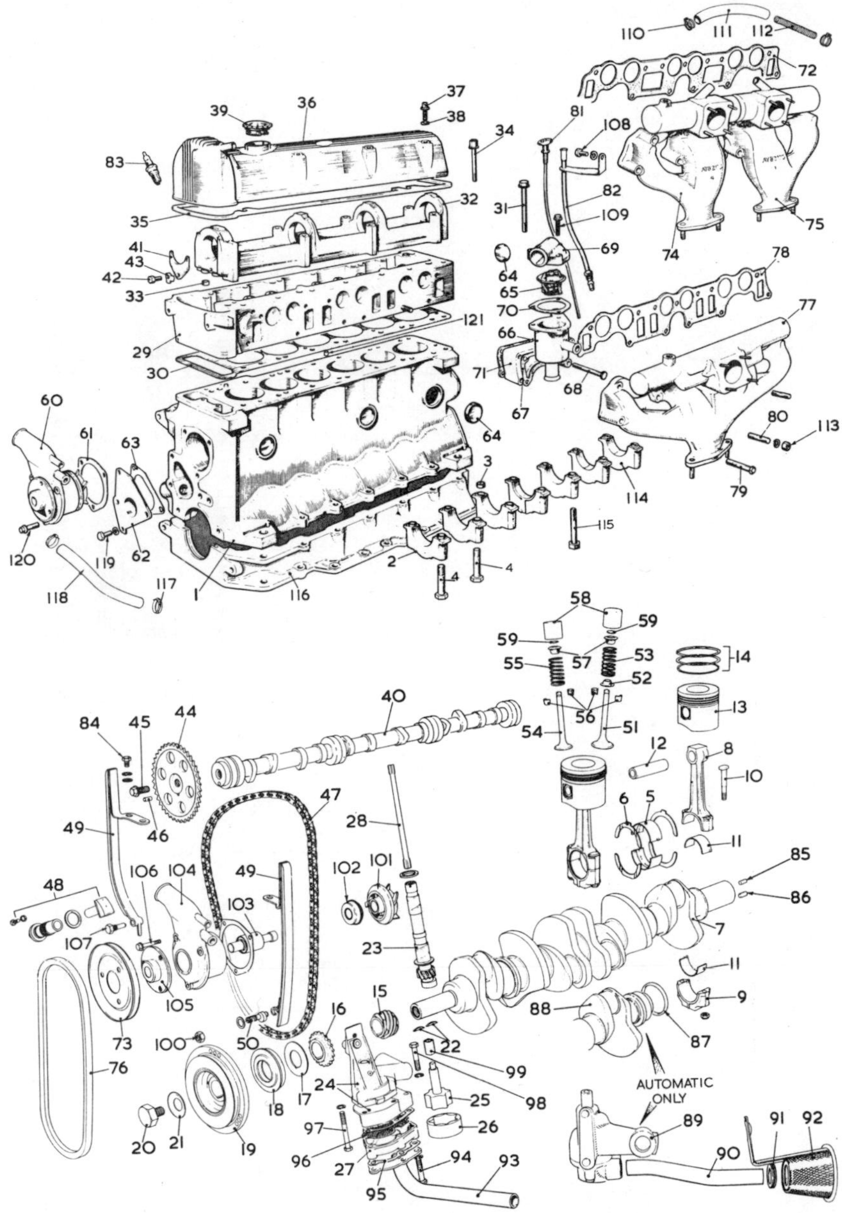

FIG 1:2 Exploded view of engine components

1:3 Routine maintenance

Checking oil level:

With the car standing on level ground and preferably when the engine has been stopped for a period to allow the oil to settle, check the level with the dipstick and top up if necessary. The location of the dipstick is shown in **FIG 1:1**, withdraw it and wipe it clean with unsoiled absorbent paper or a lint free cloth. Note that the word 'OIL' on the dipstick knob must be the correct way round when dipping from a position at the front of the car. Ensure that the stick is pushed fully home at all times as leakage from this point could effect the sealed breathing system and consequently the engine idling. Top up to the correct level but do not overfill, wait a few minutes after topping up and check the level again, allow time for the oil to settle.

Renewing the engine oil:

Every 3000 miles (5000 km) or every three months, whichever is the sooner, drain off the old oil and replenish with new. The drain plug is situated on the lefthand rear lower corner of the sump. A magnetized section is

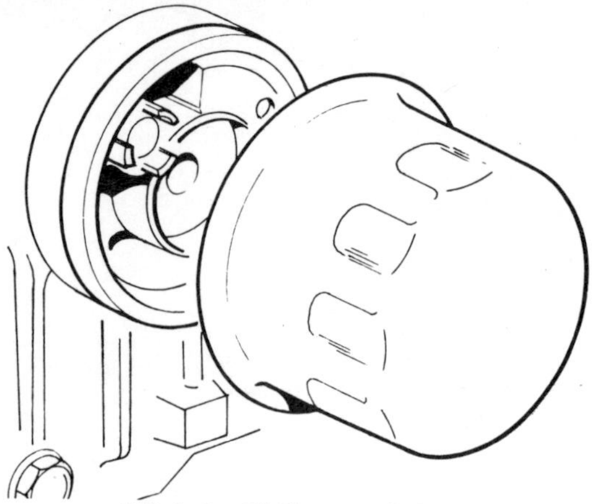

FIG 1:3 Oil filter—sealed type

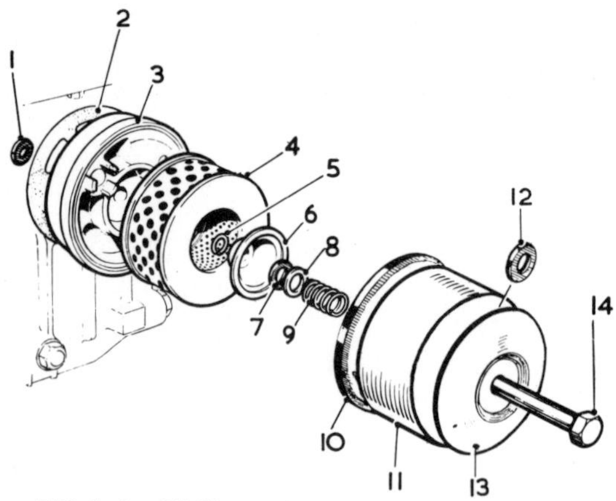

FIG 1:4 Oil filter—detachable element type

Key to Fig 1:4 1 O-ring—base to transmission 2 Gasket—base to transmission 3 Base 4 Element 5 Wire clip—bolt 6 Cone—element retaining 7 O-ring—bolt to cone 8 Washer 9 Spring 10 Seal—bowl to base 11 Bowl—filter 12 O-ring to backing plate 13 Backing plate 14 Bolt—retaining

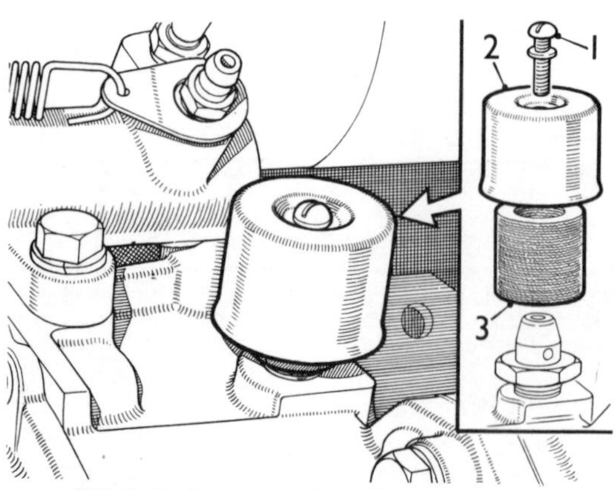

FIG 1:5 Location of air filter assembly

Key to Fig 1:5 1 Cover screw 2 Cover 3 Element

pressed into the end of the plug to collect small metal particles, remove these and wash the plug before refitting. Vehicles that operate in very dusty areas or suffer immoderate stop:start conditions should have the oil changed more frequently. Use only the well-known propriety brands of oil and consult your local dealer regarding the grade. Engine condition, atmospheric temperatures or other known local factors may make some of the more commonly used grades unsuitable.

Transmission oil:

With synchromesh transmission models the engine oil lubricates and cools both units because they are integral, but automatic transmission models are not and the transmission oil level is checked with a separate dipstick (see **FIG 1:1**). The system of dipping is quite different and the oil should not be renewed as a routine maintenance procedure. Refer to **Chapter 7** for instructions on checking.

Renewing oil filter:

The engine oil filter should be renewed every 6000 miles (10,000 km). One of two types may be fitted, either a sealed disposable unit or an unsealed type of which only the filter element and rubber seals are renewed.

Sealed type:

1 Refer to **FIG 1:3** to identify the filter which is screwed onto an aluminium base plate on the transmission case. A special tool is used for this operation but any universal strap-wrench will do.

2 Unscrew the unit from the block and replace with a new unit and two new sealing rings. First tighten the new unit by hand only, as far as possible, mark the filter case and then tighten with the strap wrench a further $1\frac{1}{2}$ turns only. Start the engine and check for oil leaks.

3 Stop the engine, allow the oil to settle and recheck the oil level.

Unsealed type:

1 Refer to **FIG 1:4** and unscrew the centre bolt 14. A certain amount of oil will be released when the seal is broken and the filter is detached. Leave the base plate in position in the transmission case, but examine it for lack of adhesion. If it is loose, remove it and examine the surfaces for fractures or distortions. If the base plate is removed the O-ring 1 and the gasket 2 must be renewed.

2 Rnew the filter element 4 and all gaskets and seals, 7, 10 and 12. Tighten the centre bolt to a torque of 20 lb ft (2.77 kgm). Start the engine and check for oil leaks.

3 Stop the engine, allow the oil to settle and recheck the oil level.

Engine breather filter:

Referring to **FIG 1:5**, which illustrates a synchromesh transmission model, air is drawn into the transmission case through an air filter mounted on the clutch housing. On the automatic transmission models air enters the crankcase only through an air filter mounted on the dipstick tube. The air filter elements must be changed every 12,000 miles (20,000 km) or possibly earlier if the vehicle is operating in dusty conditions.

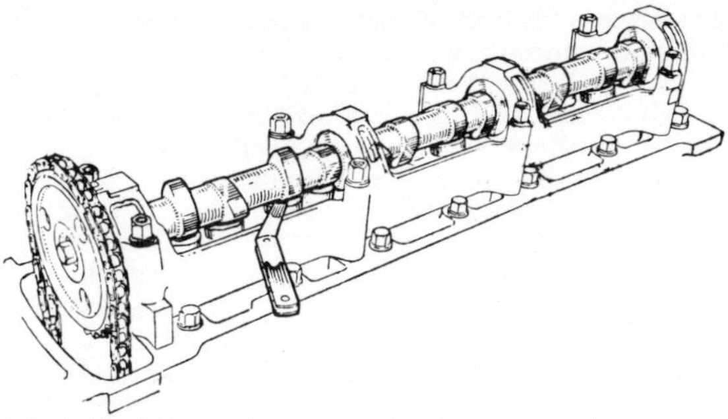

FIG 1:6 Using feeler gauge to check valve clearances. Note position of cam when gap is measured

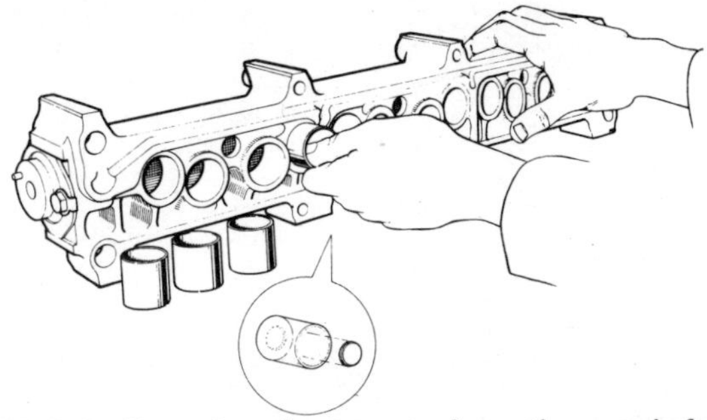

FIG 1:8 Removing the tappets from the camshaft carrier, inset shows location of shim

Testing:

To test the air breathing system first run the engine until it reaches normal operating temperature. Take off the oil filler cap and note the engine idling speed. If the engine speed decreases noticeably it denotes that the air filter is performing satisfactorily, but if the engine speed remains constant the filter element should be renewed.

Renewing:

1 Remove the screw and cover 1 and 2, lift off the filter 3 and discard it. Do not attempt to clean it.

2 Clean the cover and element container, fit the new element and replace the cover and screw.

1:4 Adjusting valve tappet clearances

1 Refer to **FIG 1:6**. Check the clearances every 12,000 miles (20,000 km or 12 months) Do the following: Disconnect the breather hose and distributor vacuum pipe. Remove eight screws and lift off the camshaft cover and gasket.

2 Scribe a location mark on the camshaft boss and sprocket, loosen the sprocket bolt approximately $\frac{3}{8}$ inch (9·5 mm) and pull the sprocket forward to just clear the dowel. Take care to prevent it from coming off the boss. Turn the camshaft with the hexagon spanner fitting provided. Check with feeler gauges as shown and in the following sequence. No. 1 is at the sprocket end. Record with pencil and paper the actual valve clearances enumerating them as per sequence.

3 Check tappet No. 1 with valve No. 12 fully open
" " " 7 " " " 6 " "
" " " 9 " " " 4 " "
" " " 2 " " " 11 " "
" " " 5 " " " 8 " "
" " " 10 " " " 3 " "
" " " 12 " " " 1 " "
" " " 6 " " " 7 " "
" " " 4 " " " 9 " "
" " " 11 " " " 2 " "
" " " 8 " " " 5 " "
" " " 3 " " " 10 " "

4 Adjustment is necessary only if the clearance (inlet and exhaust) is less than .012 inch (.31 mm). Correct clearances are .016 to .18 inch (.41 to .46 mm) for inlet valves and .020 to .022 inch (.51 to .56 mm) for exhaust when cold. If new parts have been fitted or valves reground, set the clearances to the correct figures just given.

Adjustment:

5 Retighten the camshaft sprocket to the scribed mark. Turn engine until cylinder No. 1 (nearest to water pump) is on the compression stroke. Align the flywheel or crankshaft pulley mark with TDC indicator (see **FIG 1:7**). Align the hole in sprocket boss and carrier mark.

6 Plug the sprocket aperture with lint free cloth. Remove the sprocket and chain and support them in tension with string or wire tied to the bonnet.

7 Slacken the camshaft carrier diagonally to release the valve spring tension, then take off the bolts. Carefully

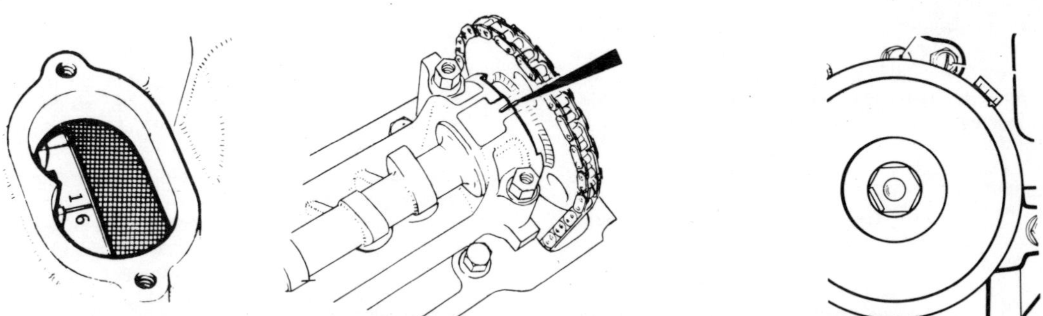

FIG 1:7 Aligning the timing marks on manual and automatic transmission models

raise the carrier only enough to allow the tappets to clear the valves, then push the tappets back into the carrier. Slowly clear the carrier from the head and invert it as soon as possible to prevent the tappets from sliding out and the shims from falling out of the tappets.

8 Remove tappets needing adjustment in turn. Check the thickness stamped on the shim inside tappet (see **FIG 1:8**). The correct shim thickness will be given by adding together the clearance, as checked, to the thickness of the shim removed and taking away the dimension for the correct clearance. Shims are available as follows:

9 97 .097 inch (2.47 mm) 13 .113 inch (2.87 mm)
99 .099 inch (2.52 mm) 15 .115 inch (2.93 mm)
01 .101 inch (2.56 mm) 17 .117 inch (2.98 mm)
03 .103 inch (2.62 mm) 19 .119 inch (3.03 mm)
05 .105 inch (2.67 mm) 21 .121 inch (3.08 mm)
07 .107 inch (2.72 mm) 23 .123 inch (3.13 mm)
09 .109 inch (2.77 mm) 25 .125 inch (3.18 mm)
11 .111 inch (2.83 mm) 27 .127 inch (3.23 mm)

10 Smear shim with petroleum jelly and insert it into the recess in the tappet. Refit tappets into their correct bores, lubricating them before insertion. Refit carrier to the locating dowels in the head and tighten the bolts in the alphabetical sequence shown in **FIG 1:9**. Take care to prevent the shims from falling out of the tappets during carrier location. Tighten the carrier bolts to a torque of 20 lb ft (2.77 kgm).

11 Fit camshaft sprocket and align marks, tighten the bolt to a torque of 35 lb ft (4.8 kgm). Do not apply gasket cement to the cover joint gasket. Tighten the screws to 6 lb ft (.80 kgm). Refit remaining parts in reverse order to dismantling.

1:5 Servicing cylinder head and camshaft

Removing head:

This operation can be completed with the engine in the car but it is advisable to either support the bonnet securely or remove it completely to allow for a comfortable working clearance. To remove the bonnet refer to **Chapter 12**.

1 Disconnect the battery leads and refer to **Chapter 4** to drain the cooling system.

2 Disconnect the top hose from the thermostat housing and the bottom hose from the water pump. Detach the heater hoses from the thermostat housing and the water pump.

3 Detach the thermal transmitter wire from its connection in the thermostat housing and pull the breather hose from the camshaft cover.

4 Disconnect the brake servo hose from the inlet manifold and pull the vacuum advance pipe from the carburetter.

5 Disconnect the engine steady bracket from the cylinder head and refer to **Chapter 2** to remove the air cleaner from the carburetter(s). Detach the fuel inlet pipe from the carburetter and plug the end to prevent the entry of dirt.

6 Disconnect the leads from the sparking plugs and take off the camshaft cover. Remove the throttle and choke cables from the carburetter(s) and uncouple the throttle return spring(s) (see **Chapter 2**).

7 Refer to **Chapter 12** to identify the jacking points under the car and raise the front end. From underneath the car release the exhaust pipe manifold clamp(s) and slacken the lower mounting bracket on the transmission case. Lower the front end.

8 Refer to **Section 1:4**, item 5 and reset the position of the crankshaft and camshaft to the valve timing marks. Ensure that No. 1 piston is at the firing position.

9 Refer to **FIG 1:10** to identify the timing chain tensioner which is situated under the alternator adjacent to the petrol pump. Remove the screwed plug and with an Allen key retract the chain tension and lock it by turning it in the direction indicated by the arrow.

10 Unscrew the camshaft sprocket securing bolt and disengage the sprocket from the chain. Allow the chain to disengage from the crankshaft sprocket and hang on the timing chain guides.

11 Refer to **FIG 1:9** and slacken the cylinder head bolts in the reverse numerical order, starting with number 14. Extract the cylinder head bolts and lift off the head and gasket.

12 Note that two location dowels position the cylinder head on the block face, they are situated next to the front bolts at each end of the cylinder head.

Dismantling and servicing head:

13 Refer to **Chapter 2** and remove the carburetter(s).

14 Withdraw the heat shield, distance piece(s) and gaskets.

15 To remove the manifolds on the Tasman, unscrew the two socket head cap screws and the four hexagon setscrews on top of the inlet manifold and two setscrews at the bottom of the manifold. Lift off the inlet manifold. Remove the exhaust manifold. Lift off the gaskets.

16 To remove the manifolds on the Kimberley, take off the rubber balance hose, unscrew the top seven bolts and washers then detach each manifold separately by unscrewing the remaining three bolts from each manifold. Lift off the gaskets.

17 Remove the thermostat housing, spacer by-pass and gaskets.

18 Refer to **FIG 1:9** and slacken the camshaft carrier bolts evenly in the reverse alphabetical order, starting with H. Extract the bolts and position the cylinder head on its side with the combustion chambers facing the operator. Tilt the head away to bring the camshaft carrier nearer the workbench and push the carrier off the head ensuring that the tappets and shims remain in position in the carrier.

19 Extract the tappets and shims from the carrier ensuring that they stay in the same numerical order of one to twelve (see **FIG 1:8**). Withdraw the camshaft from the rear of the carrier. If necessary remove the camshaft retaining plate at the front of the carrier and check it for wear.

20 Compress the valve spring with a suitable compressor and remove the valve collets (see **FIG 1:11**). Release the spring and take off the spring cup, spring and (inlet valve only) the spring seat and seal. Remove all the valves by this method and keep them and their associate parts in the same numerical order from which they were removed.

21 Wash all the parts in petrol or another solvent, clean the carbon from the head combustion chambers with a hardwood or plastic scraper. Remove the carbon from the valves using the same tool but if the carbon is stubbornly adhesive use a wire brush or buffing wheel. Clean also the piston crowns and block face with a 'soft' scraper, the engine may be turned freely as the timing chain is disengaged from the crankshaft sprocket.
When scraping the head or cylinder block, plug all the water ways with lint free cloth.
Scrap all gaskets and obtain new ones.

22 Inspect the camshaft, carrier bores and the tappets and cams for wear or pick-up. Check the journal diameters against the figures given in Technical Data.

23 Examine valves and scrap those that are cracked, badly pitted, burned, have worn stems or a thin seat edge.

24 Worn valve guides in the cylinder head or badly pitted valve seats should be rectified by the service garage. Worn guides will require reaming to a specific diameter and oversize valves fitted. Badly pitted seats may be restored and trued-up by seat grinders and cutters but if they are unrestorable new inserts must be fitted.

25 Check the valve springs against the figures given in Technical Data, a common practice now is to renew all valve springs on an overhaul of this nature as the engine will presumably have done a considerable mileage. Scrap the inlet valve seat and seal and obtain new ones. Examine the collets for wear.

26 To grind in the valves, use a fine or medium grade grinding paste and work the valve on its seating with a suction tool. A light coil spring under the head will assist in the process. Obtain a dull, matt, even finish on the valve seat and insert face. Make sure all trace of carborundum is cleaned off the faces and local areas after completion.

Reassembling:

27 Reassemble the head and refit in the reverse order of dismantling, lubricating all rubbing or sliding surfaces. Before the head is fitted to the block check the tappet clearances as described in **Section 1:4**. Fit the cylinder head gasket dry and tighten the bolts and carrier bolts in the order given in **FIG 1:9**. Tighten carrier bolts to 20 lb ft (2.77 kgm) and cylinder head bolts to 60 lb ft (8.3 kgm).

1:6 Valve timing

Manual transmission:

1 Disconnect the breather hose from the camshaft cover and the vacuum advance pipe from the carburetter. Remove the camshaft cover.

2 Refer to **FIG 1:7** and remove the flywheel housing timing cover. Mark on the distributor body the relative position of the No. 1 spark plug lead in the cap. Remove the the distribution cap.

3 Turn the engine to bring the rotor arm pointing to the mark on the distributor body, this is to ensure that No. 1 cylinder firing and not No. 6. Align the 1.6 (TDC) mark on the flywheel with the pointer on the flywheel housing. The alignment should be done by turning the

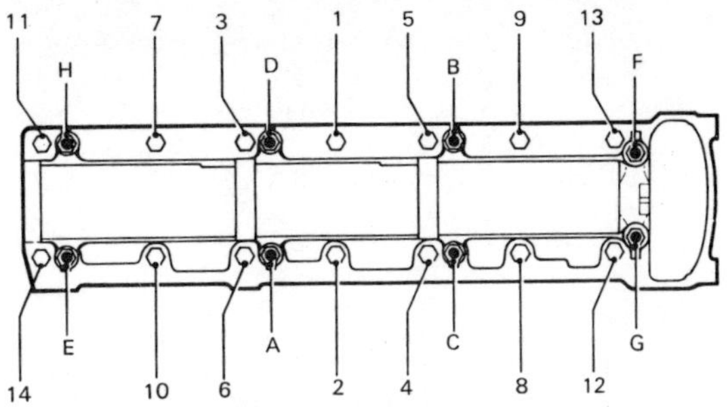

FIG 1:9 **Camshaft carrier (letters) and cylinder head (numbers) tightening sequences**

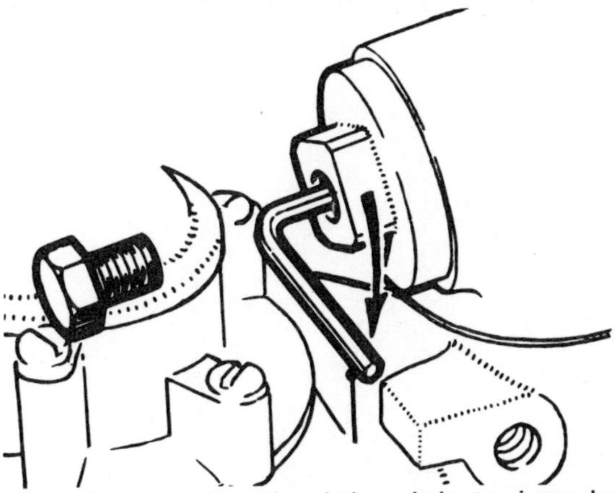

FIG 1:10 **Retracting the timing chain tensioner by turning the Allen key in direction of arrow**

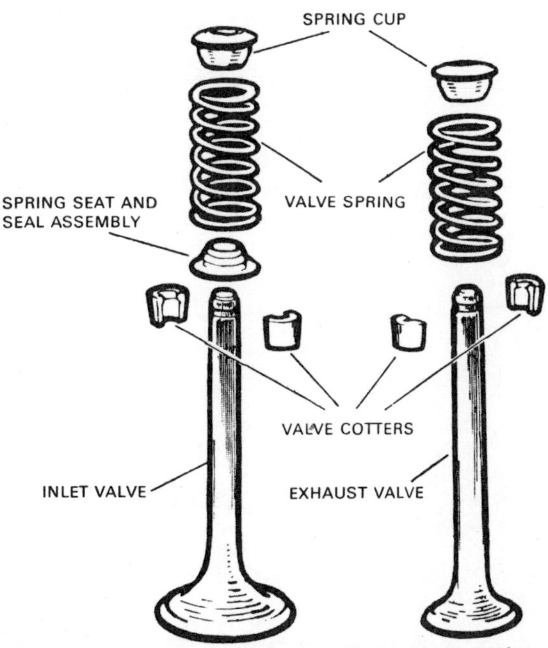

FIG 1:11 **Inlet and exhaust valve with associate components**

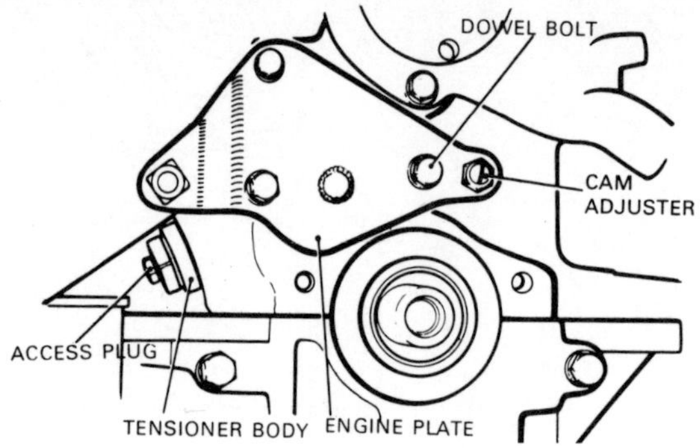

FIG 1:12 Timing chain adjusting components

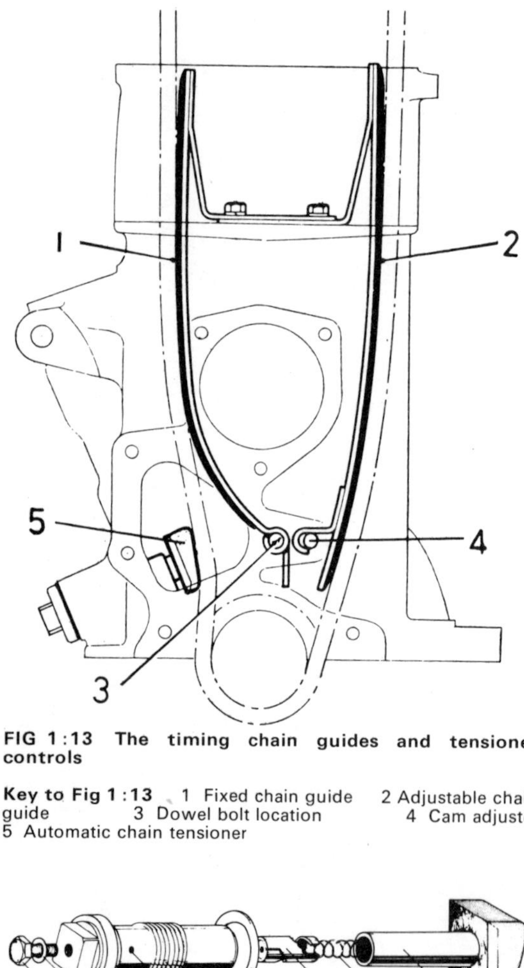

FIG 1:13 The timing chain guides and tensioner controls

Key to Fig 1:13 1 Fixed chain guide 2 Adjustable chain guide 3 Dowel bolt location 4 Cam adjuster 5 Automatic chain tensioner

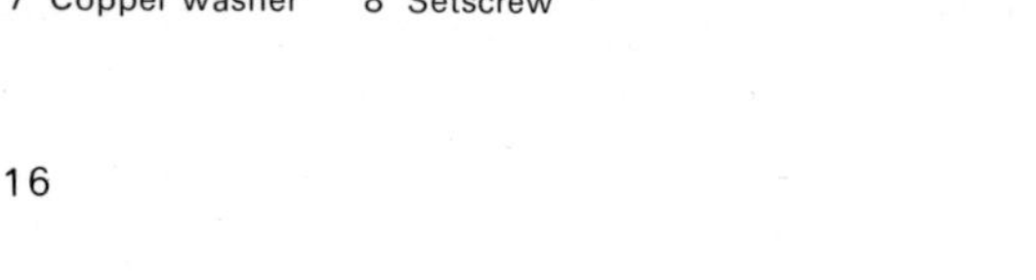

FIG 1:14 Components of automatic chain tensioner

Key to Fig 1:14 1 Slipper assembly 2 Spring 3 Plunger 4 Washer 5 Tensioner body 6 Oil hole 7 Copper washer 8 Setscrew

engine in the normal direction of rotation, this is clockwise looking from the timing chain end. Do not turn the engine backwards to align.

4 With the flywheel marks set, check that the hole in the camshaft sprocket boss is aligned with the groove on the top of the camshaft carrier.

5 If adjustment is necessary, refer to **FIG 1:10** and operation 9 of **Section 1:5**. Retract the tensioner and lock it.

6 Without disturbing the setting of the camshaft remove the camshaft sprocket and disengage it from the timing chain.

7 Check the camshaft and flywheel alignment again, refit the sprocket to align the hole and groove. Remove the sprocket without disturbing the alignment.

8 Position the camshaft sprocket in the timing chain with the non-drive side, the side that runs on the tensioner slipper lead, taut. The dowel hole in the sprocket should be in a position to line up perfectly with the dowel on the camshaft. During this operation the camshaft and flywheel alignment should not be disturbed.

9 Fit the sprocket to the camshaft with the chain engaged and taut on the non-drive side.

10 Any degree of slackness on the drive side of the chain should now be taken up by the chain guide cam adjuster (see **FIGS 1:12** and **1:13**).

11 Refit the remaining parts in the reverse order of removal. Unlink the automatic tensioner by inserting the Allen key and turning in a clockwise direction. Do not apply jointing compound to the camshaft cover gasket.

Automatic transmission:

The method of operation to adjust the timing is basically the same as that for the manual transmission models, except for the initial setting in operation 3. From 2 proceed as follows:

1 Remove the sparking plugs.

2 By the hexagon fitting on the camshaft and with a suitably sized spanner turn the camshaft and the crankshaft against the normal direction of rotation, until the notch on the crankshaft pulley just passes the TDC mark on the plate. Then turn the engine in the normal direction to align the TDC mark with the notch. This is to ensure all slackness has been taken up in the chain.

3 Follow the operations for the manual transmission models, substituting in all instances 'pulley' for 'flywheel'.

1:7 Servicing the timing gear

Timing chain tensioner:

The components of the tensioner are shown in **FIG 1:14**. When the engine is running, pressurized oil from the lubrication system enters the hole 6 in the side of the body 5 and passes through the Allen key recess in the base of the plunger 3, to lubricate the timing chain through a hole in the slipper pad. The pad is held against the chain to keep it taut under the influence of the spring and oil pressure. Progressive slack in the chain is therefore automatically taken up, however, to prevent the slipper and plunger assembly from retracting under certain stresses from the chain, as the plunger rises a limiting peg rotates the plunger through the spiral slot. The pin bearing edge of the slot has locking recesses which engage with the pin and prevent the plunger from turning in the opposite direction and retracting itself into the body.

Removing:

Manual transmission:

1 Refer to **Chapter 4** or **Chapter 11** to remove the alternator drive belt.

2 Unscrew completely the crankshaft pulley bolt and withdraw the pulley.

3 Refer to **Chapter 2** to remove the fuel pump and pushrod.

4 Refer to **Section 1:5**, operation 9, and retract the tension.

5 Refer to **FIG 1:15** and remove the engine plate. Note the position of the dowel bolt.

6 Turn the chain guide cam adjuster to provide a maximum slackness in the chain.

7 Lever the chain away from the slipper assembly, turn the slipper approximately 180 deg., push the chain inwards and withdraw the slipper through the engine plate orifice. Unscrew and remove the tensioner body.

8 In some cases the crankshaft sprocket may have to be removed to allow sufficient slack in the chain to complete operation 7.

Automatic transmission

1 Disconnect the battery earth (—) lead.

2 Release the exhaust pipe(s) from the manifold and detach the steady bracket from the engine.

3 With a jack, interspaced by a block of wood, support the weight of the power unit on the lefthand side.

4 Kimberley only. Refer to **Chapter 12** and remove the radiator grille. Refer to **Chapter 11** and remove the lefthand inner head lamp.

5 Refer to **Chapters 3** and **11** to remove the distributor and alternator respectively.

6 Remove the front and rear lefthand engine mountings. Lift the engine until the crankshaft pulley just clears the longitudinal body member.

7 Move the petrol pipe downwards to enable the crankshaft pulley to be removed.

8 Continue from operation 1 for the manual transmission models.

Inspection:

9 Clean the tensioner components in petrol and blow out the oil holes with compressed air. Measure the internal diameter of the body bore near the mouth. If ovality exceeds .003 inch (.076 mm) renew the whole unit assembly. Check the slipper head for wear and renew if at least suspect. Refit the plunger and lock it in position with the Allen key.

Reassembling:

10 Reassemble and fit in the reverse order of dismantling. To unlock the tensioner after assembly, insert the Allen key and turn it clockwise until the slipper head takes up the tension. Do not attempt to force the key anticlockwise nor force the slipper head on to the chain by external pressure. Oil pressure, when the engine is running, assists in loading the tensioner.

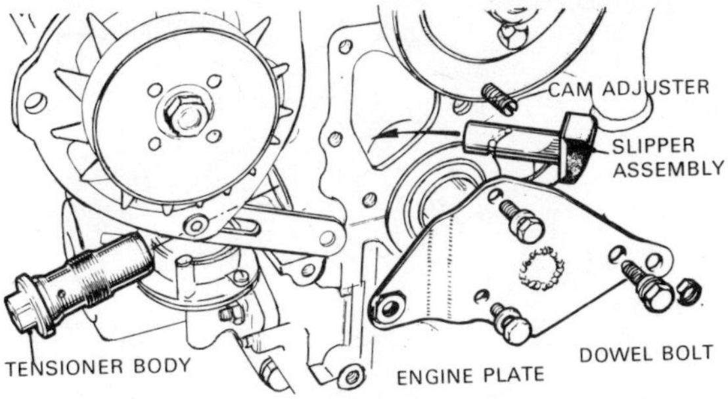

FIG 1:15 Slipper assembly removal method

Timing chain and sprockets:

The old timing chain must be parted in situ with a special link remover, Renold Part No. 311006, and the new chain must be riveted together in situ using a special anvil and three punches under the collective Part No. 18GA017. If these tools are not available to the operator the work must be entrusted to an authorized service garage.

Removing:

Manual transmission:

1 Complete operations 1 and 2 in **Section 1:7**.

2 Remove the camshaft cover as described in **Section 1:4**, operation 1 and align the timing marks as described in **Section 1:6**.

3 Refer to **Section 1:5**, operation 9 and retract the automatic chain tensioner.

4 Without distrurbing the timing mark alignments remove the camshaft sprocket.

5 Refer to **FIGS 1:12** and **1:13** and turn the chain guide cam adjuster to provide a maximum slackness in the chain.

6 Place a piece of clean, lint-free cloth in the camshaft sprocket aperture but leave a section of the chain exposed.

7 With the special tool as shown in **FIG 1:16** force out both pins in a selected link but secure the ends to prevent them falling through the aperture.

8 If the chain is badly worn the camshaft and crankshaft sprockets should be renewed also. It is at this stage, before removing the chain completely, that the crankshaft sprocket should be removed (see end of section).

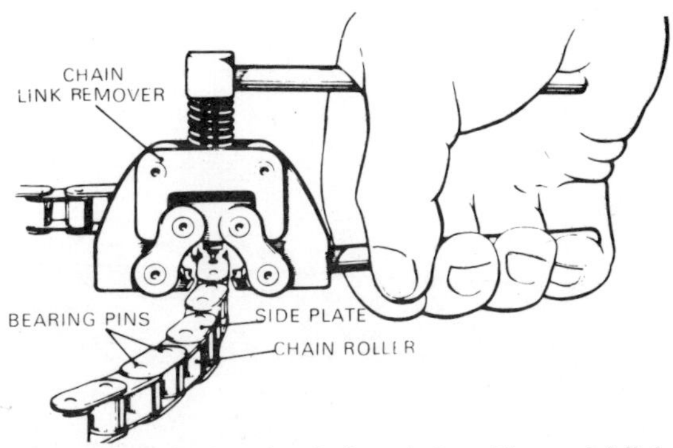

FIG 1:16 Splitting the timing chain with special link removing tool

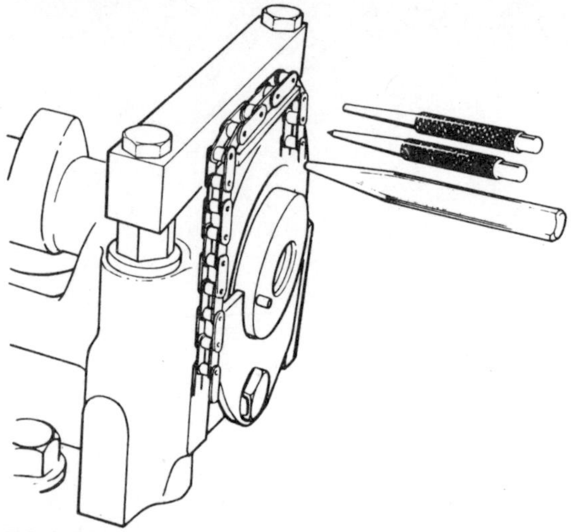

FIG 1:17 Method of rivetting link to timing chain with special anvil and punches

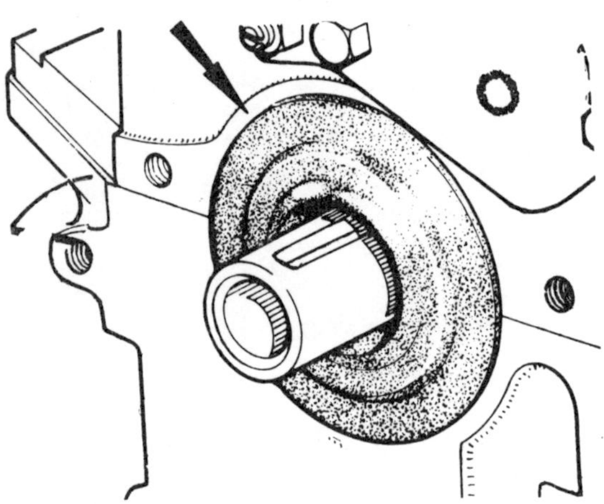

FIG 1:18 Lever between the seal flange and block (arrowed) to extract the front seal

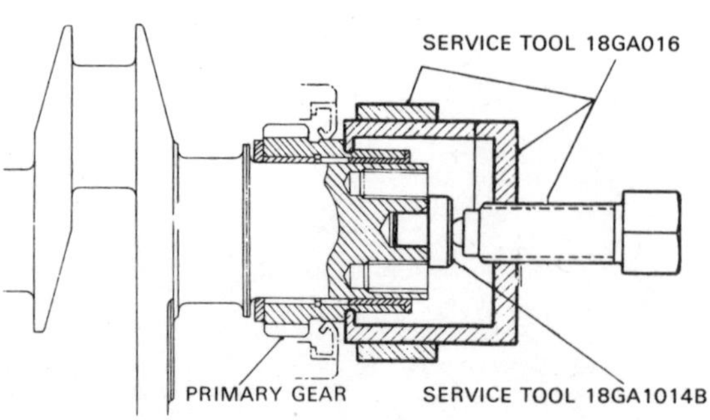

FIG 1:19 Withdrawing the primary gear and oil seal with the special service tools

9 Remove the cloth from the aperture, attach one end of the new chain to the old chain with wire and use the old chain to pull the new chain through its circuit, around the guides, tensioner and crankshaft sprocket.

10 Replace the cloth in the aperture and fit the special tool anvil to the camshaft carrier bolts as shown in **FIG 1:17**. Connect the new link to the chain and use the centre punch to spread the ends of the pins, peen the ends of the pins with the concave punch. Ensure, after rivetting, that the link has sufficient side clearance. If it is too tight tap the side plates to free it.

11 Replace the remaining parts in the reverse order of dismantling and check and adjust the valve timing.

Automatic transmission:

Refer to **Section 1:7** and complete operations 1 to 8 listed under the same heading, then continue as for manual transmission as described in this section.

Due to the limited clearance at the crankshaft sprocket it will be difficult to disengage the chain from the sprocket. Secure the new chain to the old chain with wire as described for the manual models but turn the crankshaft to thread the new chain through the circuit.

Removing crankshaft sprocket:

If the sprocket is to be removed it can be extracted from the crankshaft after the seal has been taken off. A suitable puller or the use of a lever through the engine plate aperture will be necessary to withdraw the sprocket from the keyed shaft.

Refit the sprocket with the dimples facing outwards. With the timing set for No. 1 cylinder firing, the dimple should be aligned with the bottom face of the cylinder block on the righthand side when viewed directly facing the sprocket.

1:8 Crankshaft oil seals

Removing, refitting pulley seal:

Manual transmission:

1 Remove the crankshaft pulley as described in operations 1 and 2 of **Section 1:7**.

2 Refer to **FIG 1:18** and remove the seal by levering between the seal flange and cylinder block as indicated by the arrow.

3 To fit the new seal, first lightly coat the diameter and inner flange face of the seal with jointing compound and press it squarely into position.

4 Lubricate the seal and pulley running surfaces with engine oil before refitting the pulley.

5 Tighten the pulley bolt to a torque of 60 to 70 lb ft (8.4 to 9.8 kgm).

Automatic transmission:

1 Complete operations 1 to 7 in **Section 1:7** listed under the same heading, then continue as for the manual models as described in this section.

Removing, refitting primary gear oil seal:

Manual transmission:

1 Refer to **Chapter 5** and remove the clutch assembly.

2 Using special service tools 18GA1014B and 18GA016 as shown in **FIG 1:19** pull off the old oil seal and primary gear.

3 Clean thoroughly the flywheel housing seal aperture. To protect the new seal from damage as it is being fitted over the splines fit the nylon protection sleeve, service tool 18G1152/9, over the gear splines.
4 Lubricate the new seal and sleeve and slide the seal over the sleeve and on to the primary gear. Position the primary gear on the crankshaft with the oil seal against the edge of the flywheel housing aperture, but make sure whilst doing so the seal is not accidentally dislodged on to the primary gear splines.
5 Using the screw base section of the service tool 18GA016A and two flywheel bolts, fit it to the end of the crankshaft as shown in **FIG 1:20**. Fit the outer sleeve of the same service tool on to the screw base and push the seal into its housing aperture. The flange of the outer sleeve should contact the edge of the aperture. Do not overtighten the nut.
6 Take care when removing the tool to ensure that the primary gear does not move far enough, to allow the oil seal to move off the machined surface of the primary gear.
7 Refit the flywheel and clutch assembly.

Primary gear end float:

During the operation of renewing the seal check also the primary gear end float. This must be done by using Plastigage (12 type PR-1 red) or a measuring gauge such as a depth micrometer or vernier.

1 Separate the flywheel from the clutch assembly (see **Chapter 5**) and clean the mounting faces of the flywheel and crankshaft with solvent. Take note also of the serviceability of the flywheel location dowels (see end of this sub-section).
2 Remove any burrs or marks from the mounting surfaces with a fine abrasive stone to ensure the measurements will be accurate.
3 Plastigage method:
Refer to **FIG 1:21** and place a strip of Plastigage on the end of the primary gear as indicated. Carefully fit the flywheel and tighten the bolts to a torque of 60 lb ft (8.4 kgm). Remove the flywheel and measure the now compressed width of Plastigage. The measured width is the existing end float. The correct end float should be between .003 and .007 inch (.076 and .178 mm). If the measured Plastigage is either below or above this tolerance fit a selective size of thrust washer at 'A' to obtain an end float within the tolerance. These washers are available in several thicknesses.
4 Depth gauge method:
With a depth micrometer or vernier measure the distance from the end face of the crankshaft to the primary gear bush flange (B), ensure that the primary gear is correctly positioned against the thrust washer. Make a note of the measurement. Now measure the depth of the flywheel counterbore (C). Subract (C) from (B) to find the existing end float. Correct the end float, if necessary, as described for the Plastigage method.

Crankshaft dowels:

The flywheel location dowels consist of one large master dowel and three smaller dowels. The dimensions and fitted height are shown in **FIG 1:22**. Standard dowels are available if it is necessary to change them, but any worn dowel holes must be reamed to an accurate size if oversize dowels are to be fitted. This will entail the removal of the crankshaft and the holes must be jig reamed. This type of work should be given to the authorized service garage.

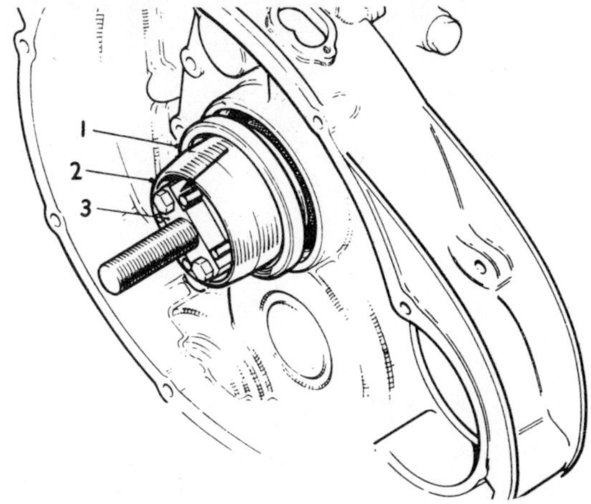

FIG 1:20 Fitting a new primary gear oil seal

Key to Fig 1:20 1 Oil seal 2 Seal protector sleeve 18G 1152/9 3 Screw base tool 18GA 016A

Removing, refitting adaptor plate and oil seal:

Automatic transmission:

1 Refer to **Section 1:10** and remove the power unit from the car. Separate the automatic transmission from the engine as described in **Chapter 7**
2 Unscrew and take out the six setscrews that secure the drive plate to the crankshaft flange. Withdraw the drive plate and two packing rings.
3 Unscrew and take out the five setscrews that secure the adaptor plate and remove the oil seal.
4 Refit in the reverse order of dismantling noting the following points:
Renew the adaptor plate gasket and use jointing compound.
When fitting the new seal ensure that the spring section is facing inwards. Lubricate the seal lips.
Refit one packing ring, then fit the drive plate with its concave face inwards. Fit the second spacer ring and lockplate.
Tighten the six drive plate setscrews to a torque of 8 to 13 lb ft (1 to 1.8 kgm) and lock them into position.

1:9 Servicing oil pump

Manual gearchange:

1 Disconnect the battery and remove the alternator drive belt. Drain engine oil, wipe magnet and refit drain plug. Turn crankshaft to TDC with No. 1 cylinder firing (see **Section 1:6**). Remove distributor (see **Chapter 3**).
2 Refer to **FIG 1:23** and push split tube or tool 18G.1147 over pump shaft and withdraw it. Raise and support front of car. Remove crankshaft pulley (see **Section 1:7**). Remove gearbox cover (8 setscrews and one countersunk screw with lockwasher).

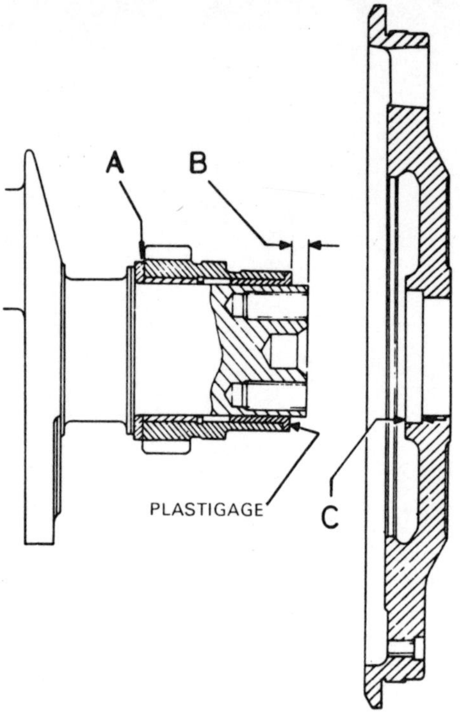

FIG 1:21 **Checking the primary gear end float**

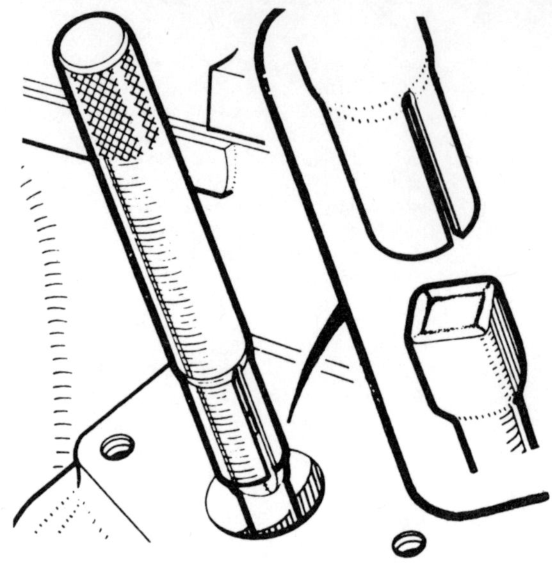

FIG 1:23 **Removing quill shaft with tool 18G 1147**

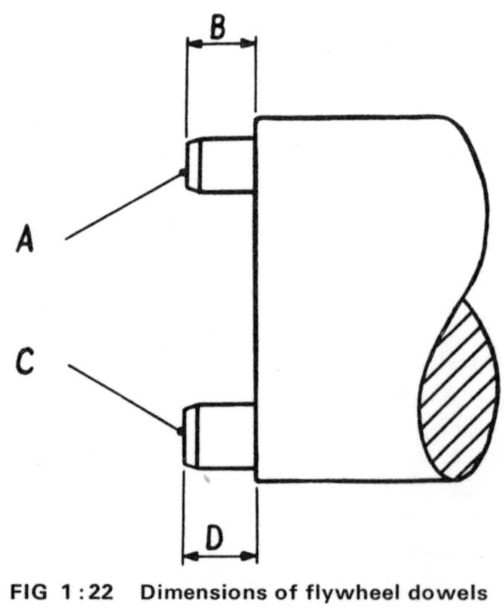

FIG 1:22 **Dimensions of flywheel dowels**

Key to Fig 1:22 A $\frac{5}{16}$ in dia. (7.941 mm) dowels B .43 to .36 in (10·92 to 9.14 mm) C $\frac{3}{8}$ in dia. (9.525 mm) dowel D .43 to .39 in (10·92 to 9.9 mm)

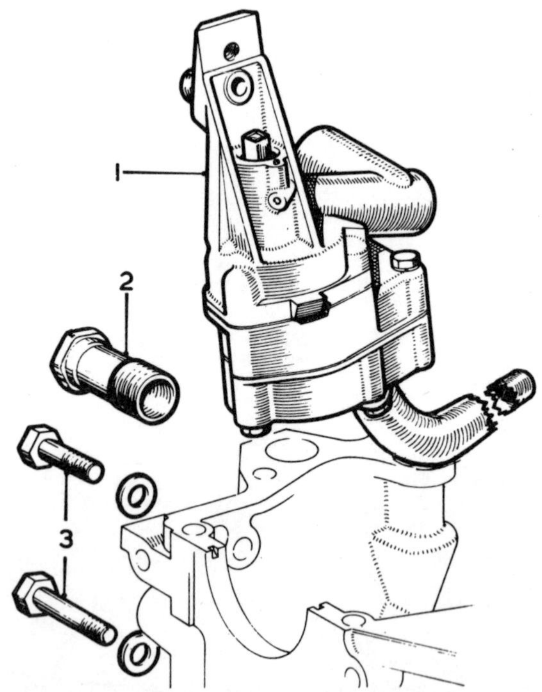

FIG 1:24 **Oil pump connection and securing bolts**

Key to Fig 1:24 1 Pump body 2 Outlet connection 3 Securing bolts

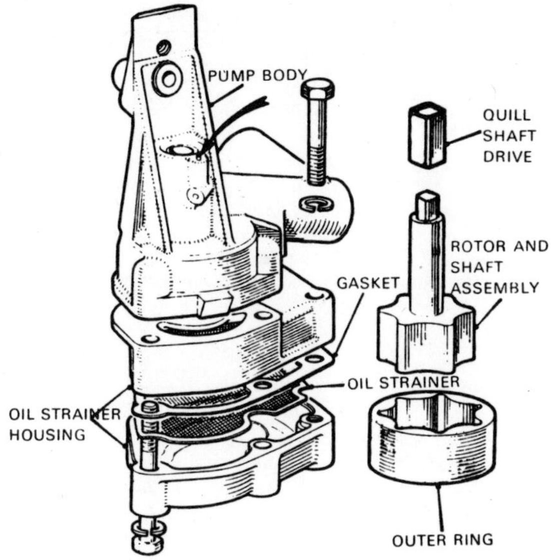

FIG 1:25 Oil pump components (manual transmission)

3 Remove filter and head, catching draining oil (see **Section 1:3**). Refer to **FIG 1:24** and unscrew pump outlet 2. Remove pump pick-up pipe by extracting the two securing screws. Remove pump bolts with sealing washers 3. Refer to **Chapter 2** and remove the fuel pump and pushrod.

4 Manoeuvre the pump down, tilt it back and withdraw it with the fuel pump oil deflection plate. Dismantle pump as shown in **FIG 1:25**. Although renewed only as an assembly it may be inspected for wear.

After cleaning check end float of outer ring and rotor using a straightedge and feelers as shown in **FIG 1:26**. Outer ring end float .004 to .005 inch (.10 to .12 mm).

Inner rotor end float .0045 to .0055 (.11 to .14 mm).
Outer ring clearance in body (C) .011 inch (.28 mm).
Rotor lobe clearance (B) .0035 inch (.089 mm).
Renew pump if worn beyond limits.

Reassemble pump after oiling internal parts.

When refitting pump, locate it in position and loosely fit bottom bolt (2.25 inch or 57 mm long) and pump outlet connection. Fit dowel and top bolt leaving fixings .25 inch (6 mm) slack. Fit suction pipe with long central bolt. Tighten pump bolts to 20 lb ft (2.8 kgm). Tighten pump outlet to 25 lb ft (3.4 kgm). Reverse rest of dismantling procedure and refill with oil. Tighten front cover setscrews to 10 lb ft (1.4 kgm) and pulley bolt to 60 to 70 lb ft (8.3 to 9.7 kgm).

Automatic gearchange:

Complete operations 1 to 7 in **Section 1:7** relating to automatic, but also drain the engine oil and remove the oil filter (see **Section 1:3**). After removing the distributor, extract the quill shaft as described in operation 2 for the manual transmission.

1 Take off the crankshaft pulley and the lefthand side engine mounting plate.

2 Remove the fuel pump, pushrod and adaptor (see **Chapter 2** if necessary).

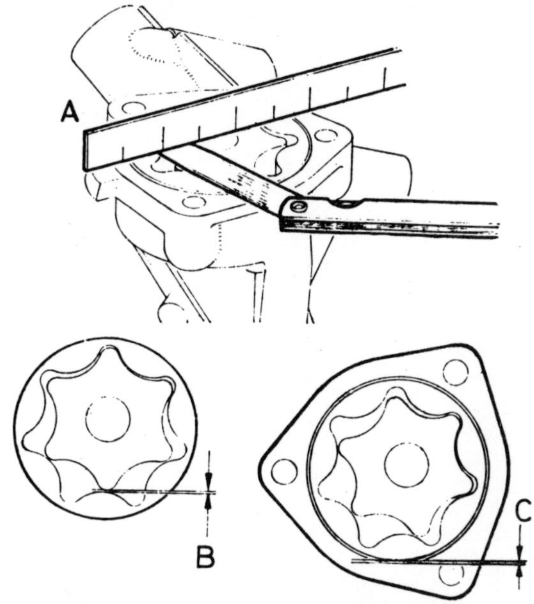

FIG 1:26 Checking oil pump rotor clearances

Key to Fig 1:26 (10 to 13 mm) (11 to 14 mm) mm) maximum maximum

A Outer ring end float .004 to .005 inch
Inner rotor end float .0045 to .0055 inch
B Rotor lobe clearance .0035 inch (.089
C Outer ring to body .011 inch (.28 mm)

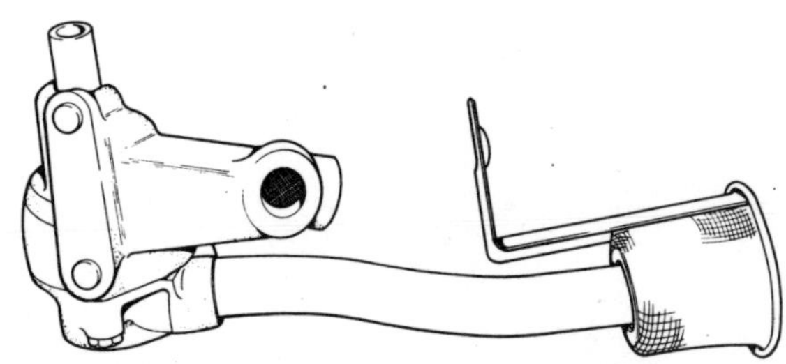

FIG 1:27 Oil pump, automatic transmission models

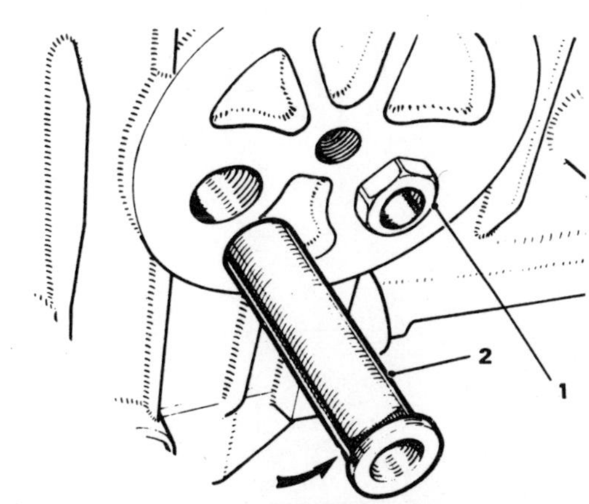

FIG 1:28 Oil pressure relief valve

Key to Fig 1:28 1 Oil pump connection 2 Relief valve

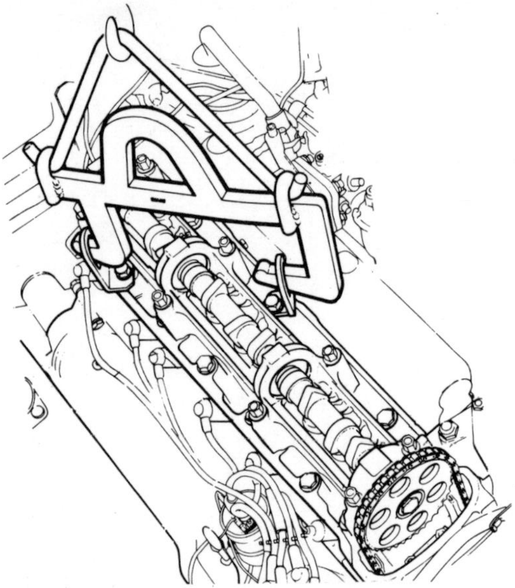

FIG 1:29 Lifting the engine out of the frame with the special sling and attachments. Note the position of the two lifting brackets for the manual transmission model illustrated

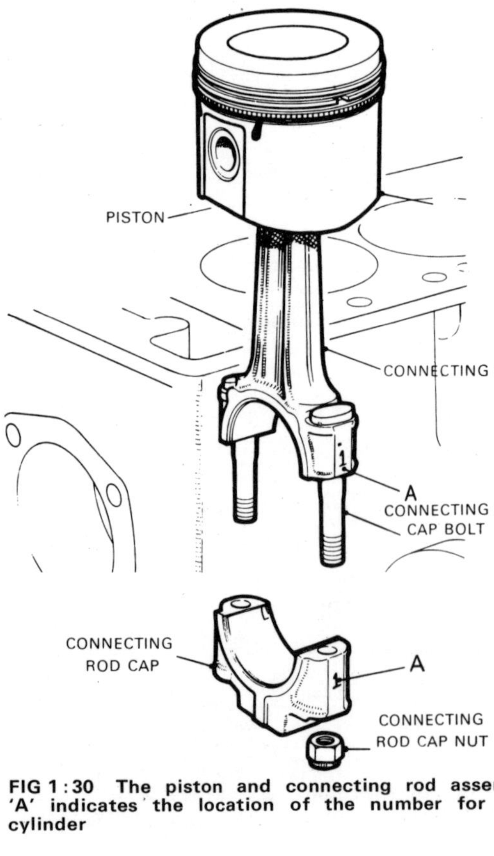

FIG 1:30 The piston and connecting rod assembly. 'A' indicates the location of the number for each cylinder

3 Remove the extension housing from the adaptor plate (item 116 in **FIG 1:2**) and the transmission case.

4 Refer to **FIG 1:24** and unscrew completely the outlet connection 2. Remove the securing screws 3 complete with sealing washers. Withdraw the pump (see **FIG 1:27**).

Dismantling:

5 Remove the three bolts from the oil pump base and disconnect the base and pick-up pipe from the body.

6 Check the oil pump components as described for the manual transmission bearing in mind that any defect cannot be rectified by fitting a new component part. The whole unit must be renewed.

Reassembling and refitting:

7 Assemble and refit in the reverse order of dismantling ensuring that the oil filter grommet is not displaced. Check and adjust the ignition timing.

Servicing oil pressure relief valve:

Refer to **FIG 1:28**. Remove valve as follows:

On cars with automatic transmission, drain the engine oil. Remove oil filter and head, catching draining oil (see earlier in this Section). Withdraw valve. This is not adjustable and must be serviced as an assembly.

Refit valve 2 with relief hole downwards. Refit filter. Refill with oil (automatic), run engine and check for leaks. Check oil level.

Oil pump drive:

Details of this are given in **Section 1:13**. See also. **FIG 1:2**.

1:10 Removing and refitting power unit

Removing (manual gearchange):

1 Remove bonnet. Drain oil, clean magnet and refit plug. Drain cooling system and remove cylinder block drain plug (see **Chapter 4**).

2 Remove battery, tray and carrier. Disconnect fan leads and remove radiator assembly after disconnection all the hoses. Do not lift the assembly with the cowl. Disconnect all wiring to engine including engine earth strap.

3 Remove air cleaner and disconnect throttle and mixture cables. Disconnect fuel pipe to the carburetter and servo hose to the manifold. Release oil pipe and clip from block. Disconnect heater hoses at the heater and remove the vacuum pipe and breather pipe from carburetter.

4 Release clutch slave cylinder and move it aside. Release exhaust pipe from the manifold. Lift front of car and fit stands.

5 Extract pin and detach engine steady rod. Release exhaust pipe from transmission case and support it. Disconnect speedometer cable. Release drive shafts. Remove the six retaining bolts from each of the inner sliding joints and lever the inner drive shaft joints away from the differential drive flanges. Disconnect by sliding the inner joints outwards (see **Chapter 8**). Remove the change speed cable housing from the transmission casing. Remove the camshaft cover.

6 Take the weight of the power unit with the sling brackets and attachments 18GA019 as shown in **FIG 1 : 29**. Note the position of the two sling brackets on the head (manual models).
7 Disengage front engine mounting brackets from the body brackets, leaving the mounting on the engine. Disconnect the right and lefthand rear engine mountings from the mounting brackets. Slowly and carefully lift the power unit clear of the body making sure all connections, electrical and mechanical and fluid carrying tubes are completely detached.

Refitting (manual gearchange):

Lower the unit into place in reverse order, locating the righthand studs and fitting nuts and spring washers. Locate lefthand mountings in body brackets and tighten fixings to 30 lb ft (4.1 kgm). Tighten righthand mountings to same torque. Continue in reverse order of dismantling.

Removing (automatic transmission):

Follow the preceding instructions for cars with manual gearchange with the following additions:
1 Release the bonnet lockplate. Drain the automatic transmission or plug the drive shaft apertures if the transmission is not being dismantled.
2 Remove both horns. Disconnect the kickdown cable from throttle control and bracket. Disconnect manual control (top) and parking cables from their selector rods and bracket. Slacken adjusting nuts on selector side only (refer to **Chapter 7**).
3 Disconnect earth cable. Pull manual control cable through from below. Refer to **FIG 1 : 19** and fit the lifting brackets to bolts 4 and 6.

Refitting (automatic transmission):

Reverse the dismantling procedure. After installation check transmission selection and parking engagement (see **Chapter 7**).

1 : 11 Servicing pistons and connecting rods

Removing:

For this operation remove the power unit as in the preceding Section. Remove the transmission assembly (see **Chapter 6** or **7**). Remove cylinder head and gasket (see **Section 1 : 5**).

Lie cylinder block on distributor side. Refer to **FIG 1 : 30** and check that rods and caps 'A' are marked consecutively from the water pump end. Rods and caps must be kept together and returned to their correct journals.

Remove the big-end nuts. Withdraw caps and bottom liners or shells. Push rod and piston out from top of block after removing ring of carbon at top of bores.

Check the bolts, cap and nuts, which should run freely down threads. Fit new parts if there is pick-up or permanent stretch. Renew bearing shells if worn. Diametrical clearance may be checked with Plastigage. It must not exceed .0015 to .003 inch (.038 to .076 mm). Refer to sub-section under heading, Big-end bearing shells.

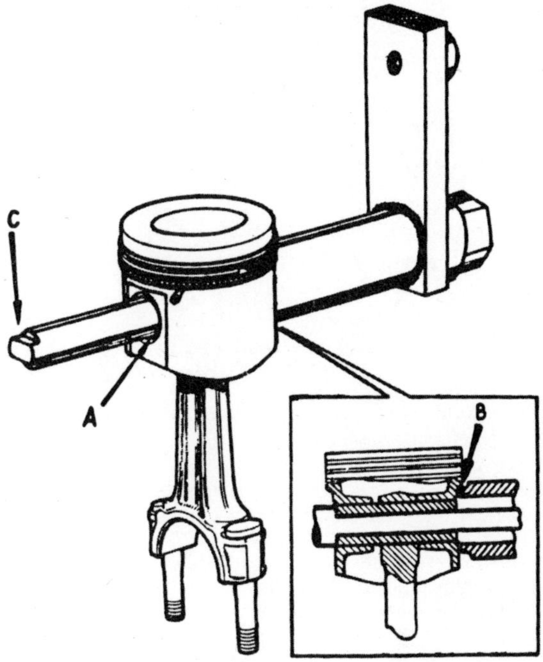

FIG 1 : 31 Removing gudgeon pin with special service tool 18GA06

Refitting:

Fit bearing shells making sure tags locate in notches in rod and cap. Lubricate piston with graphited oil (Acheson's Colloids 'Oildag'). Fit assemblies to their original bores, ensuring that the oil jet holes in the connecting rods are facing the distributor side of the engine. The big-end markings must run consecutively from the front.

Use a compressor tool on the piston rings and after fitting the assemblies, oil the crankpins and fit the big-end caps, tightening the nuts to 33 lb ft (4.6 kgm). Reverse rest of dismantling procedure, refill with engine oil and refill the cooling system.

Overhauling:

Refer to **FIG 1 : 31**. This shows the tool 18GA06 that is needed to remove and refit the gudgeon pins.

Dismantling:

Remove the rings upwards and hold the flat section bar of the tool in a vice, with the post uppermost. Remove screw from tool and pass screw through gudgeon pin to contact gudgeon pin with large diameter of shoulder (see 'A'). Position piston and screw to withdrawal post and fit the nut and withdrawal bearing. Make sure flat section of piston is squarely mounted with the cutaway of the post positioned directly below ring land (see 'B'). Mark the relative positions of piston, gudgeon pin and connecting rod to ensure subsequent assembly to original positions. Turn nut until pin is fully retracted and support connecting rod to prevent it falling. If screw rotates during withdrawal, hold end 'C' with spanner.

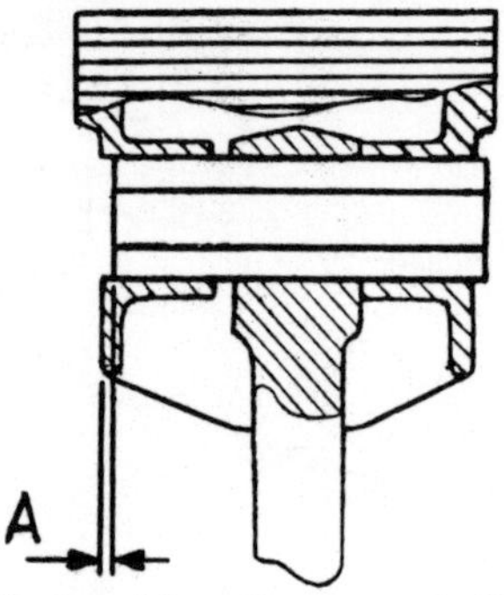

FIG 1:32 Final position of a correctly fitted gudgeon pin. A=$\frac{1}{16}$ inch (1.59 mm) depth

Reassembling:

Lubricate gudgeon pin with thin oil and position in bore on one side of piston, unless parts have been renewed the components must be of the original assembly; do not mix the parts with other assemblies. Clamp the tool in a vice with the small length boss uppermost. Fit the screw through the gudgeon pin, connecting rod and tool, fit the nut and thrust bearing and tighten the nut finger tight, make sure that the piston and rod face correctly. Ensure the cutaway portion of the tool is directly below ring land. **Never let the flange contact the piston.** Using a suitable torque wrench set at a preliminary break-off point of 10 lb ft (1.4 kgm) draw the gudgeon pin in until the shoulder of the tool enters the piston bore approximately $\frac{1}{16}$ inch (1.59 mm). This is illustrated (without tool) at 'A' in **FIG 1:32**. The small-end should now be exactly central on the pin and the piston can be aligned so that the ends of the pin are flush with the flat faces of the piston. **If the torque wrench does not break throughout the pull, the gudgeon pin fit is not acceptable.** The components must be renewed. Keep the nut and the screw well oiled.

Remove the tool and check that the piston pivots and slides freely. If tight, wash assembly in fuel or paraffin (kerosene), lubricate with graphited oil and recheck. If still tight, dismantle and check for dirt or damage. Check piston and connecting rod for alignment.

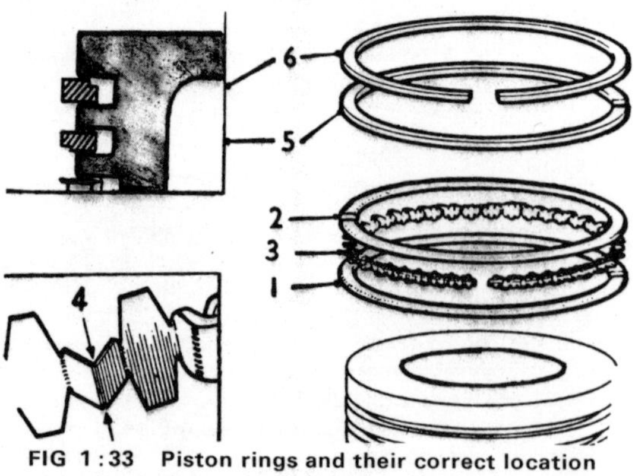

FIG 1:33 Piston rings and their correct location

Key to Fig 1:33 1 Oil ring bottom rail 2 Oil ring top rail 3 Oil ring expander 4 Expander ends butted 5 Second compression ring 6 Top compression ring

Piston rings:

Refer to **FIG 1:33**. When fitting new rings, check gap in cylinder bore as shown in **FIG 1:34**. Push ring about one inch down bore with a piston. Measured gap should be .008 to .016 inch (.20 to .40 mm) for compression rings and .015 to .045 inch (.38 to 1.14 mm) for the oil control ring pair, 1 and 2. Check side clearance as shown in **FIG 1:35**. It should not exceed .0015 to .0035 inch (.03 to .08 mm) for compression rings.

To fit rings, position bottom oil control ring 1 below lowest groove in piston. Fit expander 3 in groove. Move bottom ring into groove. Fit upper control ring 2. Ends of expander must butt (see 4). Set ring gaps and expander gap at 90 deg. to each other. Fit second compression ring with scalloped face downwards and the top ring with the inner shouldered face upwards (see inset). Set ring gaps at 90 deg. to each other and away from thrust side of piston.

Big-end bearing shells:

The correct clearance for big-end bearings is given early in this Section. If the bearing metal of the shells is scored or pitted, renew the shells. Check the crankpins for wear or ovality. If excessive, have the crankshaft reground to one of the undersizes mentioned in Technical Data and fit the appropriate size of shells. Never try to rectify excessive clearance by filing the rods or caps and do not scrape the bearings in an attempt to correct the fit. If a big-end is tight when reassembled, dismantle it and check for dirt behind the shells.

1:12 Servicing the crankshaft

Removing:

Remove power unit (see **Section 1:10**). Remove transmission assembly (see **Chapter 6** or **7**). Remove cylinder head cover (see **Section 1:4**). Remove camshaft sprocket (see operations 9 and 10, **Section 1:5**). Remove front oil seal, oil thrower, and crankshaft sprocket (see **Section 1:8**). Remove distributor drive gear and drive shaft (see **Section 1:13**).

Lie cylinder block on distributor side. Remove crankshaft lower extension from automatic transmission (ten fixings inside and four outside).

Check crankshaft end float at No. 3 bearing by levering shaft fully in one direction. Use feelers between crankshaft face and face of thrust washers 6 in **FIG 1:2**. Correct float is .002 to .003 inch (.05 to .07 mm). To rectify, remove No. 3 cap and push on one end of each half-washer in crankcase to release them. Remove tagged half-washers from cap. From the selection of thrust washer thicknesses available, select a set that will give the correct end float (see later). Push crankcase half-washers (without tag) into place round the crankshaft with oil grooves facing outwards.

To remove the shaft, remove the primary gear and thrust washer. Check that big-end and main bearing caps are numbered from water pump end. Remove all caps and lift out the shaft. If original bearing shells are to be refitted, store them in their correct order.

Refitting:

Check bearings against figures given in Technical Data. Wear and excessive clearance may be corrected by regrinding the crankshaft to one of four undersizes and refitting new shells. **Never try to adjust clearances by filing caps.** Fit new shells if the journals are satisfactory. The clearance should be correct without the need for adjustment.

Flush out the crankshaft oilways under pressure (particularly if a bearing has 'run'). Inject fresh oil. Fit top shells and thrust washer to crankcase, oil liberally and fit crankshaft. Fit thrust washer to No. 3 cap with tags correctly located. Fit and tighten this cap and check the end float with feelers or a dial guage. Selective thrust washers are available as follows:

.089 to .091 inch (2.26 to 2.29 mm)
.091 to .093 inch (2.29 to 2.36 mm)
.093 to .095 inch (2.36 to 2.41 mm)

Continue fitting the main bearing caps, tightening to 70 lb ft (9.7 kgm). Check shaft for free rotation after each tightening. If it suddenly becomes tight, remove cap and check for dirt behind shells. Fit the big-ends, tightening to 33 lb ft (4.6 kgm).

Reverse the rest of the dismantling procedure and refill with oil.

1:13 Distributor and oil pump drive shaft

Removing:

1 Remove the power unit from the car (see **Section 1:10**) and separate the transmission from the engine (see **Chapter 6** or **7**). Position and support the engine on its carburetter side.
2 Remove the oil filter and oil pump (see **Sections 1:3** and **1:9**).
3 Refer to **Section 1:8** and remove the crankshaft oil seal.
4 Turn the camshaft to align the timing marks for No. 1 firing and remove the crankshaft sprocket (see **Section 1:7**).
5 Remove the fuel pump and operating shaft.
6 Refer to **FIG 1:36** (inset 'C') and note the position of the distribution drive slot, which should be between 9 and 10 o'clock with the large offset segment uppermost.
7 Withdraw the distributor drive shaft noting that it will turn approximately 70 deg. as it is disengaged from the shaft. Pick up the thrust washer 6 if it fails to remain on the shaft during disengagement.

Refitting:

8 Fit the thrust washer to the shaft and check that the valve timing is still correctly set.
9 Fit the drive shaft initially with the segments in the 12 o'clock position (see inset 'B') so that as it meshes with the drive gear and turns approximately 70 deg. anticlockwise it will finally position itself with the segments between the 9 and 10 o'clock position (inset 'C').
10 Fit the distributor and check that the rotor is set to fire No. 1 cylinder.
11 Reverse the rest of the dismantling procedure and check the ignition timing.

1:14 Engine mountings

Front lefthand:

When removing, take the weight of the power unit, lowering it again slightly after releasing the mounting. When refitting, note that the mounting flange fits over the crossmember. Tighten bolt and nut to 30 lb ft (4.1 kgm).

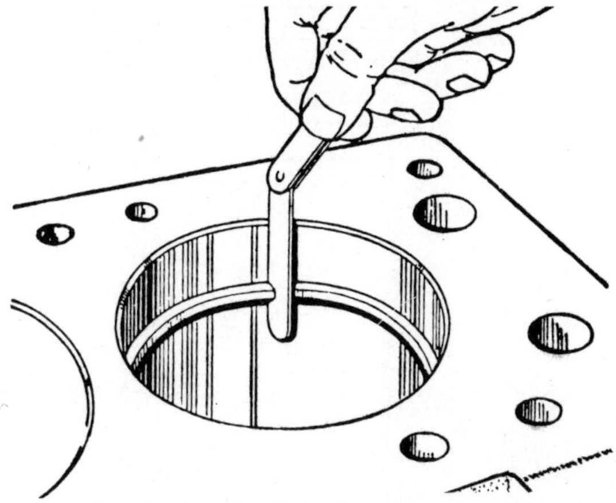

FIG 1:34 Checking the piston ring gap

Front righthand (manual gearchange):

To remove, set handbrake, raise front of car with wheels supported and fit a wedge between front tyre and bottom rear edge of wheel arch. Take weight of power unit. Remove mounting nut from crossmember. Slacken tie rod bracket from body, pull down and turn it sideways. Lift power unit slightly and release rear mounting from bracket. Remove front righthand mounting.

Refit mounting as for front lefthand. Tighten tie rod bracket bolts (two long ones at front end). Tighten tie rod to suspension arm bolt to 40 to 50 lb ft (5.5 to 6.9 kgm).

Rear lefthand (manual gearchange):

Support power unit. Lift expansion tank and set aside. Remove mounting nut at engine bracket. Release mounting from body bracket and withdraw downwards. Refit as for front lefthand mounting.

Rear lefthand (automatic):

To remove, apply handbrake, lift front of car and support power unit. Disconnect lower engine tie rod at transmission bracket. Remove bolt from mounting to body bracket. Release rear righthand mounting bracket from torque converter housing. Lower power unit and remove mounting and bracket.

To refit, reverse dismantling procedure, ensuring that mounting bracket fits easily over torque convertor housing. Distance between faces 1.68 inch (43 mm).

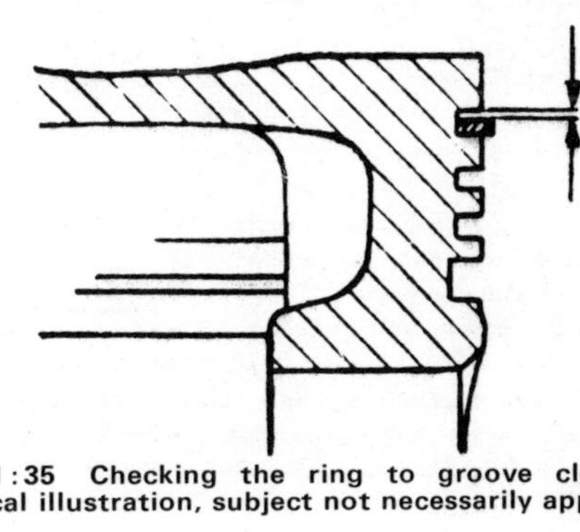

FIG 1:35 Checking the ring to groove clearance. (Typical illustration, subject not necessarily applicable)

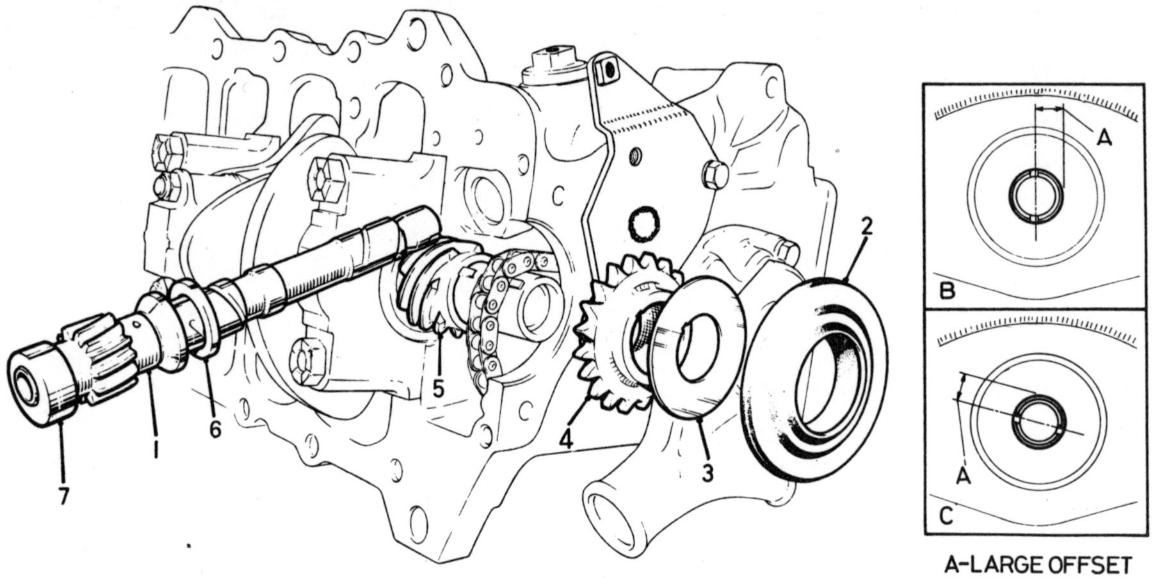

FIG 1 : 36 The distributor drive shaft and associate components

Key to Fig 1 : 36 1 Distributor and fuel pump drive shaft 2 Pulley oil seal 3 Oil thrower 4 Crankshaft sprocket 5 Drive gear 6 Thrust washer 7 Fuel pump cam

Flanges on mounting fit over top of brackets. Tighten to 30 lb ft (4.1 kgm). Position mounting assembly, engage body bracket and torque convertor and pull up into position.

Rear righthand (automatic):

Repeat the instructions for the front righthand mounting (manual gearchange) but note that two screws secure the mounting bracket to the torque convertor.

When refitting, secure the mounting bracket to the torque converer housing before the tie rod bracket bolts are fitted.

1 : 15 Reassembling a stripped engine

Provide a new set of gaskets, make sure all parts are clean and oil bearing surfaces liberally. Fit the crankshaft (see **Section 1 : 12**). Check that all camshaft and distributor drive parts are in position. Refit pistons and connecting rods (see **Section 1 : 11**). Fit head and camshaft drive and remaining parts in reverse order of dismantling. Use the torque wrench figures given in Technical Data.

When the power unit is in the car and all connections have been checked, fill with fresh oil to the correct level and refill the cooling system. Once the engine has started, check all round for leaks. Check the ignition timing (see **Chapter 3**). After a hundred miles on the road, check all bolts and fixings for tightness.

1 : 16 Fault diagnosis

(a) Engine will not start

1 Defective coil
2 Faulty distributor capacitor (condenser)
3 Dirty, pitted or incorrectly set contact breaker points
4 Ignition wiring loose or insulation faulty
5 Water on plug leads, damp distributor
6 Battery discharged, terminals corroded
7 Faulty or jammed starter. Switch defective
8 Plug leads wrongly connected
9 Vapour lock in fuel pipes due to heat
10 Defective fuel pump to float mechanism
11 Overchoking or underchoking, sticking carburetter piston
12 Blocked petrol filter or carburetter jet
13 Leaking valves, broken springs
14 Sticking valves
15 Valve timing incorrect
16 Ignition timing incorrect

(b) Engine stalls

1 Check 1, 2, 3, 4, 5, 10, 11, 12, 13 and 14 in (a)
2 Sparking plugs defective or gaps incorrect
3 Retarded ignition
4 Mixture too weak
5 Water in fuel system
6 Petrol tank vent blocked
7 Incorrect valve clearances

(c) Engine idles badly

1 Check 2, 4 and 7 in (b)
2 Air leak at manifold joints
3 Carburetter jet wrongly positioned
4 Air leak in carburetter
5 Over-rich mixture
6 Worn piston rings
7 Worn valve stems or guides
8 Weak exhaust valve springs

(d) Engine misfires

1 Check 1, 2, 3, 4, 5, 8, 10, 12, 13, 14, 15 and 16 in (a); 2, 3, 4 and 7 in (b)
2 Weak or broken valve springs

(e) Engine overheats (see **Chapter 4**)

(f) Compression low

1 Check 13 and 14 in (a), 6 and 7 in (c) and 2 in (d)
2 Worn piston ring grooves
3 Scored or worn cylinder bores
4 Breakdown of head gasket

(g) Engine lacks power

1 Check 3, 10, 11, 12, 13, 14, 15 and 16 in (a); 2, 3, 4, and 7 in (b); 6 and 7 in (c) and 2 in (d)
2 Leaking joint washers
3 Fouled sparking plugs
4 Automatic ignition advance not operating

(h) Burnt valves or head seats

1 Check 13 and 14 in (a); 7 in (b); 2 in (d) and also check (e)
2 Excessive carbon build-up round valve seats and head

(j) Sticking valves

1 Check 2 in (d)
2 Bent valve stem
3 Scored valve stem or guide
4 Incorrect valve clearance

(k) Excessive cylinder wear

1 Check 11 in (a) and see **Chapter 4**
2 Lack of oil
3 Dirty oil
4 Piston rings gummed up or broken
5 Badly fitting piston rings, gaps too small
6 Bent connecting rod

(l) Excessive oil consumption

1 Check 6 and 7 in (c) and check (k)
2 Ring gaps too wide
3 Oil control rings defective
4 Scored cylinders
5 Oil level too high
6 Leaking oil seals, filter, joints
7 Ineffective inlet valve stem oil seals

(m) Crankshaft or connecting rod bearing failure

1 Check 2 in (k)
2 Restricted oilways
3 Worn journals or crankpins
4 Loose bearing caps
5 Very low oil pressure
6 Bent connecting rod

(n) Internal water leakage (see **Chapter 4**)

(o) Poor water circulation (see **Chapter 4**)

(p) Corrosion (see **Chapter 4**)

(q) High fuel consumption (see **Chapter 2**)

(r) Engine vibration

1 Loose alternator bolts
2 Mounting rubbers loose or ineffective
3 Exhaust pipe mountings defective
4 Engine steady loose or faulty
5 Misfiring due to mixture, ignition or mechanical faults

NOTES

CHAPTER 2

THE FUEL SYSTEM

2:1 Description

Fuel pump:

A Goss mechanical fuel pump is fitted to the Kimberley and Tasman and it is mounted on the front of the transmission casing below the alternator. There is a slight difference in the pump fitted to an automatic transmission model, but nothing that effects its working similarity with that fitted to a manual model. The slight difference between the two pumps can be seen in **FIGS 2:1** and **2:2**. The pump fitted to the automatic model has a different spacer block and an oil seal and retainer are fitted under the diaphragm spring. Also the pump is mounted horizontally instead of vertically.

The pump is operated by an eccentric cam on the distributor drive shaft (see **FIG 1:36**) which bears against and activates a pushrod and short rocker arm. The rocker arm is linked to an operating lever that is connected to the diaphragm pushrod. When the pushrod is actuated the diaphragm is pulled downwards and creates a depression in the pump chamber, petrol is then drawn in through the inlet valve. When the cam lobe on the distributor drive shaft passes the rocker arm, the diaphragm is unrestrained and it returns to a normal position under the influence of the return spring. The upsurge forces the fuel from the pump chamber, through the outlet valve and into the carburetter. The inlet and outlet valves are the pressure operated one-way type.

When the correct fuel level is reached in the carburetter float chamber, the needle valve is closed by the rising float. The back pressure in the fuel lines and pump chamber is sufficient to overcome the tension of the diaphragm spring and the diaphragm remains in the pulled down position. The operating lever also is retained in this position and the rocker arm idles on the cam lobe, until the carburetter needle valve opens again to admit more fuel. The pressure of fuel delivered is directly related to the predetermined strength of the diaphragm spring.

The carburetters

These are SU type HS6. Refer to **FIGS 2:3** and **2:4**.

The air intake bore through body 1 is fitted with a butterfly valve 39 in throttle spindle 38 to control the volume of mixture passing to the engine. The piston rises and falls inside chamber assembly 8 and when at rest vitually blocks the air intake. Its movement is due to the depression in the air intake system associated with engine load and throttle opening. This depression affects the space above the piston, causing the piston to rise and fall,

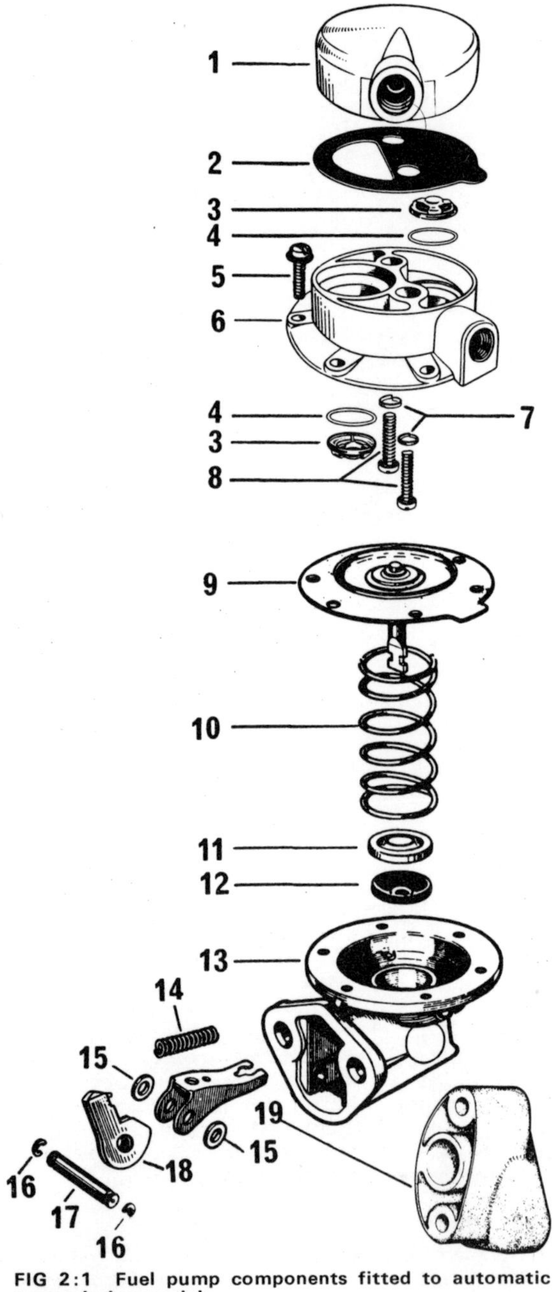

FIG 2:1 Fuel pump components fitted to automatic transmission models

Key to Fig 2:1 1 Top cover 2 Pulsator diapharagm 3 Valve assembly 4 Valve gasket 5 Screw 6 Upper casting 7 Washer 8 Screw 9 Diaphragm assembly 10 Diaphragm spring 11 Oil seal retainer 12 Oil seal 13 Lower casting 14 Spring 15 Spacer washer 16 Rocker pin clip 17 Rocker pin arm 18 Rocker arm 19 Spacer block

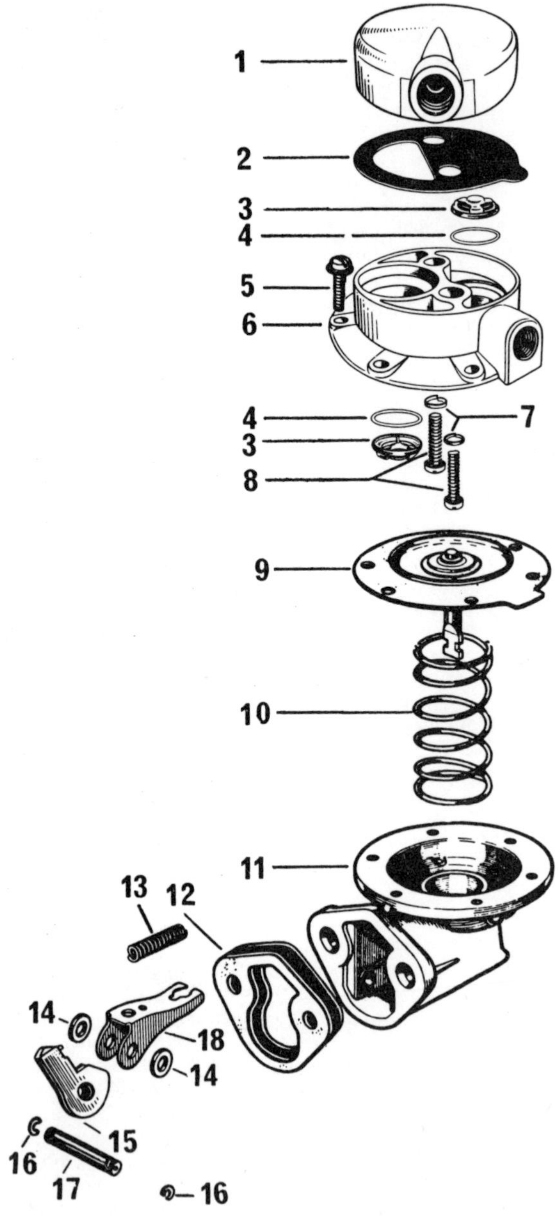

FIG 2:2 Fuel pump components fitted to manual transmission models

Key to Fig 2:2 1 Top cover 2 Pulsator diaphragm 3 Valve assembly 4 Valve gasket 5 Screw 6 Upper casting 7 Washer 8 Screw 9 Diaphragm assembly 10 Diaphragm spring 11 Lower casting 12 Spacer block 13 Spring 14 Spacer washer 15 Rocker arm 16 Rocker arm pin clip 17 Rocker arm pin 18 Rocker arm

thus producing a variable choke aperture in the body. This constantly changing volume of air which is drawn into the engine demands a variable quantity of fuel to produce the correct mixture. Tapered needle 24 is attached to the underside of the piston so that it also rises and falls inside a jet 14. The smallest diameter of the needle is in the jet when the piston is fully raised, so that there is maximum air and fuel when required. Rapid fluctuations of the piston and needle are damped out by hydraulic damper 10.

Rich mixture for starting from cold is obtained by pulling the jet down to a smaller diameter of the tapered needle. Fuel is supplied to the jet by the usual system of a float controlled needle valve 34 or 60 in chamber 32. The cam on lever 51 comes into play when the choke control is pulled out. It provides for a small throttle opening at the same time as the rich mixture needed for easy starting from cold.

2:2 Routine maintenance

Refer to **FIG 2:5**. Every 6000 miles (10,000 km or six months) remove the damper(s) and add engine oil until the level is $\frac{1}{2}$ inch (13 mm) above the top of the hollow rod of piston as shown by the arrows. At the same time oil the throttle linkages and pedal fulcrum.

Every 12,000 miles (20,000 km or 12 months) renew the air cleaner elements. Change more frequently if conditions are very dusty (see **Section 2:10**).

Every 6000 miles (10,000 km or six months) make a visual check of all fuel pipes and connections. At the same mileage check the carburetter idling speed and mixture settings (see **Section 2:4**).

2:3 Servicing the fuel pump

Removing:

The fuel pump is below the level of the fuel tank, be prepared when the fuel line is disconnected to either plug the line or secure it in an upwards position to bring it above the fuel tank level.

1 Disconnect both fuel lines at the pump.

2 Unscrew and remove the two bolts and washers from the pump flange.

3 Detach the pump assembly, spacer block and two gaskets.

4 Remove the pump pushrod.

Refitting:

5 Refitting is the reversal of removal, but discard the old gaskets and fit new ones. Do not use gasket cement or other jointing compound on the gaskets.

Overhauling:

1 After removal, thoroughly clean the exterior of the pump and scribe a mark across the upper and lower body mounting flanges. This is to ensure correct relocation when assembling.

2 Unscrew and remove the six flange securing screws and separate the two castings.

3 Referring to **FIGS 2:1** and **2:2** press and turn the diaphragm through 90 deg. to free it from the operating lever. Remove the diaphragm assembly and spring.

4 Remove the circlips 16 from the rocker arm pin, carefully mount the flange in a soft-jawed vice and extract the rocker pin 17, rocker arm, spring and operating lever.

5 **FIG 2:1** types only. Remove the retainer 11 and seal 12. Clean off any burrs that might be around the cavity.

6 Unscrew and remove from inside the top cover 6 the two screws 8, collect the washers 7. Lift off the top cover 1 and pulsator diaphragm 2. Access can now be made to the outlet valve 3 and, if necessary, its removal. If the valves are removed, they will be damaged during the process and new ones must be obtained. Clean off the burrs around the seating recesses.

Inspection:

7 Examine the diaphragms 2 and 9 for any signs of deterioration, such as cracking, fraying or hardening. The spring 10 should be checked for wear and distortion but if the pump has done considerable service reflect upon the probability of renewal. Examine the operating lever, pin and rocker arm for wear or fractures. Renew all suspect parts but renew the valves 3, gaskets 4 (retainer 11 and seal 12—automatic) and the mounting gaskets whatever the condition.

Reassembling:

8 Reassemble in the reverse order of dismantling but note the following points:
Restake the valves in their seats and the seal retainer, if applicable.
Fit the pulsator diaphragm 2 with the crescent cut-out over the inlet chamber. When fitting the rocker arm and its associated components, use a dummy pin to retain them in position initially.
Ensure that the diaphragm pullrod is securely clipped to the operating arm and the screw holes align.
Fit the castings to the scribe marks and tighten the screws with finger pressure only. Work the rocker arm to settle the diaphragm then tighten the screws.

Refitting and testing:

9 Refit to the engine and if test equipment is available refer to Technical Data for operating pressures and delivery rates.

2:4 Tuning carburetters:

Setting idling speed (twin carburetters):

Refer to **FIG 2:6**. Do the following:

1 Provide a reliable tachometer (revolution indicator) and a twin-carburetter balancing device. If system must confirm to laws governing exhaust emission it will also be necessary to use an exhaust gas analyzer.

2 Remove air cleaners and top up dampers (see **Sections 2:10** and **2:2**). Check that throttle operates correctly at 2 and that mixture control (choke) cables 3 return fully and have $\frac{1}{16}$ (2 mm) free play. Also check for slight clearance between fast-idle screws 2 and 4 and their cams.

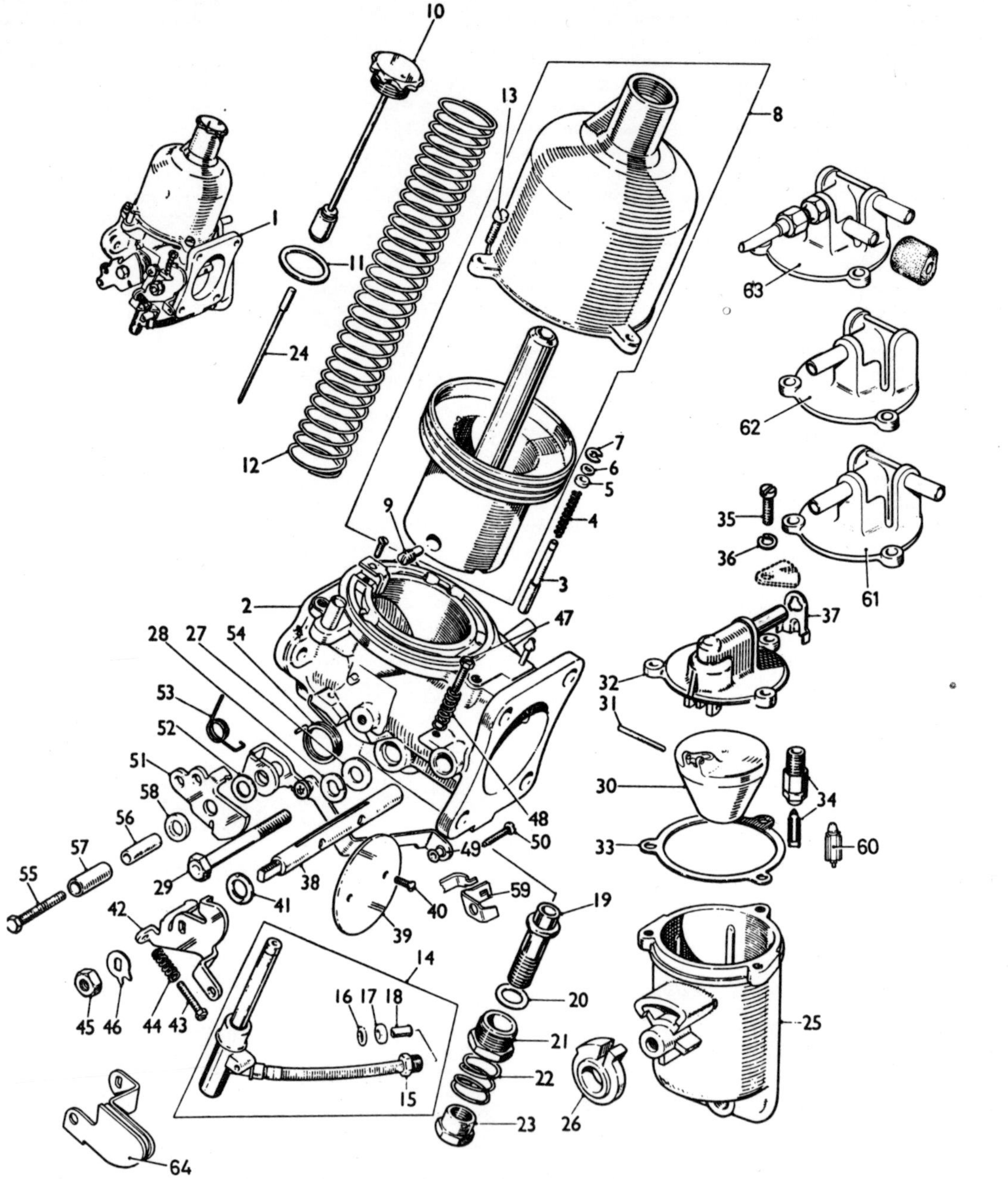

FIG 2:3 Components of SU.HS6 carburetter including the different patterns of float chamber cover and linkage levers

Key to Fig 2:3 1 Carburetter assembly 2 Carburetter body 3 Piston lifting pin 4 Spring and pin 5 Neoprene washer 6 Brass washer 7 Circlip—pin 8 Chamber and piston assembly 9 Needle locating screw 10 Piston damper 11 Fibre washer 12 Piston spring 13 Screw—chamber to body 14 Jet assembly 15 Nut 16 Washer 17 Gland 18 Ferrule 19 Jet bearing 20 Brass washer—jet bearing 21 Jet locking nut 22 Jet locking spring 23 Jet adjusting screw 24 Needle 25 Float chamber 26 Adapter 27 Plain washer 28 Spring washer 29 Bolt—float chamber to body 30 Float 31 Hinge pin—float to lid 32 Float chamber lid (Tasman models—1st type) 33 Float chamber lid gasket 34 Needle and seat assembly (2nd type) 35 Screw 36 Spring washer 37 Baffle plate lid (Kimberley models) 38 Throttle spindle 39 Throttle disc 40 Screw-disc to spindle 41 Brass washer—spindle 42 Throttle return lever 43 Cam stop screw 44 Spring—screw 45 Throttle spindle nut 46 Tab washer—nut 47 Throttle adjusting screw 48 Spring—screw 49 Pick-up lever and links (Tasman models) 50 Screw-link to jet 51 Cam lever 52 Washer—cam lever 53 Cam lever spring 54 Pick-up lever spring 55 Pivot bolt 56 Pivot bolt tube 57 Outer tube 58 Distance washer 59 Pick-up lever and link (Kimberley models) 60 Needle (1st type) 61 Float-chamber lid (Kimberley models—front) 62 Float-chamber lid (Kimberley models—rear) 63 Float chamber lid (Tasman models—2nd type) 64 Throttle linkage (Tasman models)

3 Raise lifting pins 5, release them and check that pistons fall freely (see Centralizing the jet' in **Section 2:6**). Connect the tachometer and select 'P' on cars with automatic transmission. Run the engine up to working temperature and then for five more minutes. Run engine up to 2500 rev/min for thirty seconds. If adjustments cannot be completed in three minutes, increase engine speed to 2500 rev/min for thirty seconds and then recommence tuning. Repeat this procedure every three minutes if necessary.

4 Set idling speed to 600 rev/min for manual transmission and 550 rev/min for automatic transmission turning adjusting screw 9 equally as required. Set up the balancing meter. If balance is incorrect, adjust by turning one screw 9 as required. Reset the idling speed by turning both screws equally and again check the balance. Check fork clearance (see 14). Slacken clamping bolts and use feeler gauge to set clearance to .012 inch (.31 mm) between link pin and fork as shown by arrows in inset on left. Tighten clamp bolts.

5 If a smooth idle is not obtainable, adjust mixture as follows:

6 Stop engine and remove suction chambers and pistons (see **Sect on 2:6**). Turn adjusting nuts (see 10) until jets are flush, but not above, bridge in intake bore (see 11 lower left). If just below bridge, make sure both jets are in same position. Turn nuts down by two complete turns. Refit pistons and suction chambers and top up damper oil (see **Section 2:2**).

7 Run engine at idling speed. Achieve fastest speed on tachometer by turning nuts up or down. Turning up will weaken mixture and turning down will enrich it. Now turns nuts up slowly and evenly until speed just starts to fall and then turn them equally downwards by the minimum amount until the maximum speed is regained. Recheck the idling speed and balance, adjusting at screws 9 as required.

8 Check the fork clearance as described in operation 4. Make sure that mixture control cables 3 have the necessary free movement (see operation 2). Slacken screws 2 and 4 until well clear of cams (see 6). Pull out mixture (choke) control knob until jet heads are about to move (see **FIG 2:4**). Lock the control in this position.

9 Turn each fast-idle screw (2 and 4) until it just touches the cam and then turn each screw equally to obtain a fast-idle speed of between 800 and 1000 rev/min. This completes the tuning.

Single carburetter:

1 Connect a reliable tachometer to the engine and on automatic vehicles, select 'P' and apply the handbrake.

2 Start the engine and when it has reached normal working temperature adjust the throttle screw to give an idling speed of 550 or 600 rev/min for an automatic or manual model respectively.

3 To check the mixture strength lift the piston pin approximately $\frac{1}{32}$ inch (.8 mm) and compare the result with the following:

(a) If the engine speed increases and continues to run faster with the piston pin raised, the mixture is too rich.

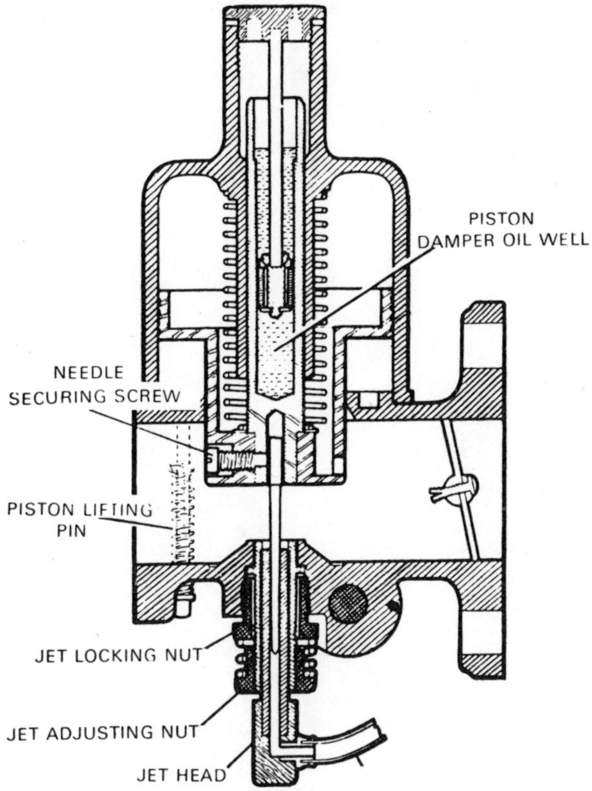

FIG 2:4 **A sectional diagram of the SU carburetter**

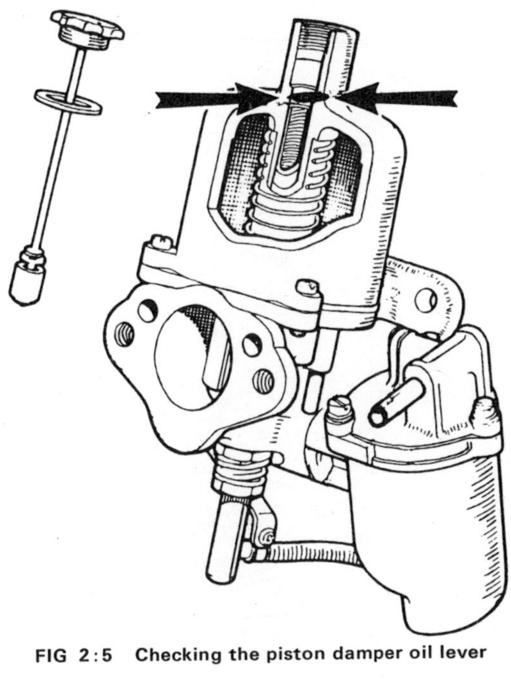

FIG 2:5 **Checking the piston damper oil lever**

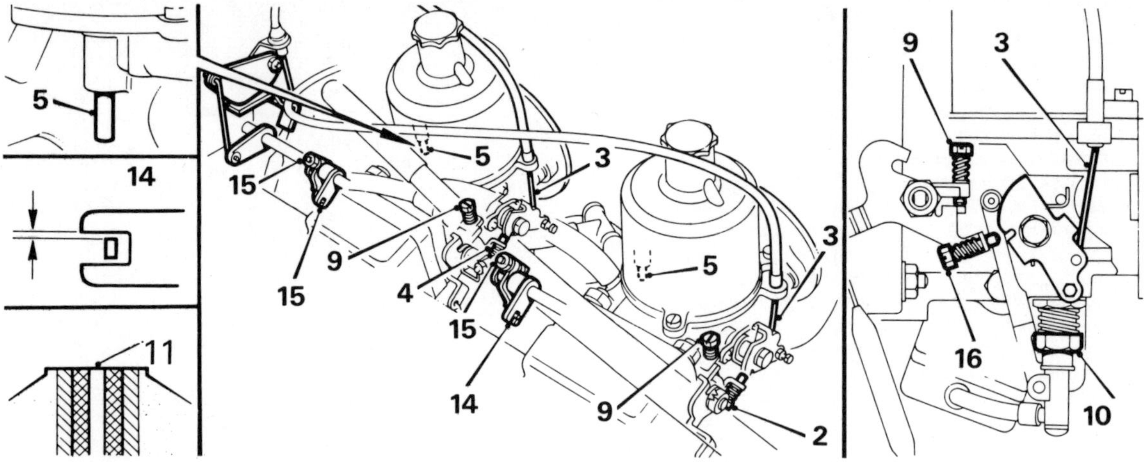

FIG 2:6 A pictorial illustration of the controls and adjustments, relating to a twin carburetter version

Key to Fig 2:6 2 Throttle fast idle screw 3 Mixture control cable 4 Throttle fast idle screw 5 Lifting pins 9 Throttle adjusting screw (normal idling) 10 Jet adjusting nut 11 Jet flush with bridge of carburetter 14 Link pin setting=.012 inch (.31 mm) 15 Progressive throttle link 16 Clearance between fast idle screw and cams=$\frac{1}{16}$ inch (2 mm)

(b) If the engine speed decreases immediately as the piston pin is raised, the mixture is too weak.

(c) If the engine speed rises only momentarily with a very slight increase and then levels off, the mixture is correct.

4 Referring to **FIG 2:7**, the jet adjusting nut controls the mixture strength. If it is turned upwards it will weaken the mixture and turning it downwards will enrich the mixture. Turn the nut in the appropriate direction to achieve the desired result and note the tachometer reading and the rhythm of the engine. Obtain, during adjustment, a regular and even note in conjunction with the gastest idling speed. The adjustment is sensitive to one flat of the hexagon nut.

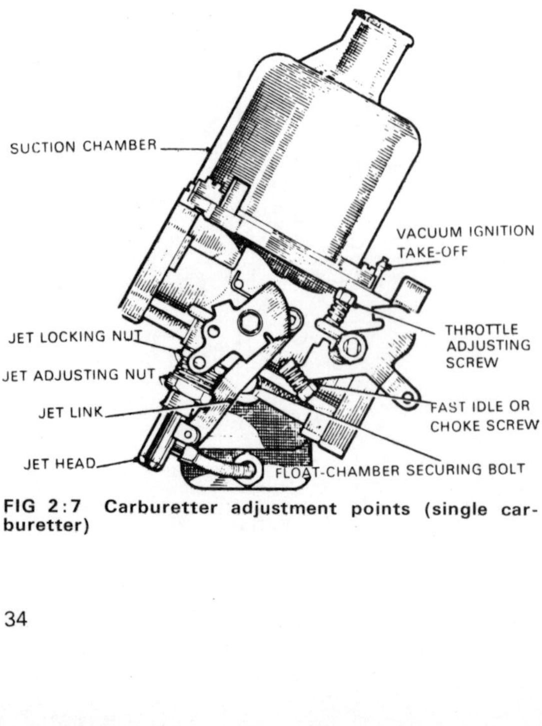

FIG 2:7 Carburetter adjustment points (single carburetter)

5 Readjust the throttle screw to obtain the correct idling speed.

6 Adjust the fast idling speed as described in operations 8 and 9 for the twin carburetters. Ignore the reference to the fork clearance.

2:5 Removing and refitting carburetter(s)

1 Disconnect the battery earth lead and remove the air cleaners.

2 Disconnect the choke and accelerator cables. Release the petrol feed pipe, engine breather pipe and vacuum advance pipe.

3 Automatic models only: Disconnect the kickdown cable.

4 Remove the carburetter mounting flange nuts—four on each carburetter—and lift off the assembly.

5 Kimberley models. Very carefully lift off both carburetters together and remove the heatshield and spacers.

Refitting:

When refitting, renew the joint washer fitting one on each side of distance pieces. Reverse dismantling procedure. Check and adjust settings (see proceding Section). Fit air cleaners. Check the kickdown cable adjustment on automatic transmission models (see **Chapter 7**).

2:6 Overhauling carburetters

Separate the carburetters by disconnecting the choke and throttle connecting rods. Refer to **FIG 2:3**. Clean outside of carburetter. Mark rim of suction chamber 8 and body 2 to ensure correct replacement. Remove damper 10. Remove screws 13 and lift off chamber. Remove spring 12, lift piston straight out and pour off oil inside rod. Remove screws 9 and withdraw needle 24. Do not bend the needle.

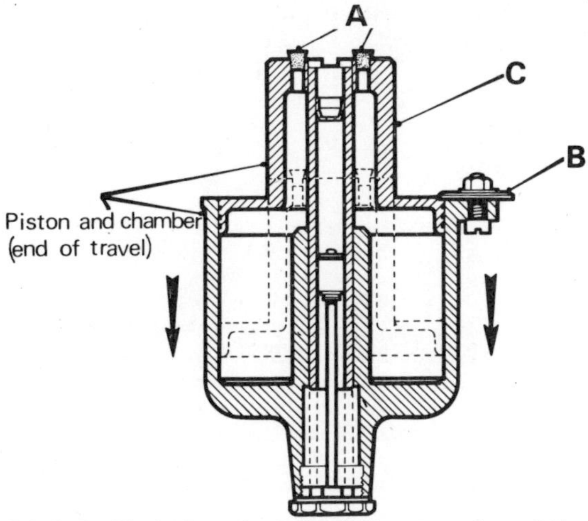

FIG 2:8 Method used to check the operation of the piston and suction chamber. The piston spring is taken out for this test
Key to Fig 2:8 **A** Plugged holes **B** Large washer fitment **C** Piston

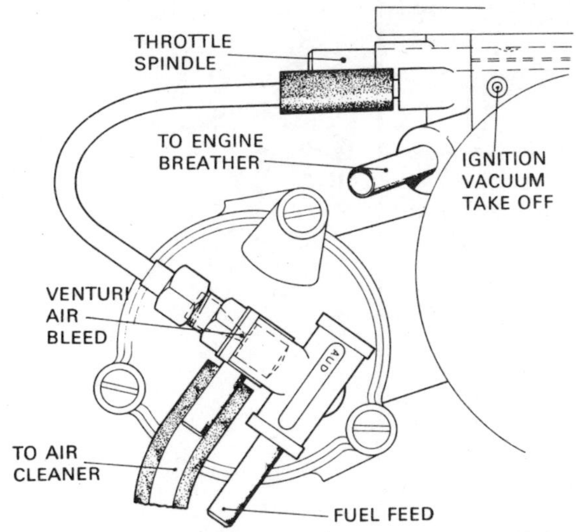

FIG 2:9 The additional mixture weakening device fitted to the Tasman models

Release hooked end of spring 54. Support head of jet 14 and remove screw 50. Unscrew nut 15 from flat chamber 25, withdraw the jet downwards and take care of parts 16, 17 and 18.

Remove nut 23 and spring 22, unscrew locating nut 21 and remove jet bearing 19. Remove pivot bolt 55 to release cam lever 51. Make a note of the location of all the associated parts.

Release float chamber (bolt 29). Mark lid 61, 62 or 63 for correct reassembly and detach it. Pull out pin 31 by the serrated end to release float 30. Withdraw needle 34 or 60. Unless worn, there is no point in removing throttle butterfly disc 39. If it must be removed, mark its position in relation to the intake bore, squeeze the split ends of screws 40 together, unscrew them and push disc out of spindle 38. Note location of lever 42 before removing nut 45. When refitting disc, snap throttle shut to centralize it in bore and then fit the screws, spreading the split ends just enough to stop them turning.

Inspecting:

Clean the parts in fuel. Check fit of spindle 38 in body and renew if slack. Check float needle and seat 34 or 60. Flooding of the carburetter may have been due to a worn needle (look for groove on needle seating). Renew both parts if suspect. Renew all other worn parts. Clean inside of float chamber. Check needle and spring against Technical Data.

Check the piston and suction chamber without fitting the spring. The parts must be clean and dry. Do not use abrasives on piston and suction chamber surfaces. Refer to **FIG 2:8** and test as follows:

1 Refit damper. Plug holes at A with rubber plugs or Plasticene. Insert piston fully.
2 Fix large washer to one lug of chamber so that it overlaps bore (see B). Turn assembly upside down as shown, hold the piston and time the fall of the chamber.
3 Total fall of the chamber should take between 5 and 7 seconds. If longer, check piston and chamber surfaces for dirt or damage. Renew assembly if time is still outside the limits.

Reassembling:

Fit needle, guide and spring into piston, with guide flush with face of piston. Tighten screw 9 against flat on guide. Refit jet bearing 19, tightening nut 21. Fit parts 22 and 23, screwing the nut on as far as possible. Insert jet 14. Fit gland parts with flexible tube projecting a minimum of $\frac{3}{16}$ inch (4.8 mm) beyond gland 17.

Reassembly the float chamber. Do not overtighten needle seat (part of 34). Fit needle, coned end first. Refit float 30, inserting pin 31 serrated end last. Refit lid on new joint washer 33. Secure assembly to body with bolt 29.

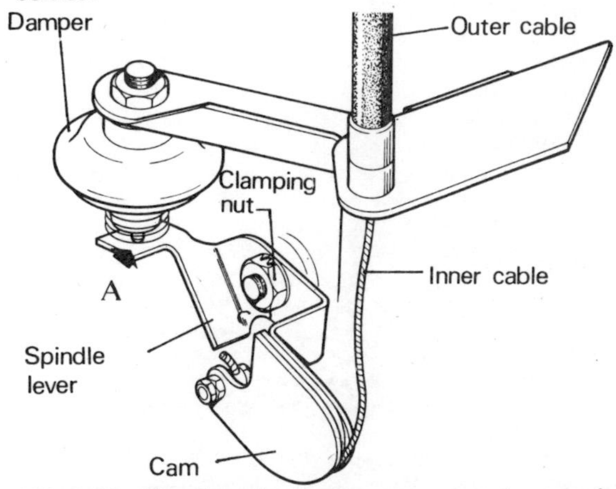

FIG 2:10 The throttle damper arrangement, second type, fitted to the Tasman models. The adjusting point is indicated at (A)

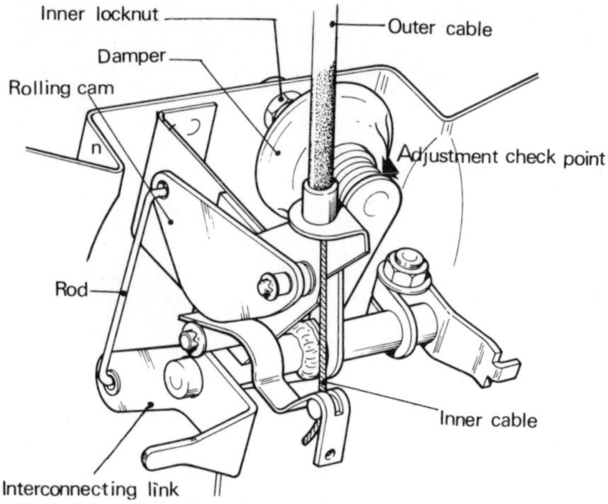

FIG 2:11 The throttle damper arrangement, second type, fitted to the Kimberley models. The adjusting point is indicated at arrow

Fit jet tube to float chamber, tightening sleeve nut 15 just enough to compress the flange. This may leak if overtightened. Refit the piston and suction chamber. Do not forget the spring and align the marks made when dismantling. Tighten screws 13 evenly. Reconnect the jet link by holding up lever 51, supporting the jet head and fitting screw 50.

Screw down adjusting nut 23 by two turns (12 flats) to give an initial setting and check the jet centralizing (see following sub-section). Refit the carburetters (see **Section 2:5**). Tune and adjust them as described in **Section 2:4** after topping up the damper oil (see **Section 2:2**).

Centralizing the jet:

The jet needle must not bind or even touch the jet whilst it is in operation or at rest. The piston must be free to fall and bottom with its plastic stop resting on the carburetter bridge. Evidence of a fouling jet is usually encountered by an engine stalling in traffic or more positively by examining the needle and noting the polished, rubbing mark on the side of the needle. To correct this the jet must be centralized and it is not necessary to remove the carburetter(s) to do so.

1 Remove the air cleaner(s) (see **Section 2:10**).
2 Unscrew the piston chamber screws and lift off the chamber, spring and piston assembly. Refit them without the spring.
3 Refer to **FIG 2:7** and screw up the jet adjusting nut to its limit, make sure the jet is pushed fully upwards.
4 Slacken the jet locking nut and tap the adjusting nut to move the jet in its holder. With the lifting pin raise the piston about $\frac{1}{4}$ inch (6 mm) and allow it to fall onto the jet bridge. There will be a distinctive metallic 'clonk' as it does so.
5 Tighten the locking nut and recheck that the piston falls freely.
6 Refit the spring, top up the piston damper and turn down the jet adjusting nut approximately twelve flats to provide an initial setting. Tune and adjust the carburetters as described in **Section 2:4**.

2:7 Mixture weakening device (Tasman)

An engine normally requires a richer mixture when running at full throttle than it does under cruising conditions. The SU carburetter automatically achieves this on the majority of engines, but certain engines demand a greater 'mixture ratio spread' during the retrogression between full throttle and cruising due to, possibly, the design of the air intake and induction passages. To prevent an over-rich mixture entering the engine under these conditions an additional weakening device is incorporated.

The rate of fuel discharged from the jet is governed by the differences in air pressure between that existing in the float chamber and the air pressure over the jet. Referring to **FIG 2:9** a weakening device is fitted which is designed to reduce air pressure—create a depression—in the float chamber and reduce the rate of flow to the jet when the throttle is partly open under cruising conditions. The device is fitted to the float chamber lid and consists of a venturi which is connected to a drilling through the carburetter body and emerges close to the throttle disc edge, but on the inner side of the disc. The other end contains a calibrated air bleed and is connected to the air intake passage by a flexible tube. A central drilling in the device connects with the float chamber.

During idling and full throttle openings the effect on the float chamber air pressure is negligible and the carburetter performs all the necessary functions to provide a balanced mixture, but it is within the cruising ranges, at part throttle openings, that the device operates at its maximum efficiency.

Servicing is confined to keeping the device clean internally and ensuring the washers and connecting tubes are maintained in a good condition.

2:8 The damper control (manual models)

Adjusting:

1 Refer to **FIG 2:10**, slacken the spindle lever and with the throttle in the shut position insert a .090 inch (2.29 mm) feeler gauge between the lever and the damper plunger (A). With the feeler gauge still inserted press down the spindle lever until the plunger bottoms, tighten the lever clamping nut.
2 Release the lever, remove the feeler and check that a small clearance exists between the lever arm and throttle spindle boss.
3 If the damping action is not suitable increase or decrease the setting in steps of .010 inch (.25 mm).
4 The Kimberley model is shown in **FIG 2:11**, adjust as described, but if a correct damping effect cannot be made remove the inner locknut and substitute thin steel washers until the correct position is obtained. Use a star washer on the outside.

2:9 Throttle linkage and cables

Tasman models:

There are two types of linkage employed, the first as shown in **FIG 2:10**.

Both types use progressive throttle opening cams and conventional cables. The outer section of the cable is held by a ferrule and the inner cable is held by a pinch bolt in the back of the cam.

The automatic transmission kickdown cable claw is positioned behind the throttle opening cam.

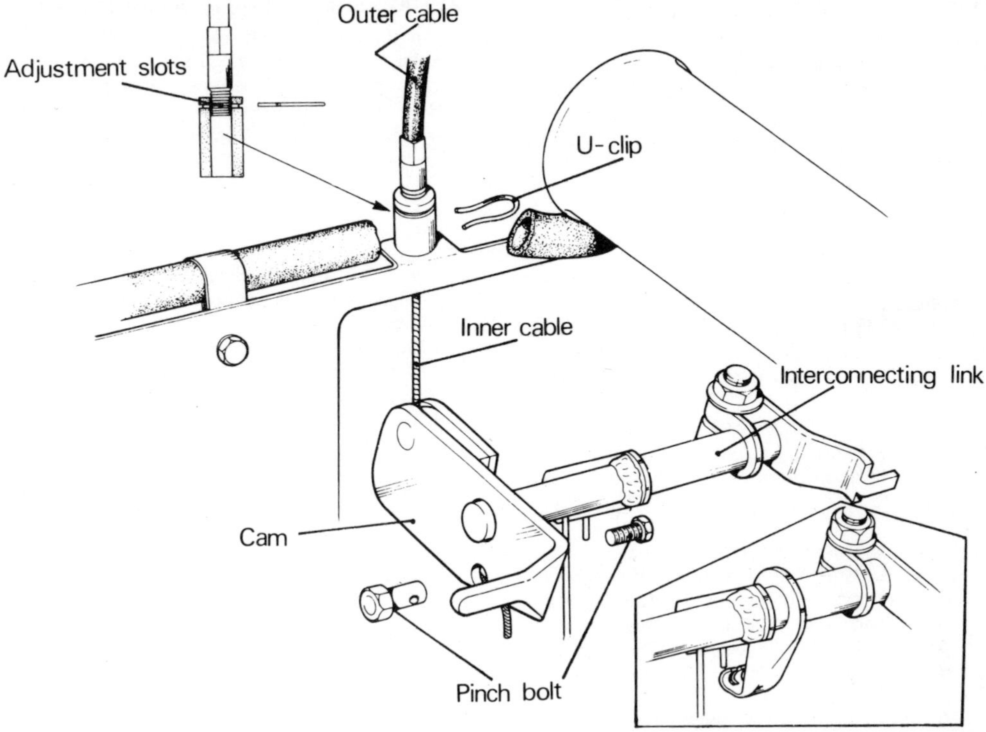

FIG 2:12 The throttle linkage adjustment to the initial Kimberley fitment. Inset shows automatic transmission models

Kimberley models:

The first type of linkage fitted to these models is shown in **FIG 2:12**. It consists of an adjustable cable connected by a pinch bolt to a progressive throttle opening cam on the interconnecting link. Adjustment is carried out by removing the U-clip and taking out any free play by lifting the outer cable and refitting the U-clip to lock into a lower slot on the outer cable.

The second type of linkage shown in **FIG 2:11** comprises a rolling cam device that is connected by a rod to the interconnecting link. Conventional operating cables are used.

Star washers hold the rod in position and these must be renewed if the rod is taken off.

The automatic models employed, originally, the type of cable shown in **FIG 2:12** with a built-in kickdown claw on the interconnecting link. Later models have a cable similar to that shown in **FIG 2:11**.

2:10 The air filters

Tasman:

The Tasman air cleaner components are shown in **FIG 2:13**. To renew the element at the appointed mileage, withdraw the cover and remove element. Do not attempt to clean and refit, scrap the element. The cover and element should not be disturbed at any other time. Clear the container before fitting new elements.

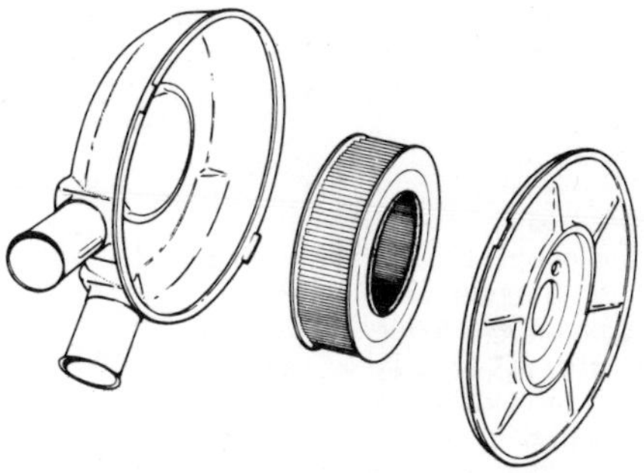
FIG 2:13 Tasman air cleaner components

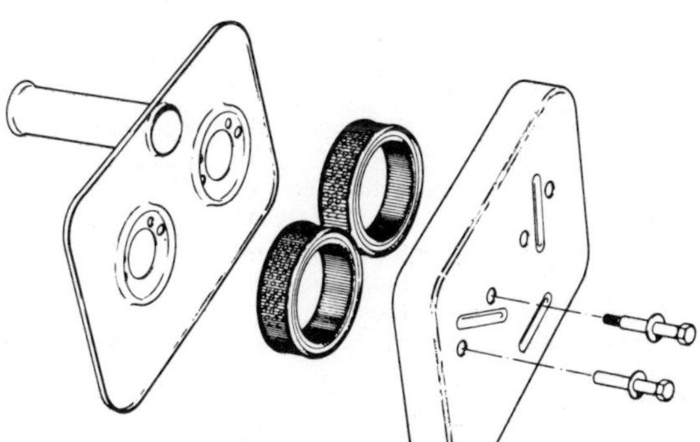
FIG 2:14 Kimberley air cleaner components

Kimberley:

Refer to **FIG 2:14** to identify the filter assembly of the Kimberley models. To renew the elements, unscrew and remove the nuts from the rear of the cleaner cover. Withdraw the assembly and remove the elements. Do not attempt to clean the elements, scrap them and obtain new ones. The elements should not be disturbed unnecessarily. Clean the container before fitting the new elements.

2:11 Fuel tank and indicator unit

Removing indicator unit:

1 Disconnect the battery.
2 Take up the boot floor mat and remove the gauge unit cover plate from the tank. Be aware of the dangers of an explosion by exposed flames, lights, smouldering tobacco and sparks.
3 Disconnect the wire at the push on terminal and release the unit locking ring.
4 Lift out the unit and sealing ring.

Removing the fuel tank:

1 Disconnect the battery.
2 With a $\frac{3}{16}$ inch Allen key and a clean container, remove the drain plug and allow the fuel to drain completely from the tank.
3 Take off the filler tube assembly, disconnect the fuel outlet pipe from the tank and the fuel gauge connector from the sender unit.
4 Support the tank and remove the six supporting bolts. Lower the tank and withdraw it.

Refitting:

Refitting the components in both instances is the reverse of the removal operations.

2:12 Fault diagnosis

(a) Restricted flow or no fuel from pump

1 Air vent in tank restricted
2 Fuel pipes blocked
3 Air leaks at pipe connections
4 Pump filter blocked
5 Pump diaphragm defective
6 Pump spring broken
7 Faulty valve assembly in pump.
8 Fuel vapourizing in pipelines due to heat

(b) Float chamber lacks fuel

1 Check (a)
2 Sticking float needle valve
3 Float level set too low

(c) Float chamber floods

1 Defective float needle valve
2 Float level set too high
3 Punctured float

(d) Excessive fuel consumption

1 Carburetters need adjusting
2 Fuel linkage
3 Sticking mixture control
4 Dirty air cleaner
5 Wrong carburetter needles
6 Engine running too hot
7 Brakes binding
8 Tyres too soft
9 Idling speed too high
10 Car overloaded

(e) Idling speed too high

1 Rich fuel mixture
2 Throttle or mixture controls sticking
3 Vacuum pipe to brake servo faulty
4 Worn throttle butterfly valves or spindles

(f) Poor idling

1 Check (c)
2 Vacuum pipe to distributor faulty
3 Vacuum pipe to brake servo faulty
4 Sticking piston
5 Worn throttle spindle and bushes

(g) Difficult starting

1 Check most of preceding Sections
2 Faulty ignition
3 Mechanical defects in engine
4 Air leaks at manifold joints

(h) Noisy fuel pump

1 Loose mountings
2 Air leaks on suction side or at diaphragm
3 Obstruction in fuel pipe
4 Clogged pump filter

CHAPTER 3

THE IGNITION SYSTEM

3:1 Description

The Lucas distributor, type 29.D6 incorporates two automatic ignition timing controls. The first operates centrifugally and the second by vacuum. These controls may be seen in **FIG 3:4**. In the centrifugal device (8 and 19), weights fly outwards against the tension of small springs as engine speed rises. This movement advances the contact breaker cams 7 relative to the distributor driving shaft 18. The contact points then break earlier to give advanced ignition timing.

The vacuum unit 9 is connected to the carburetter intake system by a pipe. Depression in this system operates on a diaphragm in the unit, the suction varying with the load on the engine. Diaphragm movement turns contact breaker plate 5. The distributor shaft is driven anticlockwise.

3:2 Routine maintenance

The following operations should be carried out every 6000 miles (10,000 km or six months). Refer to **FIG 3:1**.

Lubrication:

1 Release the cap clips and lift off the distributor cap. Lightly smear cams 2 with grease.

2 Using 20W engine oil, apply one drip to moving contact pivot 4.

3 Inject two or three drops of oil into the space indicated at 1.

4 Apply two or three drips of oil to recess in shaft 3. **Do not remove the screw.**

Make sure that oil and grease do not contaminate the points 5. Be sparing with lubricating oil at all times.

Checking:

With rotor arm fitted, turn the shaft anticlockwise and release it. It should return freely to its original position. Check the contact points 5 for dirt and pittings.

Adjusting contact breaker gap:

1 Remove the cap. Remove the rotor arm and turn the engine until the contact points are fully open. Turn the engine by operating the starter motor carefully. Alternatively, remove the sparking plugs, engage top gear and push the car forwards (not backwards).

2 With points fully open as shown in **FIG 3:2** use feelers to check the gap. Correct opening should be .014 to .016 inch (.36 to .41 mm). Make sure that the feeler blades are free from oil or grease.

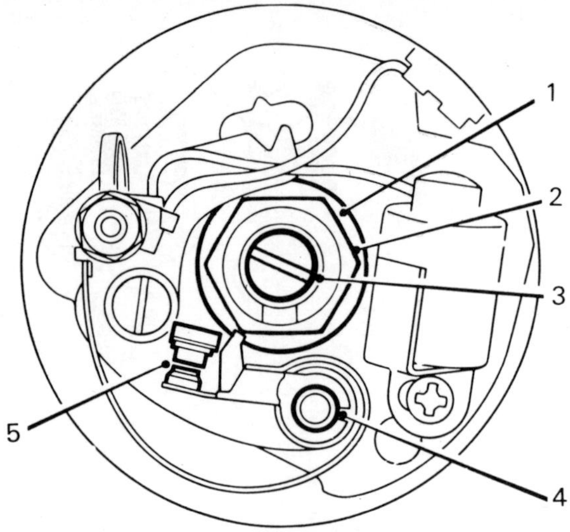

FIG 3:1 A typical plan view illustration of a Lucas distributor indicating lubrication points

Key to Fig 3:1 1 Centrifugal advance lubrication 2 Cam lobe lubrication 3 Cam bearing lubrication 4 Pivot post lubrication 5 Contact breaker points—avoid contaminating with oil

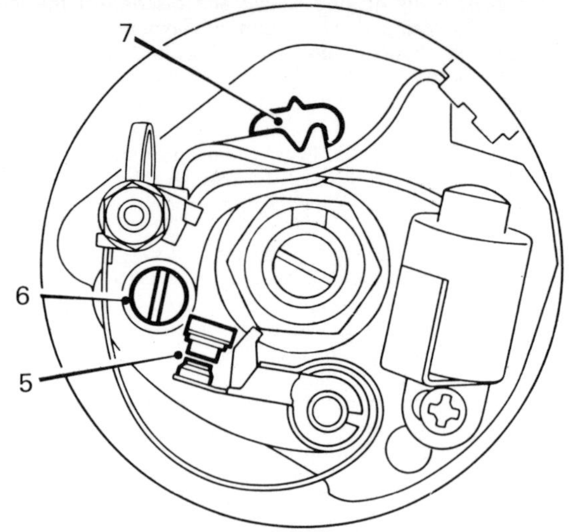

FIG 3:2 A typical plan view illustration of a Lucas distributor indicating method of contact breaker point adjustment

Key to Fig 3:2 5 Contact breaker points 6 Retaining screw 7 Adjusting notches

3 Adjust gap if necessary. Slacken screw 6 a little and insert a screwdriver blade in notches 7. Turn as required and then tighten screw. Turn the engine for a further check. If new points are fitted, increase the gap to .019 inch (.48 mm) to allow for bedding-in of the heel.

Cleaning or renewing the contact points:

If inspection shows that the points are dirty or pitted, they must be cleaned or remove for attention. Refer to **FIG 3:3**.

1 To clean the points without removal, use fine emery paper and then wipe clean with a fuel-moistened cloth.

2 To remove the contact set, remove the nut and both leads from the stud (part of 8). Remove screws 6. Lift off the contact set.

3 The contact assembly is available as a one-piece set, and badly eroded points are best serviced by fitting a new set. If the points may be cleaned up satisfactorily, use fine emery paper or a smooth carborundum stone, keeping the faces flat and square. Wipe clean afterwards.

4 When renewing a contact set, note how the bottom half of the insulating bush assembly locates the spring on the stud. The top bush is fitted above the lead terminals and the nut tightened moderately. Set the gap. Check the ignition timing (see **Section 3:4**).

The distributor cap and rotor arm:

Clean the inner surfaces of the cap. Note that slight spark erosion of the brass segments is normal. Press on the carbon brush in the centre of the cap (see 21 in **FIG 3:4**). It should spring out again quite freely and protrude about $\frac{3}{16}$ inch. Renew the cap if it is cracked or damaged.

The rotor arm is a push fit (see 20 in **FIG 3:4**). Slight spark erosion of the brass plate is normal. Renew the arm if erosion is excessive, if the arm is cracked or damaged or if it is loose on the shaft. When refitting it, make sure the key engages fully in the slot in the shaft.

Cleaning and adjusting the sparking plugs:

Remove the lead and partly unscrew the plug. Brush the seating free from dirt. Unscrew the plug. Mark leads for correct replacement.

Plugs are best cleaned on a sand-blasting machine. If this is not available, wash oily plugs in a solvent and dry thoroughly. Remove all carbon with a sliver of wood and wirebrush the threads. **Do not use a wire brush on the firing points.** Use a thin flat file to clean up the central tip till it is square with the side electrode and then restore the sparking surfaces of the side electrode until they are clean and bright. Check the gap between the electrodes, using feeler gauges set to .025 inch (.63 mm) or a Champion plug setting tool as shown in **FIG 3:5**. **Do not attempt to bend the central electrode.**

Refit the plugs by hand, screwing them down onto their gaskets. Tighten them a further quarter of a turn only. Refit the leads correctly. The correct firing order is 1, 5, 3, 6, 2, 4 in an anticlockwise direction, looking from the top of distributor.

3:3 Removing, refitting distributor

1 Adjust the crankshaft position to bring No. 1 piston to TDC at the end of the compression stroke (see **Chapter 1, Section 1:6**).

2 Take off the distributor cap and disconnect the low tension lead and the vacuum advance pipe.

3 Slacken the distributor clamp bolt and withdraw the distributor.

Refitting:

4 Refer to **FIG 1:36**, inset 'C' and note the position of the distributor drive slot, with the large offset 'A' uppermost. The engine setting should be in exactly the same position.

5 Insert the distributor into its housing so that the vacuum advance unit is facing towards the engine block. With the rotor, turn the shaft a little either way to engage the driving dogs so that the distributor drops fully into position. The rotor should be in a position to be aligned with the No. 1 segment in the distributor cap.

6 Tighten the clamp bolt, but not enough to prevent the distributor body from being turned by hand. Remove the rotor.

7 Turn the distributor anticlockwise until the points are closed and then turn it clockwise until the points are just opening. Tighten the clamp bolt and refit the rotor.

8 Reassemble the remaining parts.

3:4 Timing the ignition

The most accurate method of timing the ignition is with a stroboscopic lamp, although the method described in the previous section will suffice providing the engine is set at the TDC position with No. 1 piston at the top of the compression stroke. Another satisfactory method is the static setting in which a test lamp is wired into the ignition circuit. Stroboscopic and static are explained as follows.

Stroboscopic timing:

1 Ensure that the contact points are in good condition and set accurately (see **Section 3:2**).

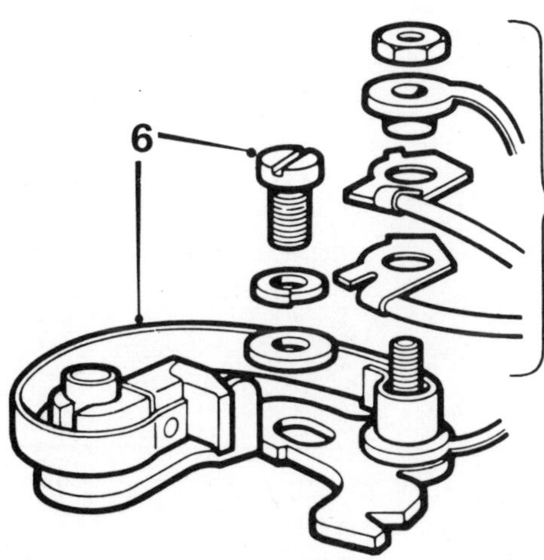

FIG 3:3 The contact breaker lead connections and method of assembling

Key to Fig 3:3 6 Retaining screw 8 Low tension lead connections

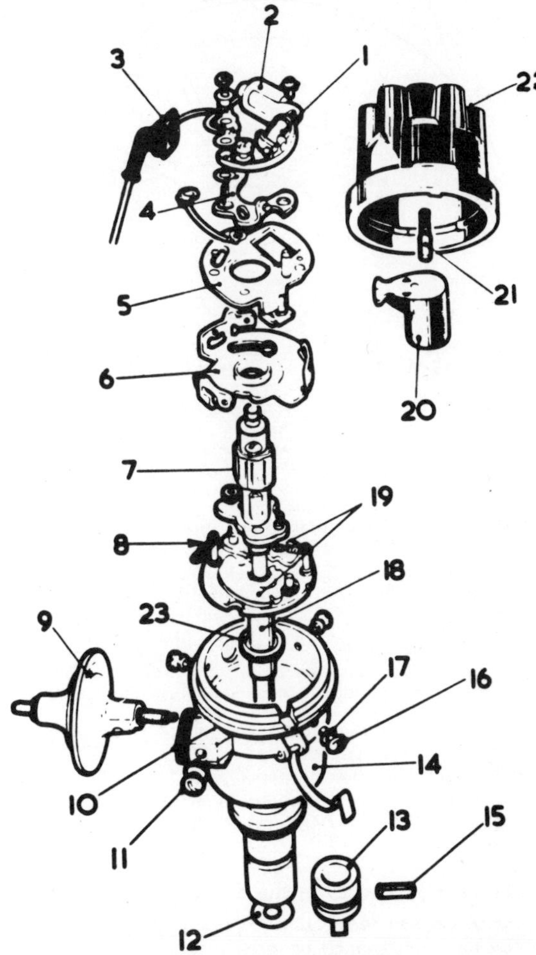

FIG 3:4 Components of a Lucas 29D6 distributor

Key to Fig 3:4 1 Movable contact 2 Condenser 3 Low tension lead 4 Fixed contact 5 Moving contact breaker plate 6 Contact breaker base plate 7 Cam 8 Automatic advance springs 9 Vacuum unit 10 Sealing grommet 11 Vacuum unit securing screw 12 Thrust washer 13 Driving dog 14 Body 15 Parallel pin 16 Base plate mounting screw 17 Spring washer 18 Shaft and action plate 19 Weight 20 Rotor arm 21 Brush and spring 22 Cap 23 Distance spacer

2 Turn the engine to bring the timing marks on the flywheel (manual) or the crankshaft pulley (automatic) in an accessible position.

3 With a very fine white dye pencil enhance the timing mark which indicates the 5 deg. BTDC setting on the flywheel or the calibrated plate behind the pulley. Mark also the tip of the pointer or the notch in the pulley.

4 Connect the timing light to the manufacturers instructions. Usually it is connected between No. 1 sparking plug and the No. 1 HT lead. Disconnect the vacuum advance pipe from the distributor.

5 Start the engine and adjust the idling speed to 600 rev/min (manual) or 550 rev/min (automatic). Point

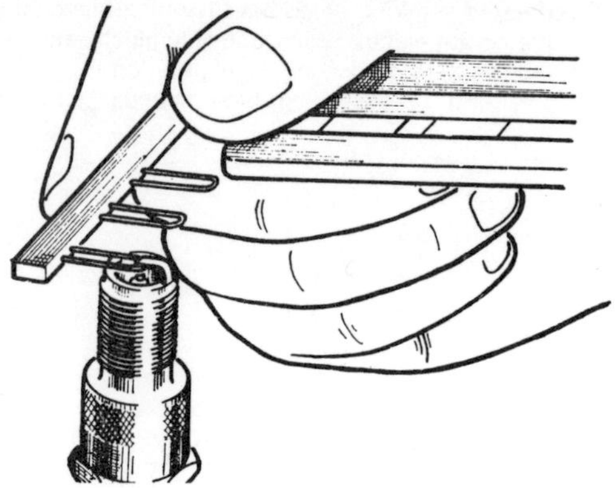

FIG 3:5 Adjusting sparking plug gap with a Champion gauge

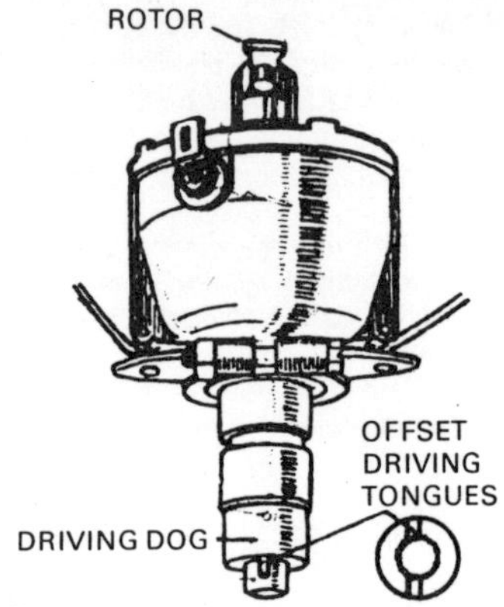

FIG 3:6 Illustrating the correct location of the distributor drive dog in relation to the rotor

the timing light at the marks which will have the effect of making the flywheel or pulley appear stationary. Note the alignment of the flywheel mark or pulley notch in relation to the pointer or calibrated plate. They should be perfectly aligned.

6 If necessary, slacken the clamp bolt on the distributor and turn the distributor body in the required direction to align the marks. Turning the body clockwise will advance the timing.

7 Tighten the clamp bolt and restore all connections and parts to their original position. Readjust the engine idling speed.

Static timing:

1 Turn the engine to bring the 5 deg. BTDC mark on the flywheel or calibrated plate aligned with the pointer or pulley notch. No. 1 piston must be at the top of the compression stroke. Confirm this by removing the distributor cap and checking the position of the rotor arm which should be aligned with the No. 1 segment inside the cap. Replace the distributor cap.

2 Connect a 12-volt test lamp with one lead to the low tension terminal on the distributor and the other lead to earth (in series). Switch on the ignition.

3 Slacken the distributor clamp bolt and turn the distributor anticlockwise a short distance, now turn the body clockwise until the lamp just lights. This is the correct setting indicating that the points have just opened.

4 Tighten the clamp bolt, disconnect the test lamp and switch off the ignition.

3:5 Dismantling distributor

Before removing and dismantling the distributor to overhaul and renew defective items, enquire through the local service garages regarding the availability of component parts for the Lucas 29D6 distributor.

1 Remove the distributor as described in **Section 3:3**.

2 Before dismantling, check the shaft end float by referring to **FIG 3:4** and inserting a feeler gauge between the driving dog 13 and the thrust washer 12. The end float should be within a tolerance of .004 and .008 inch (.10 and .20 mm). If not, the driving dog should be removed during the dismantling process and a selective thrust washer fitted to obtain the correct end float.

3 Pull the rotor arm 20 off the cam spindle. Unscrew the vacuum unit securing screw 11, uncouple the actuating link and detach the vacuum unit.

4 Unscrew and remove the three screws 16 that secure the base plate 6 to the body. Push the low tension lead grommet into the body of the distributor and lift out the whole base plate assembly and lead.

5 To dismantle the assembly take off the nut that retains the low tension lead and lift off the associate components. Remove the screw and washers that secure the breaker plate 5 to the base plate 6.

6 Note the location and remove the advance springs 8. Unscrew the cam spindle screw, mark the cam base to ensure it is refitted to the same driving post and lift off the cam spindle.

7 If the driving dog 13 is to be removed, mark the dog and shaft to ensure correct relocation. Drive out the pin 15 and take off the dog and thrust washer 12.

Inspecting:

8 Examine the contact points for pitting or signs of overheating, the leads for damage or deterioration, for indications of binding or pick-up of the moving contact breaker plate, the centrifugal springs for distortion or stretch and the vacuum unit for leaks.

9 A suspect capacitor (condenser) is usually indicated by the burning of the contact points, without the use of a suitable meter to check it the best method, to confirm its condition, is to substitute a new one.

10 Examine the distributor cap for fractures or evidence of 'tracking'. Tracking will be confirmed by the discovery of a thin black line running between the segments inside the cap.

11 Examine for wear in the drive shaft and the bush in the shaft housing.

12 Renew all parts having any of the faults mentioned on any that are at all suspect.

Reassembling:

13 Reassemble the parts in the reverse order of dismantling noting the following points:
Lubricate the automatic advance mechanism, the centre of the cam spindle and the contact point pivot post with oil.
Ensure when refitting the driving dog it is located to the original markings. Refer also to **FIG 3:6** to confirm its location and relative position with the rotor.
Reset the points gap as described in **Section 3:2**.

14 Refit the distributor to the engine as described in **Section 3:3**.

3:6 Sparking plug leads and plug condition

The leads are readily removable by pulling them off the sparking plugs and the distributor cap. If renewal is attempted, change the leads one at a time to avoid mistakes in the firing order (see end of **Section 3:2**).

The condition of the firing end of sparking plugs will give some indication of engine tune as follows:

A normal deposit should be brown to greyish tan in colour, this being the result of correct carburation and a mixture of high-speed and low-speed driving. If the deposits are white or yellowish they indicate greater heat due to long periods of constant speed driving, probably rather fast. Black, wet deposits are caused by oil entering the combustion chamber past worn pistons and bores or down valve stems. If the black deposits are dry and fluffy they usually indicate running with a rich mixture, but they may also be due to incomplete combustion through defective ignition or excessive idling.

Overheated sparking plugs have a white, blistered look about the centre electrode and the side electrode may be badly eroded. The cause may be poor cooling, wrong ignition tuning or sustained high speeds with heavy loads.

3:7 Fault diagnosis

(a) Engine will not fire

1 Battery discharged
2 Distributor contact points dirty, pitted or badly adjusted
3 Distributor cap dirty, cracked or 'tracking'
4 Carbon brush inside cap not touching rotor
5 Faulty cable, switch, or loose connections in low-tension circuit
6 Distributor rotor arm cracked
7 Faulty coil
8 Broken contact breaker spring
9 Contact points stuck open
10 High-tension lead from coil to distributor detached or broken

(b) Engine misfires

1 Check 2, 3, 5 and 7 in (a)
2 Weak contact breaker spring
3 High-tension plug or coil leads cracked or damaged
4 Loose sparking plug(s)
5 Sparking plug insulation cracked
6 Sparking plug cap incorrectly set
7 Ignition timing too far advanced

NOTES

CHAPTER 4

THE COOLING SYSTEM

4:1 Description

The system is pressurized to raise the boiling point of the coolant. The rise in pressure is, however, restricted to 13 lb/sq in (.91 kg/sq cm) by a spring-loaded valve in the radiator tank filler cap.

The natural thermo-syphon action of heated water tending to rise to the top tank of the radiator, and falling down through the core to be cooled, is augmented by a centrifugal impeller pump which is mounted on the left-hand end of the cylinder block. The outer end of the pump spindle carries a pulley, the drive being by V-belt from a pulley on the crankshaft.

A thermostatically-controlled electric fan is mounted behind the forward-facing radiator (see **FIG 4:1**).

To secure a rapid warm-up from cold, there is a thermostat valve in a housing attached to the head. This is closed when the coolant is cold, thus preventing circulation through the top hose to the radiator. When the coolant heats up, the thermostat valve opens and coolant is then free to pass through the radiator.

4:2 Routine maintenance

Topping-up radiator:

Refer to **FIG 4:1**. Note that there is pressure in the system when it is hot. In these circumstances, never remove filler cap 2 without carefully releasing the pressure first. Remove the tank cap slowly to release the pressure and take precautions against scalding from steam, by protecting the hand with a cloth. Check every 3000 miles (5000 km or three months). This is not a 'hard and fast' rule so use a little discretion.

Having removed the tank cap, check the coolant level inside either visually or with a home-made calibrated dipstick. If it is below the filler neck by more than 1 inch (25.4 mm) add fresh coolant. Use antifreeze mixture if it is in use in the system. Do not overfill. To allow for expansion maintain the level at 1 inch (25 mm) below the filler neck. Remember that topping-up with water will dilute the strength of antifreeze.

Check the system for leaks if there is a persistent need for topping-up.

Adjusting belt tension:

Refer to **FIG 4:4**. Every 6000 miles (10,000 km or six months), check belt tension midway between the pulleys on the longest run of the belt.

Deflection under moderate hand pressure should be approximately $\frac{1}{2}$ inch (13 mm).

Adjust if necessary by slackening bolts 1 and 2. To tighten the belt, push the alternator away from the engine and retighten the bolts, bolt 2 first. It is best to press on the alternator by the bracket at the drive end. Do not over tension the belt as it will lead to bearing wear.

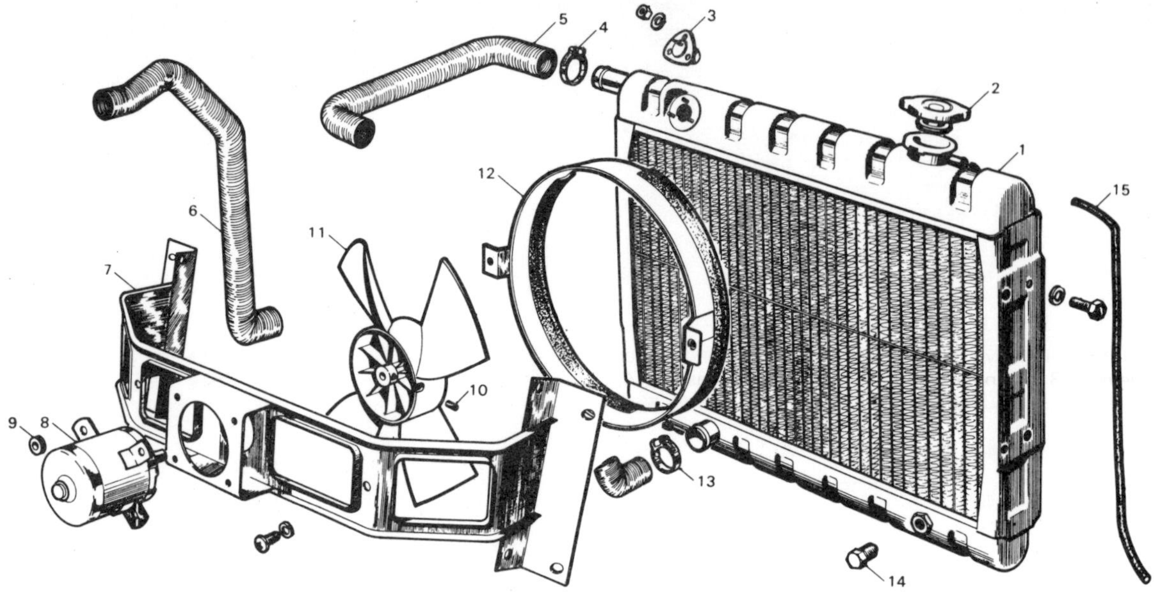

FIG 4:1 Radiator, fan and associated components

Key to Fig 4:1 1 Radiator 2 Filler cap 3 Fanstat 4 Hose clip 5 Top radiator hose 6 Bottom radiator hose 7 Fan mounting bracket 8 Fan motor 9 Rubber grommet 10 Grub screw 11 Plastic fan 12 Cowl 13 Hose clip 14 Drain plug 15 Overflow pipe

Removing, refitting belt:

1 Disconnect the battery.
2 Refer to **FIG 4:4** and slacken the bolts 1 and 2, push the alternator towards the engine to relieve all tension from the belt.
3 Unwind the belt from the pump, alternator and crankshaft pulleys. On automatic transmission models it may be necessary to lever the power unit over slightly to allow clearance between the crankshaft damper and the body.

Refitting:

4 Refit in the reverse order of removal. Adjust the belt tension. Adjust again after the first 300 miles (480 km).

4:3 Draining and refilling system

Draining:

Take note of the warning at the start of the preceding section. Refer to **FIGS 4:2** and **4:3** and do the following:

1 Remove the radiator drain plug. Remove drain plug from front righthand side of cylinder block.
Take off the radiator filler cap.

Flushing:

To ensure an efficient circulation of the coolant and to discourage the formation of scale and reduce the sediment in the radiator, it should be flushed out thoroughly with a hose inserted in the filler neck. Allow the water to run through until it comes out of the drain plugs free of sediment.

If scaling in the radiator is excessive the radiator should be removed and 'back-flushed' with clean water. Turn the radiator base upwards and insert the hose into the filler plug recess.

Refilling:

1 Refit the drain plugs and ensure that all hose connections are tight. Refill through the radiator filler neck until the water can just be seen. Start the engine and run it until it is warm, check the level again and top up to within 1 inch (25 mm) below the bottom of the filler neck. See **Section 4:7** for details of antifreeze mixtures.

4:4 Servicing fan and radiator

Removing fan and motor:

Refer to **FIG 4:1** and do the following; additionally on automatic models the bottom locking platform must be removed.

1 If system is hot, heed the warning at the start of **Section 4:2**. Remove radiator drain plug and filler tank cap. Disconnect the battery.
2 Remove cylinder block plug to drain the system. Disconnect cables from fan motor and horn relay.
3 Disconnect top hose 5 and bottom hose 6 from radiator. Remove the horn relay.
4 Remove the four bolts securing radiator assembly to the front panel. Withdraw the assembly but do not lift it by the fan cowl.

Servicing fan motor:

Remove the two bolts on each side of the radiator to release the motor carrier. Remove fan by unscrewing the grub screw securing it to the motor shaft. Release motor from carrier (4 screws and nuts).

Test motor by connecting it (without fan) to a 13.5 volt battery supply with a moving coil ammeter in series. Meter should read 3 amp (maximum) after 60 seconds from cold. The running speed should lie between 3500 and 4000 rev/min after 60 seconds from cold.

Dismantling motor:

If repairs are indicated, dismantle the motor. Refer to **FIG 4:5**. Remove bolts 2 and withdraw end cover assembly 3 complete. Remove circlip and washers 4. Withdraw armature 5, washer 6 and circlip 7. Release brush carrier (8).

Check that brushes are not less than $\frac{3}{16}$ inch (4.76 mm) long. Renew brush gear set if necessary. Clean commutator (copper segments at lefthand end of armature 5). Polish with fine glasspaper (not emery cloth). A badly worn commutator may be skimmed in a lathe. Clean swarf from between the segments **but do not undercut the insulation.**

Reassembling:

Reverse the dismantling procedure. Lubricate shaft and bearing bushes with Shell Turbo 41 oil. Line up marks arrowed, when refitting cover. Fit spring washer between shim washers at 4. Tighten through-bolts to 14 lbf in (.17 kgfm). Test the motor as described earlier. If it still does not operate it will be necessary to have the windings checked at a Service station.

Refitting motor:

Reverse the dismantling procedure, making sure that the fan grubscrew engages the dimple in the motor shaft.

Refitting radiator assembly:

This is a simple reversal of the dismantling procedure. When finished refill with coolant as described in **Section 4:3**.

'Fanstat' switch and line fuse:

The fan motor will operate only when the 'Fanstat' switch closes the circuit at a predetermined coolant temperature. The switch, acting also as a sensing unit is positioned in the radiator header tank (see 3 in **FIG 4:1**).

If the fan is not operating correctly, check that there is a voltage reading at the switch terminal, if this is in order pull off the terminal lead and short it to earth. If the motor now operates the 'Fanstat' switch is faulty.

To remove it, disconnect the battery. Disconnect the cable from the switch. Lift out the switch and joint washer after removing the three nuts and spring washers.

Line fuse:

To prevent damage to the fan motor in the event of the fan blades fouling, or an overheating of the engine if the

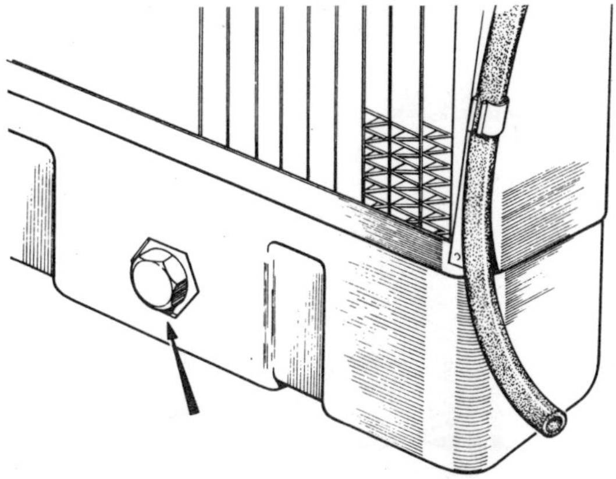

FIG 4:2 Radiator drain plug

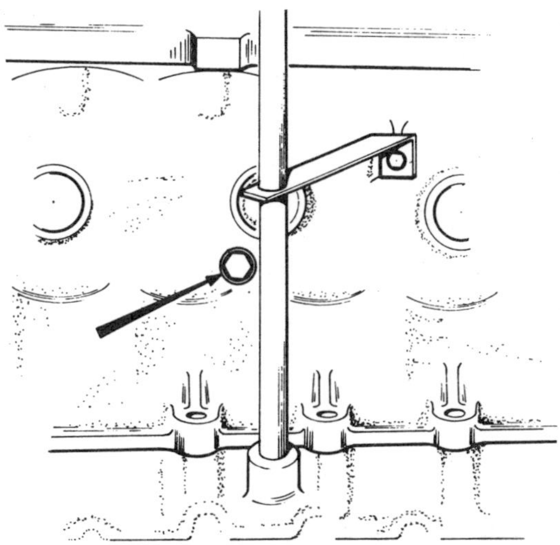

FIG 4:3 Cylinder block drain plug

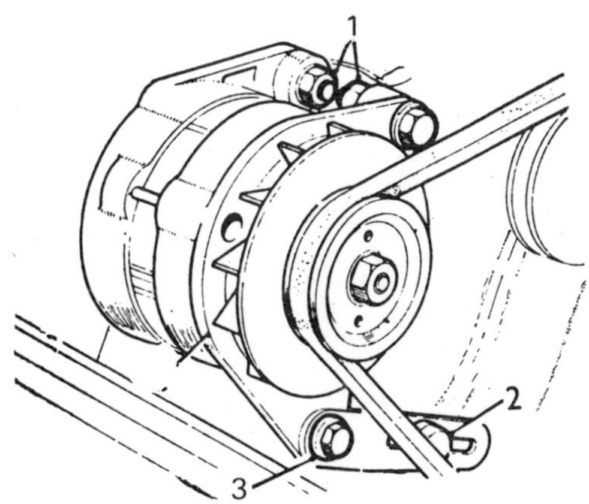

FIG 4:4 Drive belt adjustment and alternator securing bolts

Key to Fig 4:4 1 Pivot bolts 2 Adjusting link bolt (replaced by a long hexagon stud on automatic transmission models) 3 Securing bolt

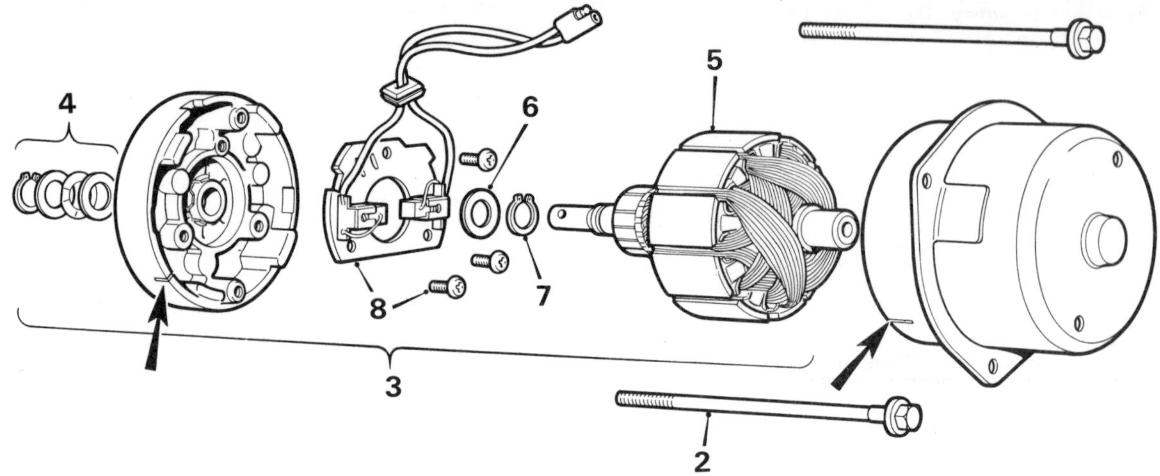

FIG 4:5 Components of typical fan motor

Key to Fig 4:5 2 Through bolts 3 End cover and armature assembly 4 Slim and bowed washers 5 Armature 6 Thrust washer 7 Circlip 8 Brush carrier screws

'A2' fuse blows, a line fuse has been added (see **FIG 4:6**). If vehicles are not equipped with this device it is recommended by the manufacturers that one should be fitted.

1 Disconnect the battery and remove the water bottle.
2 From the connector on the bulk-head, disconnect the two purple cables F3, separate and identify the one that operates the horn, fit a new terminal and replace it in the connector.
3 Disconnect the brown cable from D4 and cut off the terminal. Remove approximately $\frac{1}{2}$ inch (12 mm) of insulation from the end of the brown and remaining purple cable, twist them together and fit a new terminal. Connect the two cables into the D4 station in the connector.
4 At the fan relay cut the purple cable C1 approximately 4 inch (100 mm) from the terminal. Insert a suitable 20 amp line fuse as shown in the illustration.
5 Refit the washer bottle and reconnect the battery.

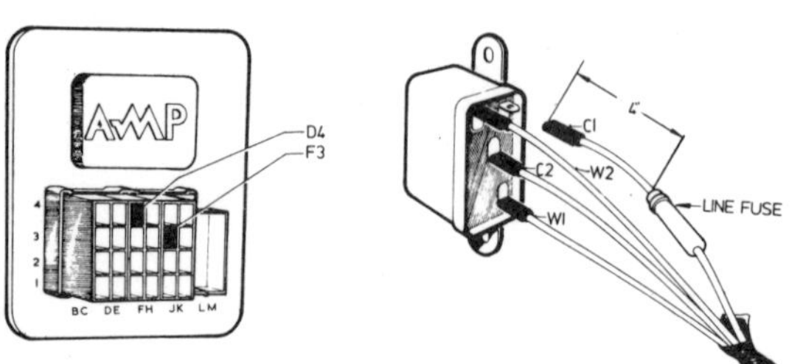

FIG 4:6 Fitting a line fuse into the fan motor circuit

4:5 Removing water pump

1 If system is hot, follow the instruction at the start of **Section 4:2**. Remove the radiator filler plug and lower the coolant level by removing cylinder block plug.
2 Slacken alternator pivot bolts and remove the drive belt.
3 Disconnect by-pass hose and heater hose. Remove pulley (3 bolts). Remove three bolts to release water pump from block. The pump is best serviced as an assembly and renewed on an exchange basis.

Refitting pump:

Reverse the dismantling procedure. Fit dished side of pulley inwards. Tighten pump securing bolts to 20 lbf ft (2.77 kgf m). Tighten pulley bolts to 8 lbf ft (1.11 kgf m). Adjust belt tension (see **Section 4:2**). Refill cooling system (see **Section 4:3**).

4:6 Servicing thermostat

If system is hot, drain it after referring to the start of **Section 4:2**. It is only necessary to remove the cylinder block drain plug to lower the coolant level. Disconnect the top hose and remove bolts to release outlet and gasket. Withdraw thermostat.

If valve is stuck open, thermostat must be renewed. To check operation, immerse thermostat in water, heat the water and note the temperature at which the valve opens. The thermostat and thermometer must not touch the container. The standard thermostat should open at 82°C (179°F). This temperature is stamped on the base of the thermostat.

Refit the thermostat on a new gasket and refill the system (see **Section 4:3**).

To remove the thermostat housing, partially drain the system as described in the preceding instructions.

Remove the battery. Disconnect the wiring from the thermal transmitter. Disconnect the top hose and the heater hose on the underside. Remove the two bolts. There is a sealing gasket between the housing and the adaptor and the cylinder head (see **FIG 1:2**).

Refit in the reverse order and then refill the system (see **Section 4:3**).

4:7 Antifreeze solution

For protection in freezing conditions, add an approved antifreeze to the cooling water. This may be Unipart Frostbeat, Bluecol antifreeze or one conforming to BS.3151 or BS.3152.

The addition of $4\frac{1}{4}$ pints (2.4 litres) gives a 25% solution that will start freezing at —13°C (9°F) and will be frozen solid at —26°C (—15°F).

$5\frac{3}{4}$ pints (3.2 litres) will make a $33\frac{1}{3}$% solution that starts freezing at —19°C (—2°F) and will be frozen solid at —36°C (—33°F).

Double the volume for 25% solution gives a 50% solution that starts freezing at —36°C (—33°F) and is solid at —48°C (—53°F).

When antifreeze is used, topping-up with plain water will dilute the solution and reduce the protection. Use antifreeze solution for topping-up.

4:8 Fault diagnosis

(a) Poor coolant circulation

1 Radiator core blocked
2 Engine water passages restricted
3 Coolant level too low
4 Loose belt
5 Defective thermostat
6 Collapsed radiator hoses

(b) Overheating

1 Check (a)
2 Faulty ignition or carburation
3 Tight engine
4 Binding brakes, slipping clutch
5 Defective fan motor or thermostatic switch

(c) Internal water leakage

1 Cracked cylinder wall or head
2 Loose cylinder head bolts
3 Faulty head gasket

(d) Corrosion

1 Impurities in water
2 Infrequent draining and flushing

NOTES

CHAPTER 5

THE CLUTCH

5:1 Description

The mechanical components of the clutch are shown in **FIG 5:1**, the hydraulics are dealt with later in the Chapter. Flywheel 6 is bolted to the crankshaft. Inside the flywheel is a pressure plate 4 and a driven plate 5. The driven plate is splined to the primary gear in the transmission, and is provided with friction linings. Lugs on the pressure plate pass through clearance holes in the flywheel and these are bolted to the flexible drive straps 7.

Diaphragm assembly 10 is also bolted to the same ends of the straps, so that pressure on the assembly can be made to force pressure plate 4 away from the flywheel against powerful spring pressure inside assembly 10.

This spring pressure, when the clutch is engaged, nips the driven plate between the pressure plate and the flywheel so that the whole assembly will rotate as one unit, transmitting drive from the engine to the gearbox.

When the clutch pedal is depressed, lever 17 presses on release bearing 13. This bearing in turn presses on plate 12 which is bolted to the diaphragm spring assembly 10. The spring is compressed and the pressure plate is pushed away from the flywheel, thus relieving the nip on the driven plate. In consequence, the plate slows down and the drive from the engine to the gearbox is disconnected. The drive is restored when the clutch pedal is released, the engagement being smoothly taken up by the friction linings on the driven plate.

5:2 Routine maintenance

Every 6000 miles (10,000 km or six months) check the fluid level in the clutch master cylinder reservoir. Note that this is the smaller of the two reservoirs. If necessary, top-up to the level indicated on the outside. It is essential to use the correct fluid. This is BLMC HBF6 Brake Fluid or a brake fluid conforming to the same specification, consult your service garage about this and do not use any other type of fluid.

Check that the vent hole in the cap is clear. Take care not to let the fluid drip onto the body paintwork as it is a solvent. Wipe the cap before unscrewing it so that dirt cannot fall inside.

At the same mileage, check the condition of the pipe and hose in the clutch hydraulic system.

5:3 Bleeding the clutch system

This will be necessary if the clutch hydraulic system has been dismantled or if there is a 'spongy' feel to clutch pedal operation, with the possibility of the clutch not fully disengaging.

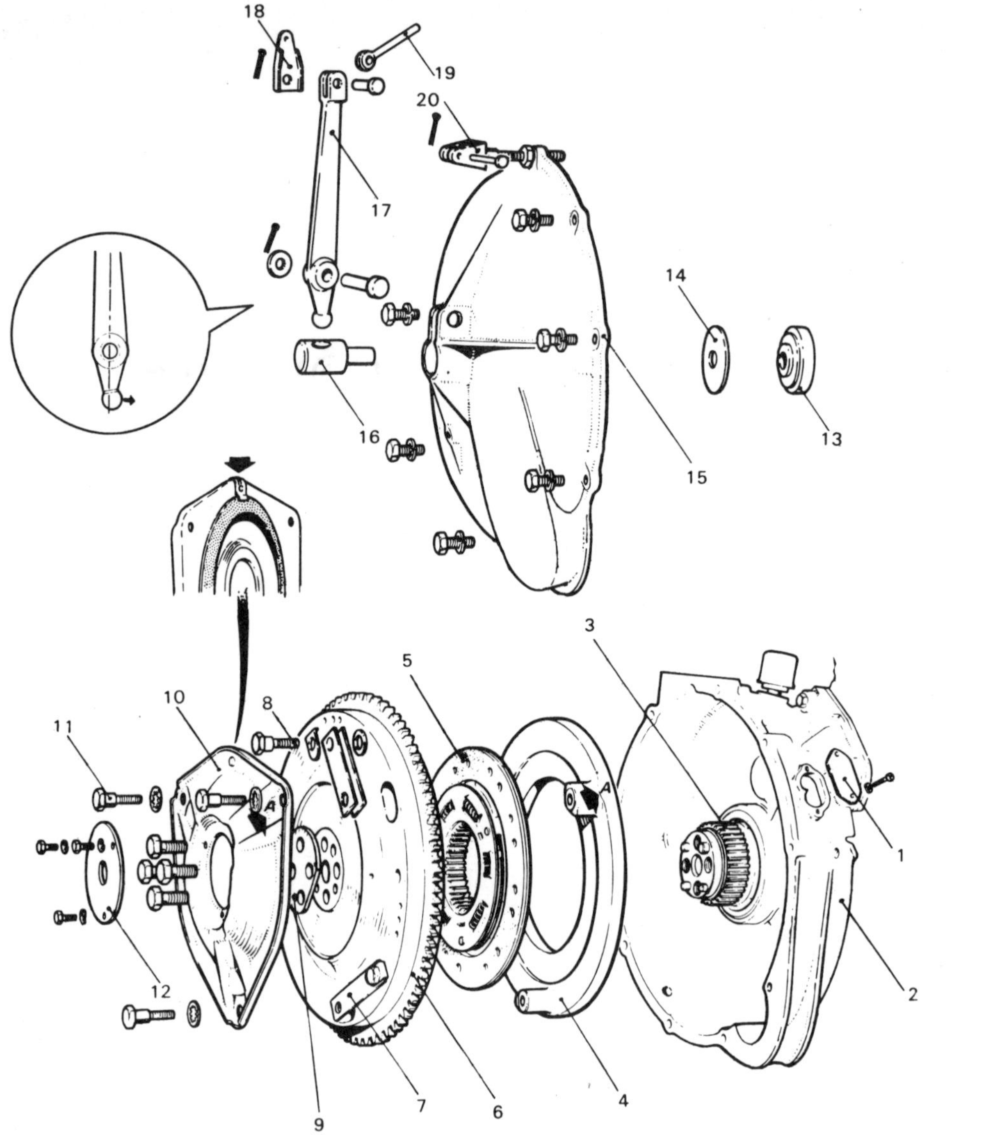

FIG 5 : 1 Components of clutch mechanism

Key to Fig 5 : 1 1 Timing hole cover 2 Flywheel housing 3 Crankshaft primary gear 4 Clutch pressure plate 5 Clutch driven plate 6 Flywheel 7 Driving strap 8 Shouldered bolt—driving strap 9 Packing plate 10 Diaphragm spring housing 11 Shouldered bolt—diaphragm to pressure plate 12 Thrust plate 13 Clutch release bearing 14 Oil slinger 15 Clutch cover 16 Clutch throwout plunger 17 Clutch withdrawal lever 18 Spring retainer 19 Slave cylinder pushrod 20 Clutch adjustment fork

The bleed screw is on the clutch slave cylinder (see 10 in **FIG 5 : 7**. Remove the dust cap and attach a rubber or plastic tube to the nipple. Immerse the free end of the tube in a small quantity of clean brake fluid in a glass jar. Make sure that the reservoir is topped-up with the correct fluid (see **Section 5 : 2**). Check this level during the operation to make sure that it has not fallen too low.

Open the bleed screw about three-quarters of a turn, get a second operator to depress the clutch pedal fully, and while it is held down, close the bleed screw. The pedal may then be released. Continue with this sequence, watching the immersed end of the tube for air bubbles. When they cease, tighten the bleed screw during a down stroke of the pedal. Check the fluid level in the reservoir. Restore the dust cap.

5 : 4 Servicing the release bearing

Refer to **FIG 5 : 2**. Note how the lever is operated by the slave cylinder. The lower ball-end engages with a throw-out plunger to press the release bearing inwards to disengage the clutch. A worn bearing is renewed as follows:

1 Take off the clutch return spring and disconnect the earth strap from the clutch cover.
2 Remove the clutch cover securing bolts and withdraw the cover.
3 Remove the clevis pin to release lever 17 (see **FIG 5:1**). Remove the clutch adjustment bolt 20 and extract the clevis pin from the adjustment fork and lever inwards. Lift the release bearing and throwout plunger assembly from the cover.
4 Press the bearing off the plunger and fit a new one. Reverse the dismantling procedure.

5:5 Servicing the clutch assembly

Refer to **FIG 5:1** and proceed as follows:

1 Remove cover and release bearing as in preceding Section. Remove thrust plate 12 and retaining plate 9. Remove the timing hole cover 1.
2 Use a lever through the timing hole to prise the flywheel and clutch assembly off the crankshaft and primary gear, working evenly all round.

Dismantling:

1 Slacken bolts 11 evenly. Mark all components including straps 7 and the shouldered setscrews for correct re-location. Remove the spring housing 10. Note the letter 'A' on diaphragm spring and pressure plate which line up with flywheel timing marks (arrowed).
2 Lift flywheel 6 off pressure plate. Remove driven plate 5. Unlock bolts 8 and remove the driving straps 7, noting the spacing washer between the straps and the flywheel.

Inspecting:

Clean the parts and check for wear or damage. Check the pressure plate for cracks or scoring. Examine diaphragm spring assembly 10 for wear or broken parts. Check the driving straps for elongated holes and the securing bolts for wear.

Check the linings on driven plate 5. They should be smooth and polished and light in colour. Renew the plate if they are worn thin or are uneven in thickness, or if they have been contamined with oil. A very dark opaque colour is a sign of burning and oil contamination.

Check for broken or loose springs in the shock-absorbing hub and for worn spring apertures in the clutch centre. Look for wear of the hub splines. It is always a good plan to renew the plate if there is any doubt about its condition.

Reassembling:

Check, and if necessary, adjust the primary gear and float (see **Section 1:8**). Place pressure plate 4 on a flat surface. Fit the driven plate 5 with springs uppermost. This side is also marked 'FLYWHEEL SIDE'.

Drop flywheel 6 into place and refit the driving straps to the flywheel with the spacers in between, see **FIG 5:3**. Use new lockwashers and make bolts fingertight.

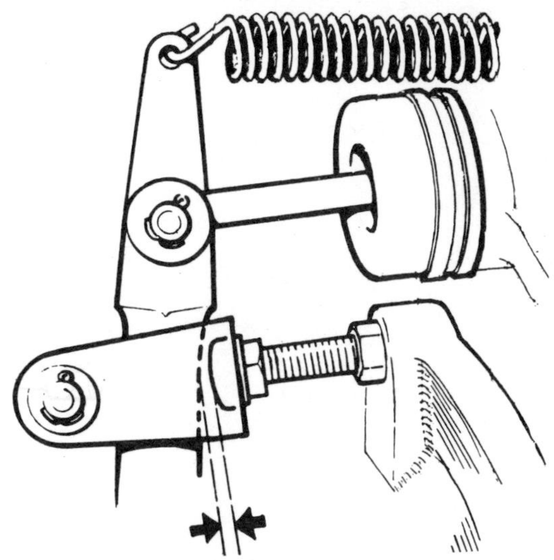

FIG 5:2 Slave cylinder connection and clutch adjustment

Fit diaphragm 10 with all marks aligned including the letter 'A' (arrowed in **FIG 5:1**) with timing marks on flywheel. Do not tighten bolts 11.

Tightening driving strap-to-flywheel bolts 8 to 18 lb ft (2.5 kgm) and turn up the locking tabs.

Refitting:

1 Fit assembly to crankshaft and tighten flywheel bolts to 60 lb ft (8.3 kgm).
2 Tighten diaphragm bolts 11 to 15 to 18 lb ft (2.1 to 2.5 kgm). Refit bearing plate 12 and tighten the bolts to 10 lb ft (1.4 kgm).
3 Refit the release bearing and cover (see preceding Section).

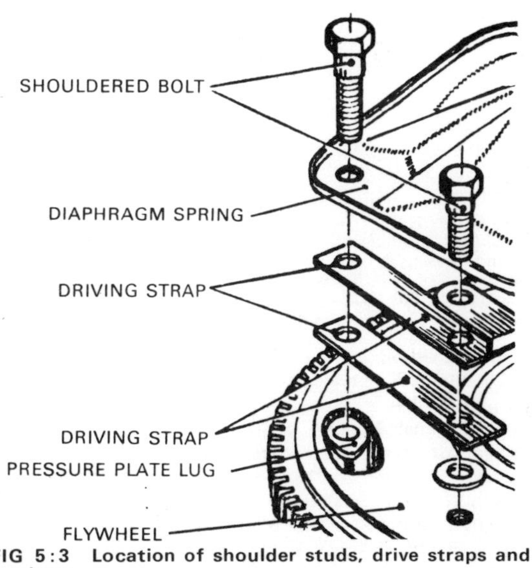

FIG 5:3 Location of shoulder studs, drive straps and washers

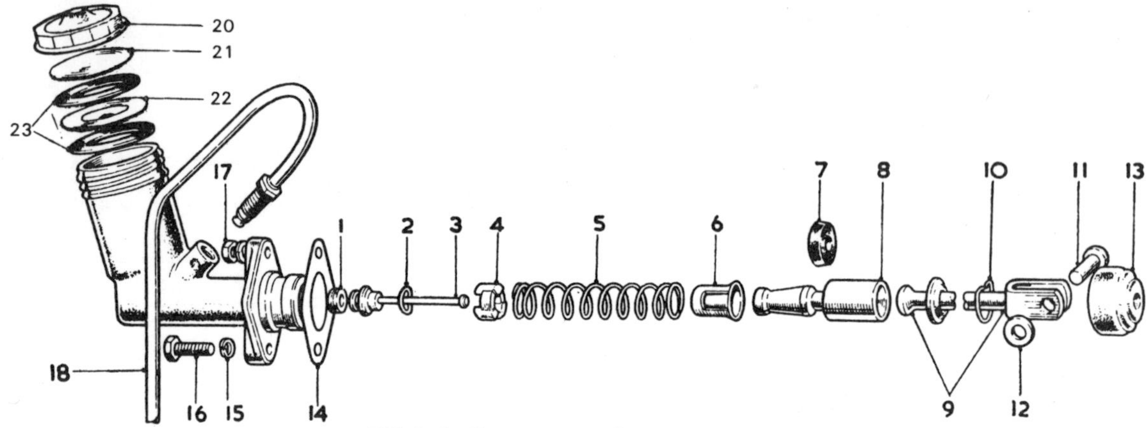

FIG 5:4 **Components of master cylinder**

Key to Fig 5:4 1 Valve seal 2 Curved washer—valve stem 3 Valve stem 4 Valve spacer 5 Spring 6 Spring retainer (thimble) 7 Plunger seal 8 Plunger 9 Pushrod 10 Circlip—pushrod 11 Clevis pin—pedal to master cylinder 12 Plain washer 13 Dust cover 14 Packing 15 Spring washer 16 Screw 17 Nut—stud 18 Master to slave cylinder pipe 19 Filler cap gasket 20 Filler cap 21 Flat plate 22 Baffle plate 23 Rubber seals

5:6 Adjusting the clutch

Referring to **FIG 5:2** it is important that a clearance of .067 inch (1.7 mm) should exist between the inner face of the lever and the stop bolt. This is to provide a clearance between the release bearing and thrust plate, which will diminish as the linings wear on the driven plate. If the adjustment is neglected clutch slip will occur.

1 Uncouple the return spring from the lever.
2 Pull the lever outwards as far as it will go and with a feeler gauge measure the gap (arrowed).
3 To adjust, slacken the locknut and turn the stop bolt in the required direction to obtain the correct clearance.
4 Tighten the locknut. Recheck the gap.
5 Refit the return spring.

5:7 Servicing the master cylinder

Refer to **FIGS 5:4** and **5:5** and proceed as follows.

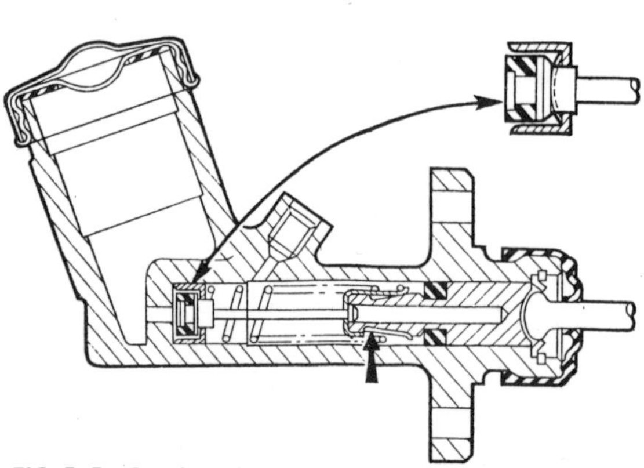

FIG 5:5 Section through assembled master cylinder enlarged valve assembly

Removing:

1 Release clutch pedal from operating fork (see **FIG 5:2**). Disconnect pipe 18 from master cylinder and plug hole and pipe end to exclude dirt.
2 Unscrew nut 17 and bolt 16. Withdraw cylinder from bulkhead, noting the adjustment shims 14 for pedal travel that are fitted under the flange.

Overhauling:

1 Remove dust cover 13. Extract circlip 10 and remove pushrod.
2 Withdraw piston assembly 8. Refer also to **FIG 5:6** and lift leaf 2 in thimble 3 and pull the piston 4 out of the thimble. Remove spacer and curved washer 2 from valve stem. Remove seal 1.

Inspecting:

Clean the cylinder in methylated spirit and all the internal parts in clean brake fluid. Use no other solvent. The cylinder bore must be smooth. If it is scored or pitted

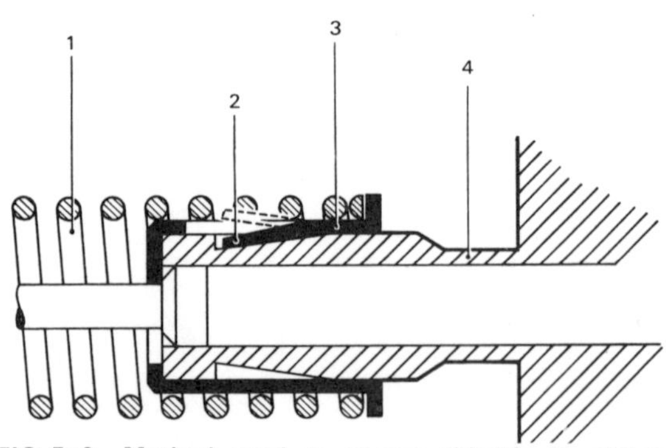

FIG 5:6 Method used to secure thimble to piston plunger

Key to Fig 5:6 1 Spring 2 Thimble leaf 3 Thimble 4 Plunger

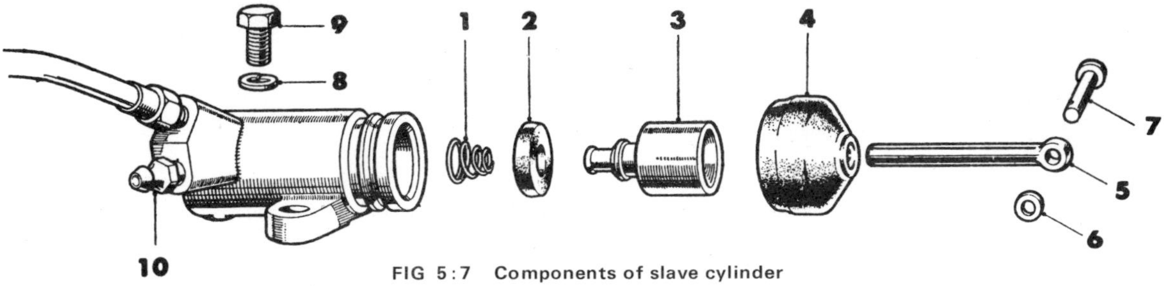

FIG 5:7 Components of slave cylinder

Key to Fig 5:7 1 Spring 2 Piston seal 3 Piston 4 Dust cover 5 Pushrod 6 Plain washer 7 Clevis pin 8 Spring washer 9 Screw—cylinder to housing 10 Bleed screw

the cylinder must be renewed. Check that all parts are clear of obstructions. Always renew the seals. These are available in kit sets. The bore diameter of the cylinder is $\frac{5}{8}$ inch (15.87 mm).

Reassembling:

1 Immerse all parts in the correct brake fluid and assemble wet. Fit seal 1 with its flat face against the valve shoulder. Fit washer 2 and spacer 4. The washer must have its domed side against the valve head. The legs of the spacer must face the valve head.
2 Fit spring centrally on spacer. Insert thimble in spring and compress spring until valve stem engages with elongated hole in thimble. Centralize the parts.
3 Fit a new seal to the piston with its flat face against the large piston shoulder. Insert piston stem into thimble and press home until the spring leaf engages behind the small shoulder.
4 Insert the piston assembly into the bore, taking care not to trap or turn back the lip of the seal. Press the assembly down the bore and refit the circlip.
5 Smear pushrod and sealing areas of dust cover with Girling rubber grease and fit the cover.

Refitting:

Reverse the removal procedure, then bleed the system as described in **Section 5:3.**

5:8 Servicing the slave cylinder

Refer to **FIG 5:7** and remove the cylinder by disconnecting and plugging the flexible pipe and removing the two securing bolts.

Leave the pushrod 5 attached to the lever and blow out piston assembly 3 with gentle air pressure at the inlet port. Drape the parts in a cloth to avoid loss or damage.

Wash the body in methylated spirit and use brake fluid to clean the internal parts. Renew the body if the bore is pitted or scored. Rnew the seal 2. The correct bore of the cylinder is $\frac{7}{8}$ inch (22.22 mm) diameter.

Reassemble the internal parts after wetting them with the correct brake fluid (see **Section 5:2**). Fit the new seal with its flat face against the piston shoulder. Refit the small end of spring 1 over piston stem.

Insert the piston assembly into the bore, taking care not to trap or turn back the lip of the seal. Refit cap if serviceable, otherwise renew it. Smear sealing areas of dust cover with Girling rubber grease and refit it.

Refit the slave cylinder and bleed the system as described in **Section 5:3**.

The slave cylinder flexible pipe:

If it is necessary to remove this pipe in situ, drain the fluid by attaching a tube to the bleed nipple on the slave cylinder and pump it into a container by operating the clutch pedal. Unscrew the pipe connections at the master and slave cylinder bosses. When a flexible pipe has been refitted it is necessary to bleed the system (see **Section 5:3**).

5:9 Fault diagnosis

(a) Drag or spin

1 Oil on driven plate linings
2 Leaking hydraulic system
3 Driven plate distorted
4 Warped or damaged pressure plate
5 Broken driven plate linings
6 Air in the hydraulic system

(b) Fierceness or snatch

1 Check 1, 2, 3 and 4 in (a)
2 Worn linings
3 Worn release mechanism

(c) Slip

1 Check 1 in (a) and 2 in (b)
2 Weak spring
3 Seized slave cylinder piston
4 Release bearing shaft tight in housing

(d) Judder

1 Check 1 and 3 in (a)
2 Warped pressure plate
3 Broken drive straps
4 Contact area of linings not evenly distributed
5 Faulty rubber mountings and steady

(e) Tick or knock

1 Worn driven plate splines
2 Worn release bearing
3 Faulty starter pinion drive
4 Defective drive straps
5 Broken shock-absorber springs in driven plate hub
6 Flywheel loose on crankshaft

NOTES

CHAPTER 6

SYNCHROMESH TRANSMISSION

6:1 Description

This transmission has a manual gearchange with synchromesh engagement for each of the four forward gears. It is housed beneath the engine to form the power unit. Integral with this unit is a pair of final drive gears and a differential assembly of which a cross-section is illustrated in **FIG 6:1**. The output shafts from the differential are coupled by drive shafts and universal joints to the front wheels.

The gearshift mechanism in the gearbox is coupled to a remote gearchange control by cables as can be seen in **FIG 6:3**.

FIG 6:2 shows the drive down to the gearbox, primary gear 103 taking the drive from the clutch driven plate 100 through the straight splines and the helical gear transmitting the drive to the input gear and shaft 34 through the idler gear 48. Refer again to **FIG 6:1**. The input or first motion shaft 34 drives the laygear 56 and this in turn drives the third motion shaft or mainshaft according to the gear selected, with the exception of top gear. Direct coupling between the first and third motion shafts gives top gear.

The action of baulk ring female cones 21 on male cones which are integral with the gear dogs to be engaged, causes the necessary speeding up or slowing down that will give synchronized speeds and silent engagement. The baulk ring cones can be seen clearer in **FIG 6:6**, the synchronizer and baulk ring assembly being items 21 and 22. One of the gear cones is clearly shown in assembly 25.

Reverse gear is obtained by sliding gear 61 (see **FIG 6:7**) into engagement with the reverse gear on the mainshaft (see 18 in **FIG 6:1**). As this sliding gear is driven by the laygear, the introduction of a third gear gives reversed rotation. A pinion on the end of the mainshaft engages with the final drive crown wheel (see 9 and 74 in **FIG 6:1**.

6:2 Routine maintenance

As the synchromesh transmission shares the same lubricating system as the engine, routine maintenance is confined to following the instructions in **Section 1:3**.

6:3 The gearchange mechanism

A remote gearshift control operates the selector rods through three adjustable cables. The selection and engagement of gears is obtained through the cable

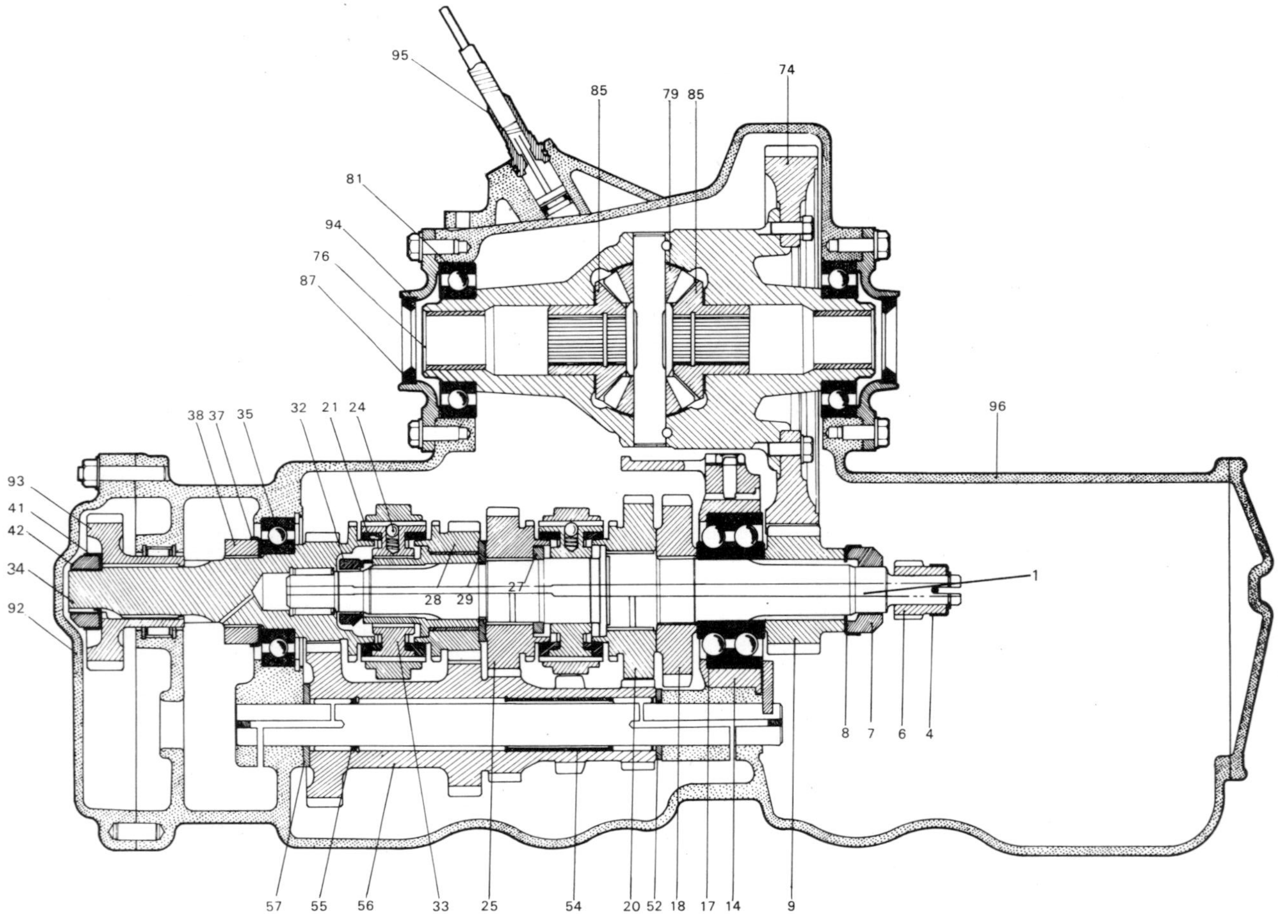

FIG 6:1 Plan section through gearbox and differential

Key to Fig 6:1 1 Mainshaft 4 Cap for speedometer drive gear 6 Speedometer drive gear 7 Pinion nut 8 Lock washer for pinion nut 9 Final drive pinion 14 Housing for ball bearing 17 Ball bearing for mainshaft 18 Reverse gear 20 1st speed gear assembly 21 Baulk ring 24 Ball for synchronizer assembly 25 2nd speed gear assembly 27 Interlocking thrust washer—2nd gear 28 3rd speed gear assembly 29 Interlocking thrust washer—3rd gear 32 Locking ring for mainshaft 33 3rd and 4th speed synchronizer assembly 34 Input shaft 35 Ball bearing for input shaft 37 Lockwasher 38 Bearing retaining nut 41 Lock washer 42 Input gear retaining nut 52 Adjustable thrust washer—laygear 54 Sleeve 55 Circlip 56 Laygear 57 Thrust washer—laygear 74 Final drive gear 76 Differential housing bush 79 Pinion gear 81 Differential bearing 85 Differential gear 87 Seal 92 Flywheel housing 93 Transmission input drive gear 94 Differential end cover 95 Gearshift cable 96 Transmission casing

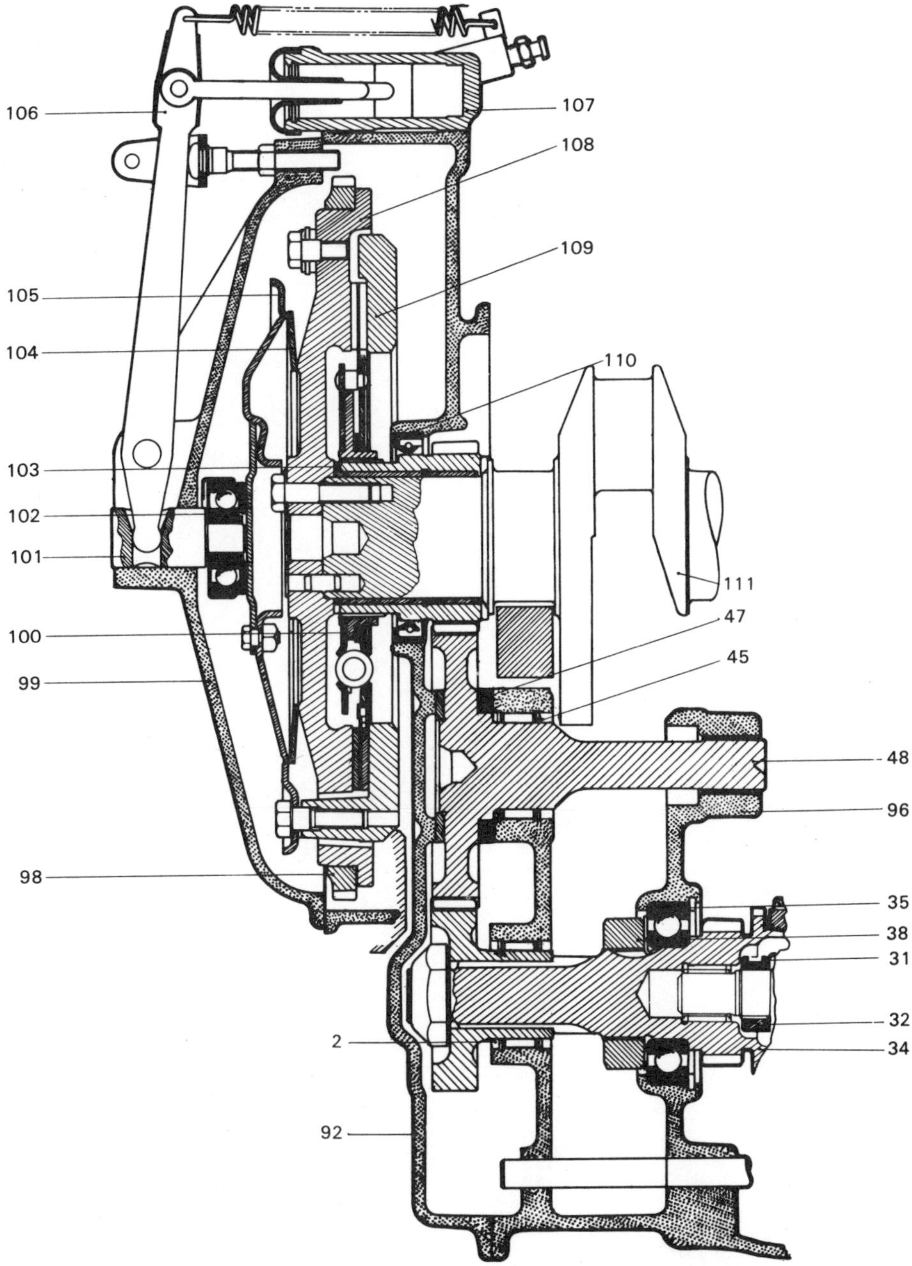

FIG 6:2 Front elevation showing part section through clutch, and primary, idler and input gears

Key to Fig 6:2 2 Needle roller bearing for input shaft 31 Lockwasher for mainshaft locking ring 32 Locking ring for mainshaft 34 Input shaft 35 Ball bearing for input shaft 38 Bearing retaining nut 45 Idler gear roller bearing 47 Idler gear thrust washer 48 Idler gear 92 Flywheel housing 96 Transmission casing 98 Starter ring gear 99 Clutch housing 100 Clutch driven plate 101 Clutch thrust race shaft 102 Clutch thrust race 103 Primary drive gear 104 Clutch diaphragm spring 105 Clutch cover 106 Clutch release lever 107 Clutch slave cylinder 108 Flywheel 109 Clutch pressure plate 110 Primary gear oil 111 Crankshaft

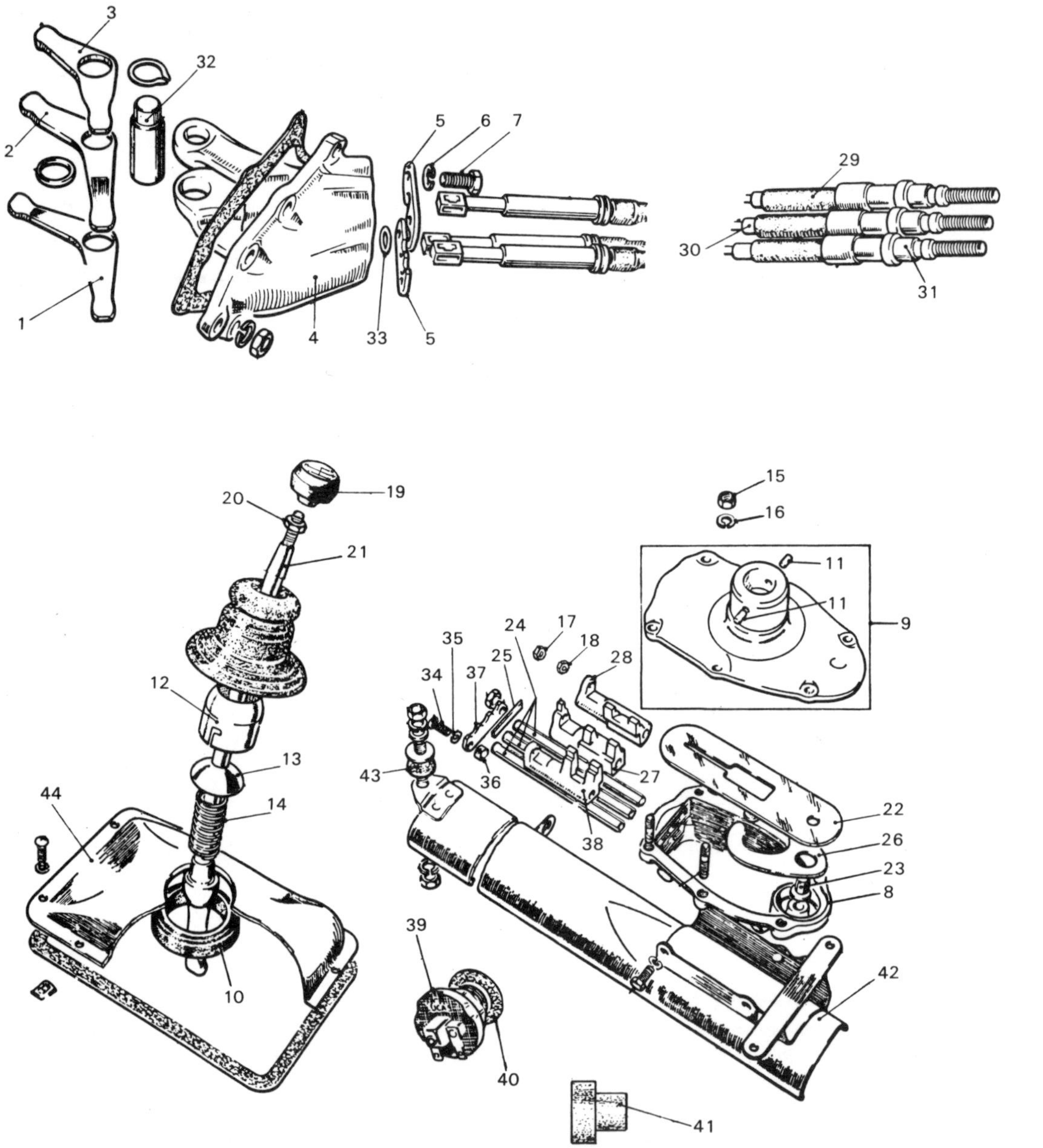

FIG 6:3 Components of gearchange mechanism

Key to Fig 6:3 1 Change speed operating lever—reverse 2 Change speed operating lever—3rd/top 3 Change speed operating lever—1st/2nd 4 Cable change housing 5 Retaining plates—change speed cables 6 Spring washer 7 Setscrew—retaining plate 8 Change speed control box 9 Top cover—change speed control box 10 Mounting ring 11 Pin 12 Spring retainer 13 Dust cover 14 Spring—reverse check 15 Nut—change speed control box 16 Spring washers 17 Locknut—cable jaws 18 Nut—cable jaws 19 Knob for lever 20 Locknut for knob 21 Change speed lever 22 Guide plate 23 Pivot pin—interlock arm 24 Shaft—jaw 25 Retaining plate—shaft 26 Change speed interlock arm 27 Change speed jaw—3rd/top 28 Change speed jaw—1st/2nd 29 Gear change cable complete—1st/2nd 30 Gear change cable complete—3rd/top 31 Gear change cable complete—reverse 32 Pivot—gear change operating levers 33 O-ring—gear change cables 34 Screw—retaining plate to control box 35 Spring washer 36 Spacer—cable retaining plate 37 Retaining plate—change speed cables 38 Change speed jaw—reverse 39 Reverse light switch (Kimberley) 40 Joint washer (Kimberley) 41 Blanking plug (Tasman) 42 Heat shield 43 Heat shield rubber mount 44 Floor cover

linkage, routed from the control box under the floor to a cable housing and relay levers attached to the differential cover.

If the adjustment of the cables is incorrect it could induce faulty gear selection and possible damage to the synchronizers and gears.

Adjusting the cables:

1 From inside the car and referring to **FIG 6:3** where applicable, raise the selector lever gaiter, depress the bayonet cap 12 and twist it to release it from the spring retainer. Withdraw the change speed lever assembly.

2 Clear the centre floor covering away from the working area. Take out the screws that retain the cover pan 44 and remove the pan and gasket.

3 Unscrew the nuts 15, collect the spring washers 16 and lift off the top cover 9 and change speed lever guide 22. Check the action of the interlock arm 26 by ensuring that it swings freely through the change speed jaws 27, 28, and 38 with .030 inch (.76 mm) clearance at each side (see **FIG 6:4**).

4 If the jaws do not line up adjust the cables as follows: Slacken the locknut and nut 17 and 18 on the cable to be adjusted and align the jaw in relation to the interlock arm 26 (see **FIG 6:4**). There is, inevitably, a certain amount of end-play in the cable and relay levers which will effect the relationship between the jaw and arm, if the end-play is not taken into consideration whilst the adjustment is being made. To do this satisfactorily, push the cable forward to take up all end-play in that direction and screw the rear adjusting nut fingertight up to the rear contact face of the jaw boss. Now pull the cable rearwards to take up all end-play in the opposite direction and finger-tighten the front adjusting nut up to the front contact face of the jaw boss. Holding the cable, equalize the play (or end float) between each nut and the jaw boss. Hold the cable in this mid-point position and tighten the adjusting nuts equally without disturbing the setting. Tighten the locknuts.

5 Replace the detached parts and check the gear selection.

Removing the control units and cables:

1 Disconnect the battery and drain the transmission oil.

2 Complete operations 1 and 2 under 'Adjusting'.

3 Refer to **FIG 6:3** and unscrew fully the three nuts that secure the heat shield 42 to the floor panel. Collect the spring washers.

4 Disconnect the reverse light switch wires (Kimberley).

5 Remove the nuts and spring washers that retain the cable housing 4 to the differential cover. Ease the housing assembly away from the cover.

6 Lower the control box 8 and heat shield 42 between the body and the exhaust pipe and withdraw the complete assembly from under the car.

Dismantling:

7 If necessary, detach the heat shield by removing the four setscrews and washers.

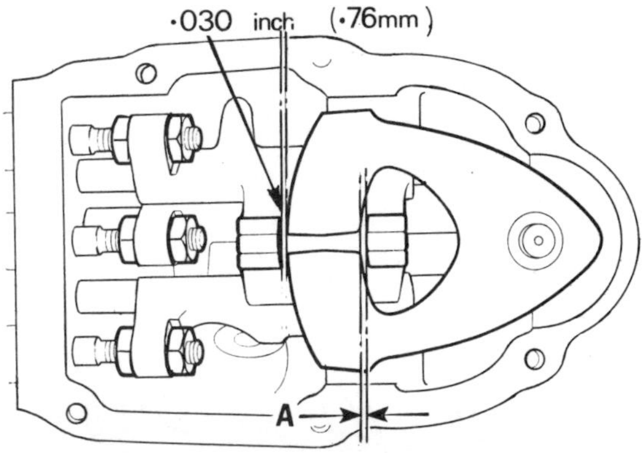

FIG 6:4 The interlock arm should swing freely through the change speed jaws with .030 inch (.76 mm) clearance at points 'A'

8 Take out the setscrews 7, washers 6, retainers 5 and release the cables from the operating levers 1, 2 and 3. Remove the circlip that retains the lever pivot 32 in the housing. Press the pivot out of the housing to detach the levers and spacers. Remove the O-rings 33.

9 Unscrew and remove the nuts 15, collect the spring washers 16 and lift off the top cover 9. Remove the change speed guide 22 and interlock arm 26.

10 Unscrew the two setscrews 34, collect the spring washers 35 and the cable retaining plate 37 with its two spacers 36. Take off the cables nuts and locknuts to release the cables from the control box.

11 Release the operating shafts' retainer 25 and press the shafts 24 out of the control box. Pick up the change-speed jaws 27, 28 and 38.

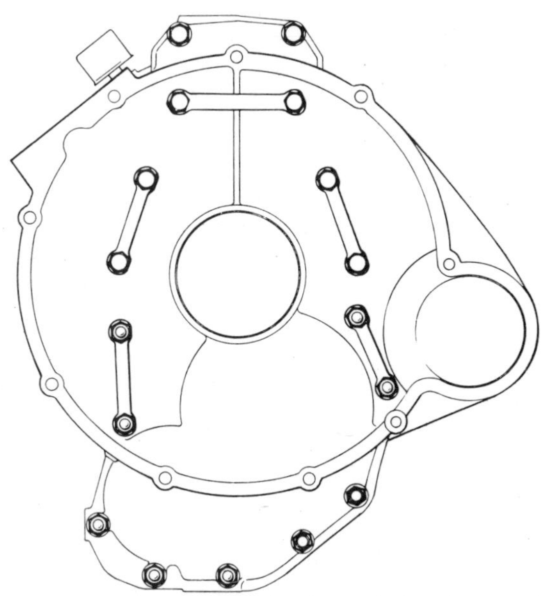

FIG 6:5 Arrangement of flywheel housing lock washers

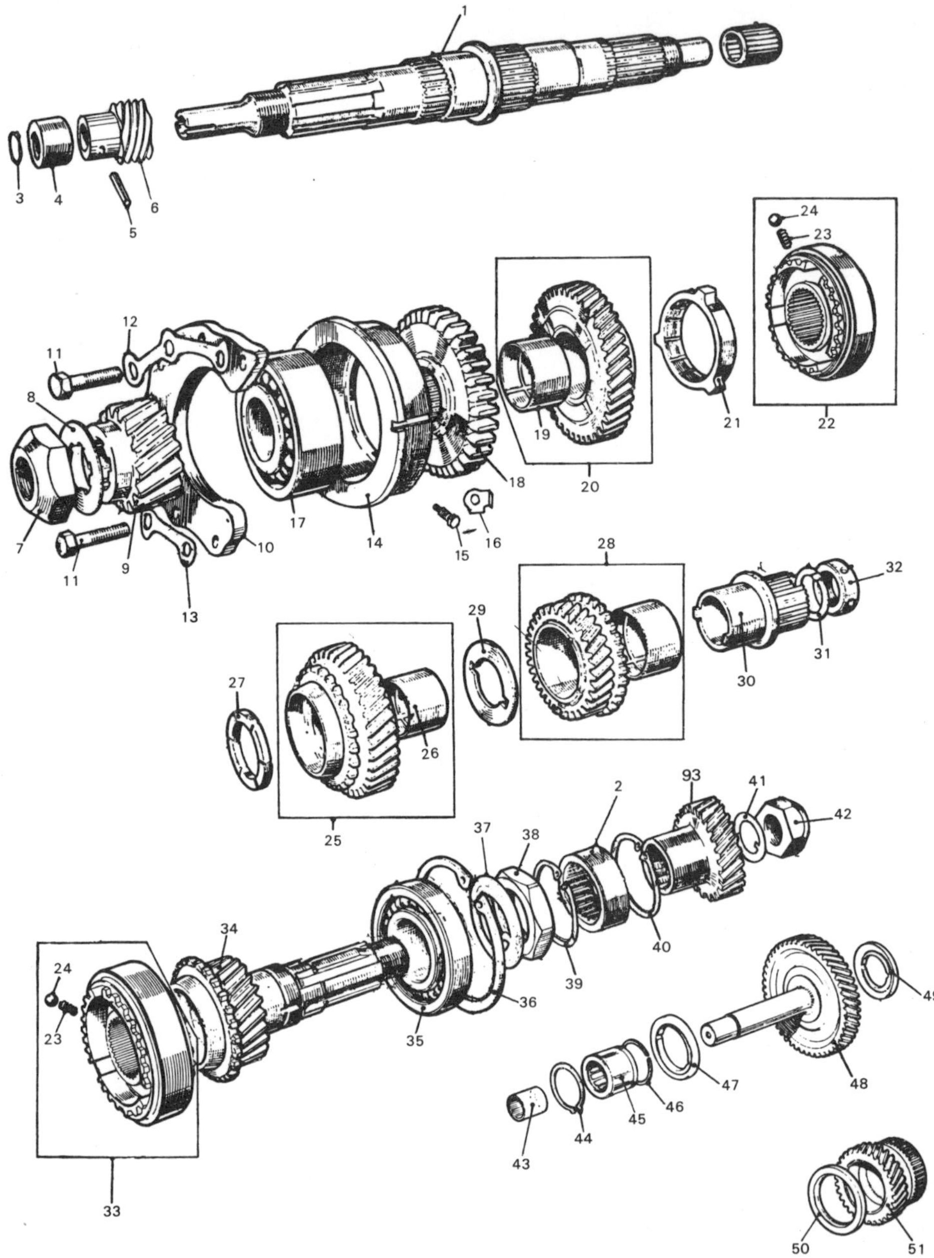

FIG 6:6 Mainshaft and input shaft components

Key to Fig 6:6 1 Mainshaft 2 Needle roller bearing for input shaft 3 Circlip for speedometer drive gear 4 Cap for speedometer drive gear 5 Roll pin for speedometer drive gear 6 Speedometer drive gear 7 Pinion nut 8 Lockwasher for pinion nut 9 Final drive pinion 10 Plate retainer for mainshaft ball bearing 11 Bolts for plate retainer 12 Lock tab upper 13 Lock tab lower 14 Housing for ball bearing 15 Dowel bolt for ball bearing housing 16 Lock tab for dowel bolt 17 Ball bearing for mainshaft 18 Reverse gear 19 Bush for the 1st speed gear 20 1st speed gear assembly 21 Baulk ring—four off 22 Synchronizer assembly 23 Spring for synchronizer assembly 24 Ball for synchronizer assembly 25 2nd speed gear assembly 26 Bush for the 2nd speed gear 27 Interlocking thrust washer—2nd gear 28 3rd speed gear assembly 29 Interlocking thrust washer—3rd gear 30 Sleeve for mainshaft 31 Lockwasher for mainshaft locking ring 32 Locking ring for mainshaft 33 3rd and 4th speed synchronizer assembly 34 Input shaft 35 Ball bearing for input shaft 36 Circlip 37 Lockwasher 38 Bearing retaining nut 39 Circlip 40 Circlip 41 Lock washer 42 Input gear retaining nut 43 Idler gear bush 44 Circlip 45 Idler gear roller bearing 46 Snap ring 47 Idler gear thrust washer 48 Idler gear 49 Adjustable thrust washer—idler gear 50 Adjustable thrust washer—primary gear 51 Primary gear

Inspection:

12 Clean all the metal parts in solvent and examine them for wear, distortion and possible fractures. Examine the cables for general wear and deterioration.
Scrap all gaskets and O-rings and fit new ones.
Ensure the gasket faces of the differential cover and cable change housing are clean, flat and free from burrs.

Reassembling:

13 Reassembling is the reverse of the dismantling operations and bearing in mind the following points:
Smear all rubbing surfaces liberally with grease. If the reverse light switch has been removed, refit and set it with its plunger just touching the contact face of the reverse jaw 38.
The reverse selector cable has a yellow band and it is longer than the other two.
Set the relay levers in the neutral position before fitting the housing to the differential cover.
Adjust the control cables as previously described.
Refill the engine transmission with oil.

6:4 Removing, refitting gearbox

1 Remove the power unit as described in **Chapter 1** and ensure that the engine:transmission oil has been drained.
2 Refer to **Chapter 4** and remove the alternator drive belt.
3 Refer to **Chapter 1** and remove the crankshaft pulley oil seal.
4 Disconnect the fuel pipe between pump and carburetter.
5 Refer to to **Chapter 11** and take off the starter motor.
6 Remove the engine steady bar.
7 Refer to **Chapter 5** and remove the clutch and flywheel assembly.
8 Refer to **FIG 6:5**, note the position of the lockwashers and remove the bolts and nuts that retain the flywheel housing to the engine and transmission.
9 Refer to **Chapter 1** and remove the primary gear and oil seal.
10 Take off the fuel pump and withdraw the pushrod, remove the dipstick and dipstick tube.
11 Refer to **Chapter 3** to remove the distributor and to **FIG 1:23** to extract the quill shaft with service tool 18G1147.
12 Remove the lefthand:rear engine mounting bracket and all setscrews securing the transmission to the cylinder block.
13 Carefully separate the transmission unit from the engine.

Refitting:

14 Reverse the dismantling operations and heed the following:
Use an approved jointing compound, i.e. Permatex No. 3, on both faces of all gaskets and joint washers.
Renew the primary gear oil seal and the crankshaft rear oil seal, fitting them as described in **Chapter 1**, and checking the end float of the gears. Before positioning the engine to the transmission remember that the setscrew above the oil filter must be screwed into the crankcase before the engine is finally mated to the transmission.
Tighten all nuts and bolts to the specified torque as listed in Technical Data.

6:5 Dismantling gearbox

Refer to **FIGS 6:1, 6:2, 6:6** and **6:7** and do the following:

1 Pull off idler gear 48 and thrust washers 47. Remove oil filter, pressure relief valve and oil pump (see **Chapter 1**). Remove transmission and cover.
2 Remove the final drive assembly (see **Section 6:11**). Unscrew speedometer drive pinion 91.
3 Remove circlip 3 and roll pin retaining cap 4. Pull or tap off speedometer drive gear 6 without removing the roll pin 5. Unlock tabs of washer 8 under pinion nut 7. Move selector forks to lock first and reverse gears together, to stop third motion shaft from moving. Unscrew the nut with an appropriate tool (18G.-1022A). **The nut has a lefthand thread.** Pull off the gear 9 and move the forks to unlock the gears.
4 Unlock tabs of washers 12 and 13. Remove bearing retainer 10. Check end float of laygear 56 at the front end with a feeler gauge. The small thrust washers 52 is at the front. Make a note if adjustment is needed during reassembling.
5 Drive out layshaft 58 leaving the laygear 56 in position but remove the thrust washer 52. Drive out reverse idler gear shaft 60. Remove selector rod retaining plate 71.
6 Cover the gearbox with a cloth to avoid losing the interlocking balls. Drive out first/second selector rod 63. Drive out third/top selector rod 65. Remove first/second fork 64 and third/top fork 66. Drive out reverse selector rod 67 and remove the fork 68. Remove reverse idler gear 61.
7 Unlock and remove locating bolt 15. Fit impulse extractor 18GA284 to third motion shaft 1 using adaptor 18GA026. Pull out the shaft (see **FIG 6:8**).
8 Remove nut 42, lockwasher 41 and first motion shaft gear 93. Remove circlip 40 and drive out the shaft 34 inwards using a soft-faced hammer.
9 Lift out the laygear 56 and thrust washer 57. Extract circlip 39. Drive out first motion shaft needle-roller bearing 2 inwards with tool 18GA284 and adaptor 18GA025.
10 Drive out the idler gear inner bush 43 using a suitable drift inserted through the idler gear needle roller bearing. Remove the bearing circlip 44. Use adaptor 18G.284.A0 and impulse tool 18G.284 to extract the bearing 45 from the housing. The bearing will be complete with outer circlip 46.

6:6 Overhauling first motion shaft

Dismantling:

Refer to **FIG 6:9**. Unlock and remove the bearing nut 38 using an appropriate tool, 18GA027 is shown in the figure. Use soft jaws when holding the shaft in a vice. Using a press, push the shaft out of the bearing 35.

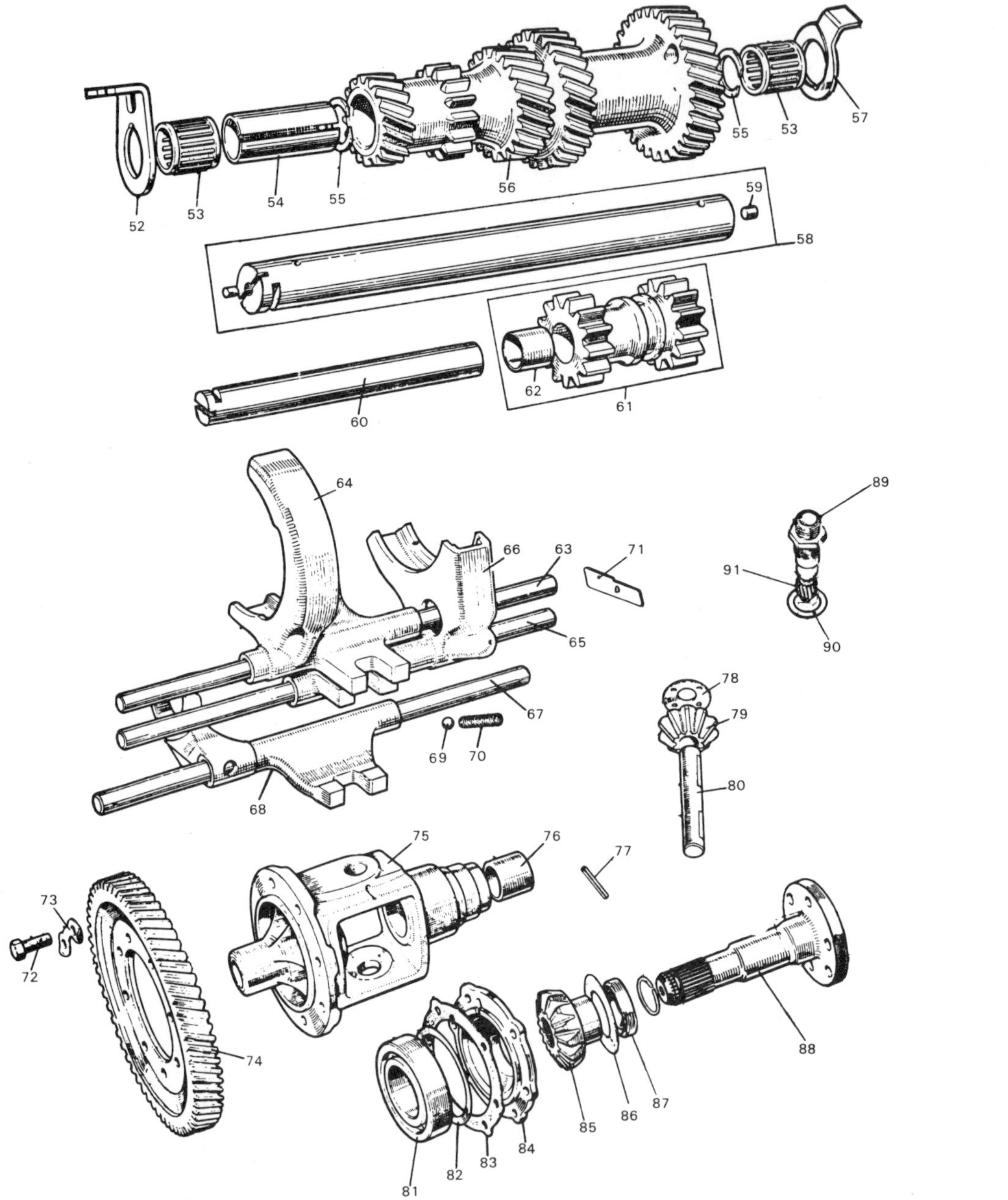

FIG 6:7 The countershaft gears, reverse idler gear, selectors and differential gear

Key to Fig 6:7 52 Adjustable thrust washer—lay gear 53 Needle roller bearing 54 Sleeve 55 Circlip 56 Lay gear 57 Thrust washer—lay gear 58 Layshaft 59 Oilway plug 60 Reverse idler gear shaft 61 Reverse idler gear 62 Reverse idler gear bush 63 1st/2nd speed selector shaft 64 1st/2nd speed selector fork 65 3rd/4th speed selector shaft 66 3rd/4th speed selector fork 67 Reverse speed selector shaft 68 Reverse speed selector fork 69 Selector shaft ball 70 Selector shaft spring 71 Selector shaft key plate 72 Final drive gear retaining bolt 73 Final drive gear lock washer 74 Final drive gear 75 Differential housing 76 Differential housing bush 77 Differential housing roll pin 78 Pinion gear thrust washer 79 Pinion gear 80 Pinion shaft 81 Differential bearing 82 Adjustable shim 83 Gasket 84 Differential housing end cover 85 Differential gear 86 Differential gear thrust washer 87 Seal 88 Differential drive shaft 89 Speedometer pinion housing 90 Sealing washer 91 Speedometer pinion

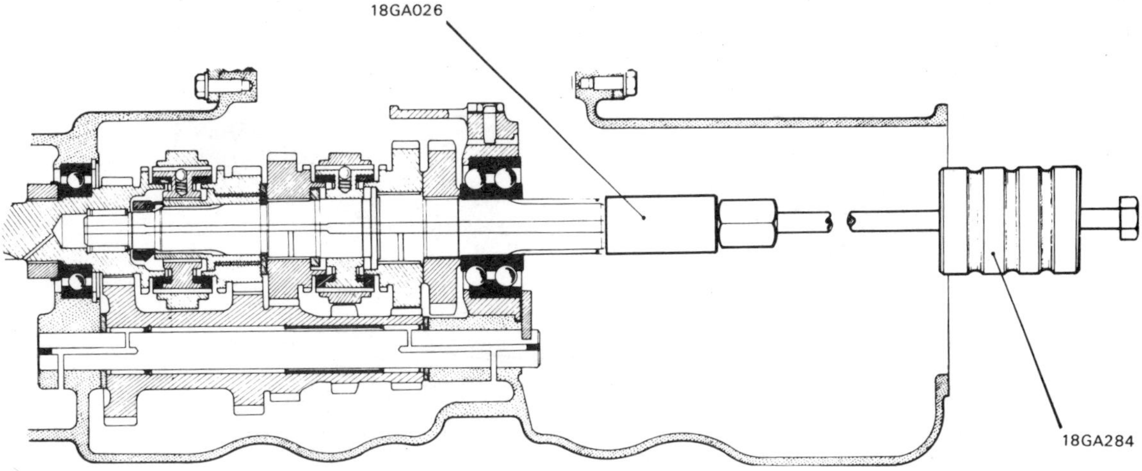

FIG 6:8 Removing mainshaft with service tool, impulse extractor 18GA284 and adaptor 18GA026

Inspecting:

After cleaning, check the gear teeth and the synchromesh cone for undue wear. Renew ball and needle roller bearings if worn, or if rough in action when turned without lubricant.

Reassembling:

Refit the bearing and tighten the nut to 120 lb ft (16.6 kg m). Turn up a tab of the locking washer 37. Drive the shaft into the gearbox casing using the needle roller bearing 2 as an alignment guide (see **FIG 6:10**).

Select and fit a circlip 36 of the maximum thickness that will fit in the groove. Circlips are available in various thicknesses from the service stores.

6:7 Overhauling laygear and reverse idler gear

The gears are shown in the top view of **FIG 6:7**. Check the bearing surfaces of both shafts for wear and renew if necessary. Renew the bearing if worn. Check the gear teeth for wear, cracks or chipping.

The laygear end float was checked before dismantling (see **Section 6:5**). Before reassembling, select a thrust washer 52 to give the correct float of .002 to .007 inch (.05 to 18 mm) Thrust washers are available in the following thicknesses:

.123 to .125 inch (3.12 to 3.17 mm)
.126 to .128 inch (3.21 to 3.26 mm)
.130 to .132 inch (3.30 to 3.35 mm)
.133 to .135 inch (3.38 to 3.43 mm)

6:8 Overhauling third motion shaft

Dismantling:

Refer to **FIG 6:6**. Use soft jaws in the vice to hold the shaft at the lefthand end. Withdraw third and fourth synchronizer assembly 33. Unlock and unscrew nut 32 using tool 18G.1024 (see **FIG 6:11**).

Withdraw sleeve 30, third-speed gear 28 and interlocking thrust washer 29. Withdraw second-speed gear 25 and thrust washer 27. Remove first- and second-speed synchronizer parts 22 and baulk ring 21. Use a press to

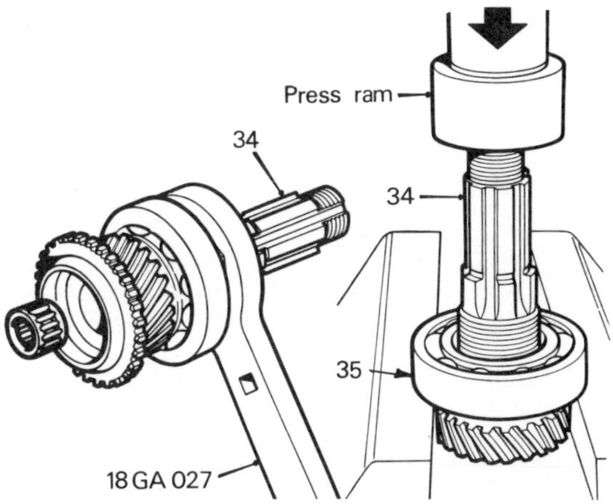

FIG 6:9 Using service tool 18GA027 and a suitable press to push the 1st motion shaft through the bearing

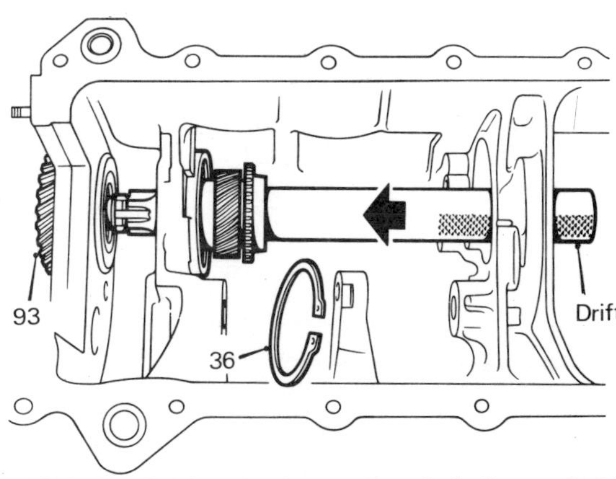

FIG 6:10 Driving the 1st motion shaft (input shaft) into position using the needle roller bearing and the input drive gear as an alignment guide

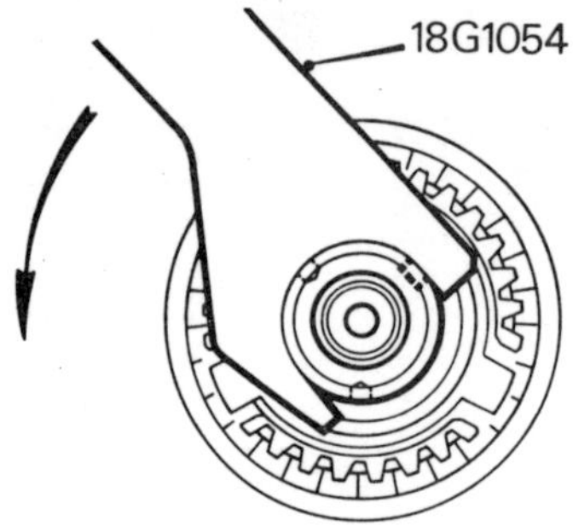

FIG 6:11 Using service tool 18G 1024 to unlock and unscrew the third motion shaft (mainshaft) locking nut

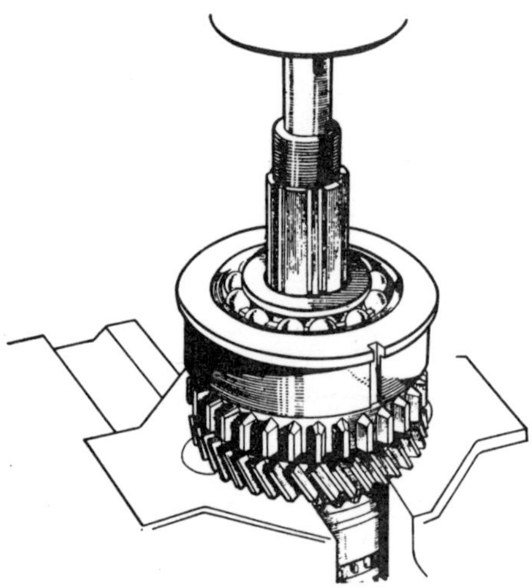

FIG 6:12 Pressing the third motion shaft from the bearing assembly

FIG 6:13 Checking the baulk ring clearance. A minimum clearance of .020 inch (.508 mm) must exist between the rings and cones at the point arrowed

force the shaft out of the bearing housing as shown in **FIG 6:12** and then remove the reverse 18 and first-speed gear 20. If the bearing 17 is worn, press it out of the housing 14.

Remove the baulk rings from the synchromesh assemblies, after wrapping assemblies in a cloth push out the hubs from the sliding couplings. The balls and springs will be retained in the cloth.

Inspecting:

Clean all the parts and check for wear. The bearing 17 should be checked when unlubricated. It must be tight in its housing 14 and be free from side play, pitting or worn cages.

Check the gear teeth for wear, cracks or chipping. Renew thrust washers if worn. Fit baulk rings to mating cones on gears (see **FIG 6:13**). If the cones do not engage before the rings contact the edge of the gear the worn parts must be renewed. A minimum clearance of .020 inch (.508 mm) must exist as shown by the arrows. Excessive wear will give rise to noisy gearchanging, due to the lack of synchronization. New components normally have a clearance of .04 inch (1.016 mm). Check all splines for wear and renew synchronizer balls and springs if unsatisfactory. Compare the springs with new ones.

Reassembling:

Press the bearing into its housing as shown in **FIG 6:14**. Note projecting boss and cutaway.

Hold tool 18G.1026 in a vice and fit a synchronizer hub and align the loading hole in the tool with one of the holes in the hub (see **FIG 6:15**). Insert a spring and ball and turn the hub while pressing on the ball. This will retain the ball and spring. Move on to the next hole. **Make sure to turn always in the same direction or a ball and spring may fly out.** Place the sliding coupling of the synchronizer on a flat surface as shown in the figure. Fit the hub and tool assembly with the cutouts aligned. Using a hammer shaft, give the hub a sharp tap to knock it into the coupling.

Continue reassembling in the reverse order of dismantling. Note that the first/second synchronizer 22 is smaller in diameter than the third/fourth one 33. Insert the sleeve into the third-speed 28, fit the thrust washer 29 with sleeve tongues located in slots and fit assembly to shaft.

Use a new lockwasher 31 and tap it into the recesses in the nut 32 after tightening. Lubricate all parts.

6:9 Reassembling gearbox

Refer to **FIG 6:6** and refit the idler gear needle roller bearing 45. Use the impact tool to fit it in position in the casing. Refit the inner retaining circlip 44. Drive a new idler gear bearing bush 43 into place until it is flush with the casing web. Lubricate all turning parts.

Refit the inner circlip 40 followed by the input shaft needle roller bearing 2 and second circlip 39.

Refer to views A, B and C in **FIG 6:16**. Use new springs and insert them, followed by the balls into the selector forks. Hold in place with tool 18G.1029 or $\frac{1}{2}$ inch (13 mm) lengths of rod (view B). The method is the same for all forks.

Drive the first motion shaft 34 into position with tools 18GA025 and 18GA284 if available, but a copper drift can be used (see **FIG 6:10**). Fit the circlip 36 as selected at the end of **Section 6:7**. Fit reverse idler 61 and laygears 56 into casing without shafts, the laygear having its large thrust washer 57 fitted.

Refer to **FIG 6:6**. Align the groove in the third motion shaft bearing housing 14 with the dowel bolt 15 locating hole in the gearbox casing and drive the bearing into place with a suitable drift contacting the outer race. Fit dowel bolt 15 and new lockwasher 16. Tighten to 6 lb ft (.8 kg m) and turn up a tab to lock.

Refit the layshaft and check the end float (see **Section 6:7**). Fit the reverse idler shaft 60 and fit the bearing retainer 10. Use new locking plates 12 and 13, tighten the screws to 18 lb ft (2.5 kg m) and lock with tabs.

Refer to **FIG 6:7**. Fit reverse fork 68, pushing the shaft 60 into place so that it displaces the loading device (see C in **FIG 6:16**). Fit forks 64 and 66, holding them in place while the rods are fitted. Retrieve the loading devices. Fit plate 71, tighten the bolt to 16 lb ft (2.2 kg m) and tap up a locking tab. Move the forks until two gears are locked.

Refit the final drive pinion 9 (see **FIG 6:6**). Tighten the lefthand-threaded nut 7 to 150 lb ft (20.7 kg m) and tap up three tabs of the lockwasher 8.

Refit the first motion shaft gear 93. Tighten the nut 42 to 120 lb ft (16.6 kg m) and tap up the lockwasher 41. Move the forks to select neutral. Refit speedometer drive gear parts 6, 4 and 3. Refit the speedometer drive pinion 91 to the casing, noting the copper sealing washer 90. Tighten to 20 lb ft (2.8 kg m).

Refit the final drive assembly (see **Section 6:11**). Continue to reassemble in the reverse order of dismantling (see **Section 6:5**).

6:10 Idler gear end float

The idler gear end float can be carried out with the engine and transmission fitted in the car but, obviously, it is much easier to do it on the bench after the engine transmission has been overhauled.

Checking and adjusting the primary gear end float with the engine in situ was described in **Chapter 1**, and it is always advisable to adjust the end float of both gears at the same time. However, to work on the idler gear the flywheel housing must first be removed, but if the housing is already removed after a transmission overhaul, start from operation 7.

1 Drain the engine oil. Place a jack interspaced with a block of wood under the righthand side of the engine and take the weight.
2 Remove the battery and battery carrier.
3 Disconnect the front and rear engine mounting brackets from the flywheel housing. Release the clutch slave cylinder by removing the two bolts, but it is not necessary to disconnect the fluid pipe.
4 Remove the clutch cover and clutch thrust plate.
5 Remove the clutch and flywheel assembly as one unit by extracting the four flywheel to crankshaft securing bolts.
6 Refer to **FIG 6:5** and take out the flywheel housing securing bolts and lockwashers. Detach the housing.

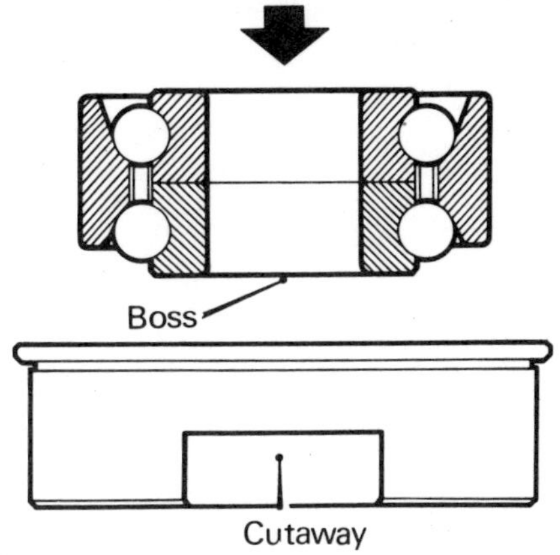

FIG 6:14 Locating the new bearing into its housing

7 Withdraw the primary and idler gears together with their respective thrust washers.
8 Place the flywheel housing on a flat bench or a machine surfaced table with the inner side of the housing uppermost. Ensure the mounting faces are clean and free from burrs.
9 Refer to **FIG 6:17** and rest the idler gear 48 with its thrust washers 47 and 49 in the normal position shown.
10 With a straightedge contacting the face of the thrust washer 47 measure with feeler gauges the gap at 'B'. It should be between zero and .004 inch (.102 mm). The required end float of the idler gear is between .002 and .007 inch (.05 and .08 mm) and it is obtained by the compressed thickness of the fitted housing gasket when assembled. The gasket compresses to .006 inch (.15 mm) when the bolts are tightened to the specified torque.
11 If there is no gap at 'B', measure the gap at 'A'. If this is between zero and .001 (.025 mm) the end float will be just on the maximum limit when assembled and should be all right. If the gap exceeds .001 inch measure the thickness of the existing thrust washers and obtain new ones of an appropriate size.
12 Tighten the flywheel housing bolts evenly to a torque of 18 lb ft (2.5 kg m).

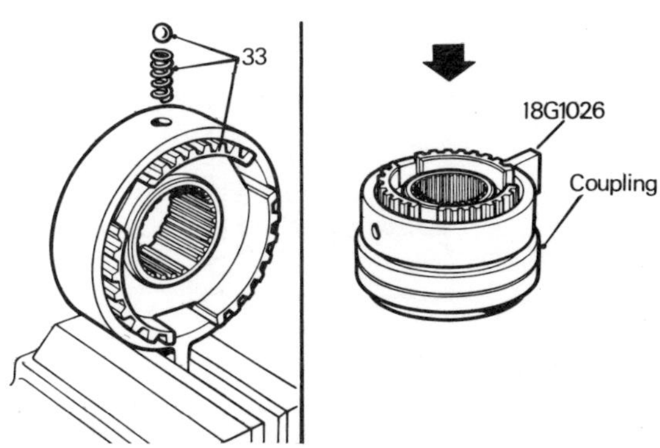

FIG 6:15 Assembling the synchronizer units using service tool 18G 1026 to secure them

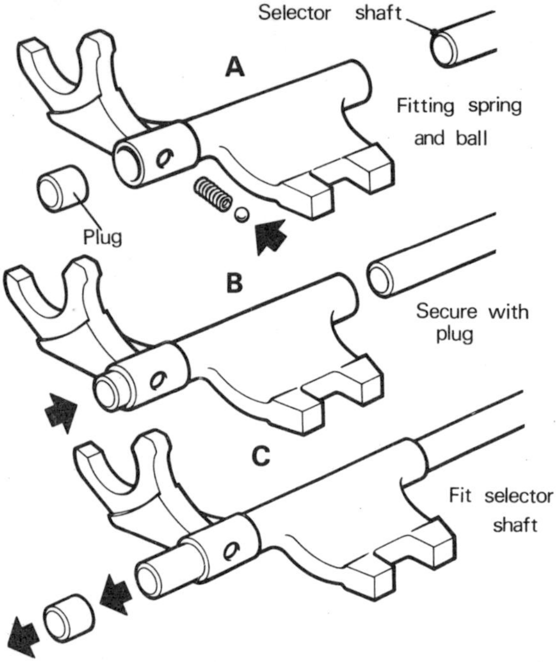

FIG 6:16 Assembling the selector shaft springs and balls using utility plugs or service tool plugs 18G 1029 to secure them temporarily in position

6:11 Removing, fitting differential

The differential housing is bolted directly onto the gearbox as an assembly and it can be removed, with a little care, without taking the engine out of the frame. The drive to the differential is taken from the pinion 9 on the mainshaft to the final drive gear 74 bolted to the differential case (see **FIG 6:1**).

The differential housing and the gearbox are a machined matched pair and should not be interchanged with other units. The final drive gear and the pinion are not machine matched as a pair, but if either requires renewal they should both be renewed.

1 Drain the engine:transmission oil.
2 Remove the complete exhaust assembly.
3 Disconnect the change speed cables from the differential cover (see **FIG 6:3**).
4 Refer to **FIG 6:18**. Disconnect the drive couplings from the drive flanges 88. Unwind the setscrews 112 and take off the end covers 84.
5 Unscrew all the nuts securing the differential cover to the transmission housing. There are two long $\frac{7}{16}$ inch studs and one long $\frac{5}{16}$ inch stud through the differential cover which must be taken out to provide clearance for the assembly to be removed.
6 Withdraw the assembly and cover away from the transmission housing.

Refitting:

7 Refit in the reverse order of removal but ensure beforehand that the mounting faces are clean and free from burrs. Fit new joint washers throughout. Locate the assembly on the transmission casing before fitting the three long studs.
Refill the engine transmission with oil.

Fitting new bearings:

1 Refer to **FIG 6:7**. Mark the crownwheel and differential cage for correct reassembly. Unlock and remove bolts 72. Lift off crownwheel 74.
2 Pull off bearing 81 with a universal extractor. Note bearing on crownwheel side is marked THRUST on its outer face.
3 Fit new bearings using tool 18G.134 with adaptor 18G.134P. Refit crownwheel in its original position. Fit new lockplates and tighten bolts in diagonal sequence to 55 to 60 lb ft (7.6 to 8.3 kg m). Tap up the locking tabs.

Overhauling the differential assembly:

1 Refer to **FIGS 6:7** and **6:18**. Drive out the two roll pins 77. Drive out the pinion pin 80.
2 Lift out the pinions 79 and thrust washers 78 and the differential gears 85 and washers 86.
3 Renew worn gears and pinion pin. Fit new thrust washers 78 and 86 and oil seals 87. The gears must be renewed as a complete set. If new differential gears are being fitted, drift new circlips into the retaining grooves. Finish assembling in the reverse order of dismantling, lubricating all running parts.

Fitting new crownwheel and pinion:

These must be renewed as a pair. After the final drive assembly has been removed from the gearbox casing proceed as follows::

1 Note that the following instructions apply exclusively to cars with manual gearchange. Expert attention is needed to remove the final drive pinion on cars with automatic transmission.
2 Remove the front cover, the oil pump, the speedometer drive pinion and gear and the final drive pinion (see **Section 6:5**).
3 Remove the crownwheel as described under 'Fitting new bearings'.

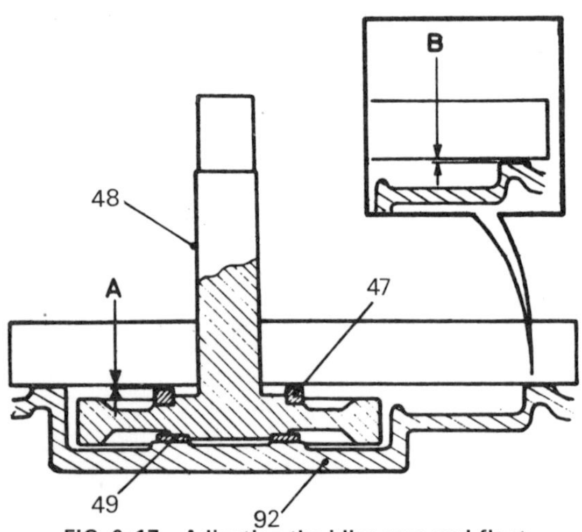

FIG 6:17 Adjusting the idler gear end float

Key to Fig 6:17 47 Thrust washer 48 Idler gear 49 Thrust washer 92 Housing **A** = zero to .01 inch **B** = zero to .004 inch

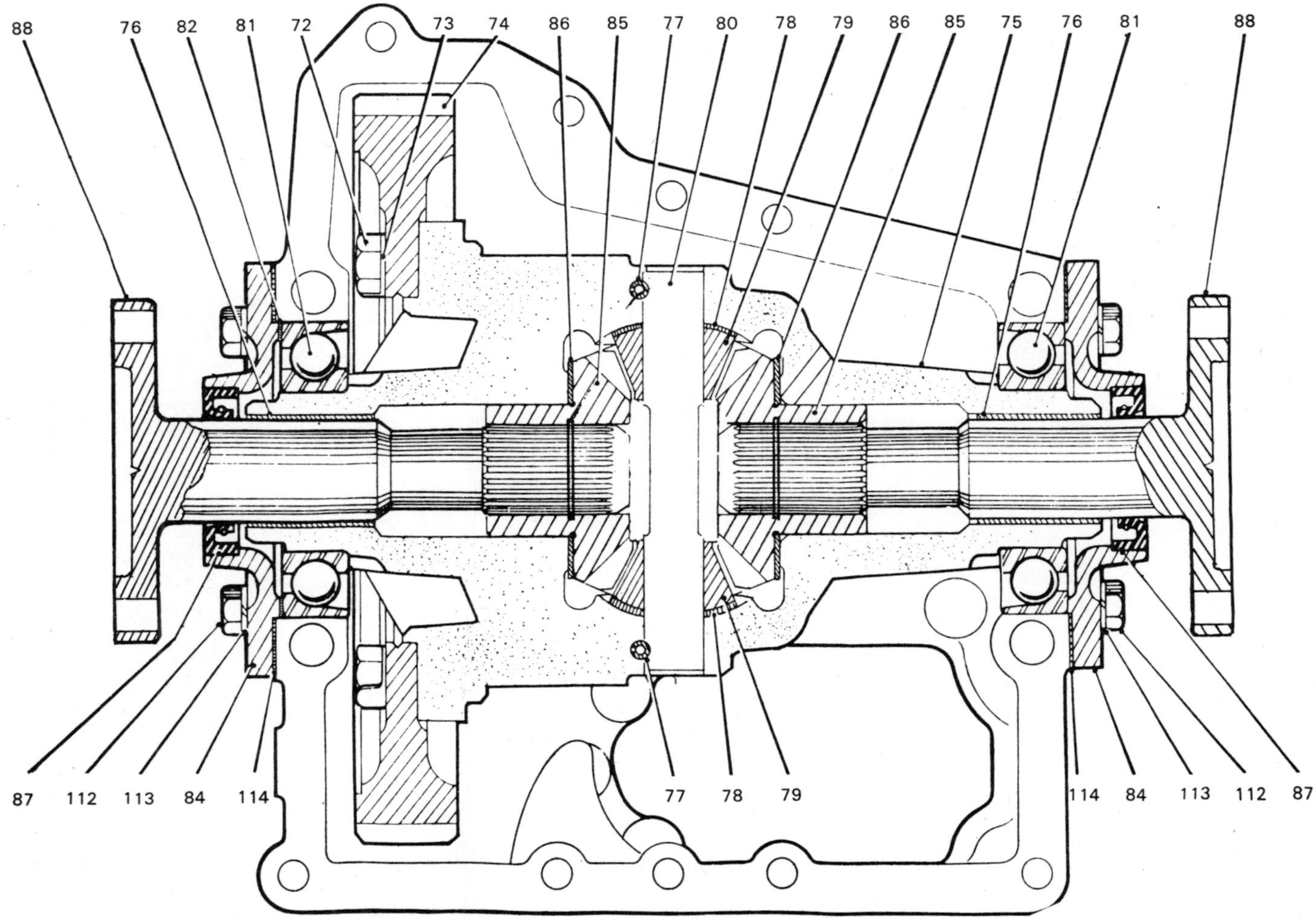

FIG 6:18 Section through differential assembly

Key to Fig 6:18 72 Bolt—final drive wheel to differential case 73 Lock washer 74 Final drive gear 75 Differential case 76 Bush 77 Roll pin—pinion centre 78 Washer for differential pinion 79 Differential pinion 80 Pinion shaft 81 Ball bearing (double purpose) 82 Shim—ball bearing to end cover 84 End cover 85 Differential gear 86 Washer for differential gear 87 Oil seal 88 Differential shaft 112 Set screw—end cover to transmission case 113 Spring washer 114 Joint washer

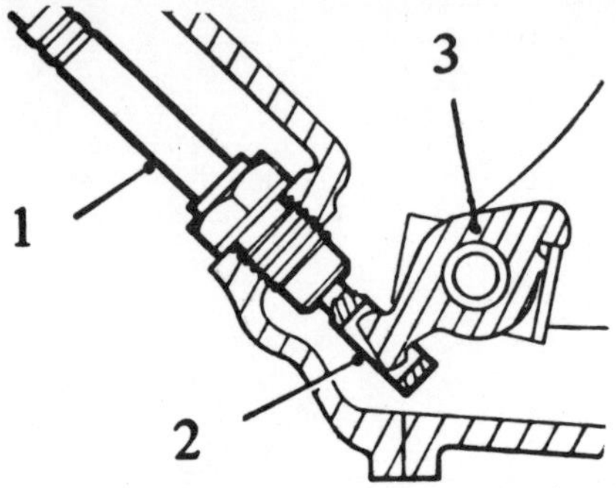

FIG 6:19 The parking pawl control cable engaged with the operating lever (automatic only)

Key to Fig 6:19 1 Cable outer casing 2 Inner cable connection 3 Parking pawl lever

4 Reverse the dismantling procedure when reassembling. If no parts of the differential assembly such as cage, covers, housing or bearings have been renewed, the operation of reassembling can proceed without adjustment. The following instructions assume the need for adjustment because new parts have been fitted.

Checking the bearing preload:

1 Fit the differential unit to the transmission casing, pressing it towards the flywheel end of the engine. Refit the final drive housing, making sure that the selectors engage with the fork assemblies in the gearbox. With automatic transmission, engage the parking pawl control cable with its operating lever before pushing the housing home (see **FIG 6:19**).

2 Tighten all nuts just enough to hold the unit firmly in place and yet allow the differential to displace sideways when the flywheel-end cover is fitted.

3 Fit the cover at the flywheel end, lining up the joint washer correctly. Tighten the bolts evenly and note that the differential unit will be displaced away from the flywheel end.

4 Adjust for bearing preload by fitting the opposite cover, without joint washer or shims. Tighten the bolts diagonally and evenly until the cover just nips the bearing outer race. Do not overtighten.

5 Refer to **FIG 6:20** and use feeler gauges to measure the gap at A. Take measurements at several places round the cover flange. If there are variations, adjust the bolt tightness until the same figure is obtained all round. If there is no gap at all, fit some shims of known thickness between the cover and the bearing at 1. This thickness must be included in preload calculations.

6 Any gap must be taken up by a new joint washer with a compressed thickness of .008 inch (.20 mm), plus shims required to give the necessary preload. For example, if the gap is .007 inch (.18 mm) and the joint washer is .008 inch (.20 mm) thick there will be an end float of .001 inch (.025 mm). If this is added to the required preload of .004 inch (.102 mm), the result of .005 inch (.13 mm) is the thickness of shims required. Do not forget to add the thickness of shims already fitted if that was necessary (see end of preceding operation 5).

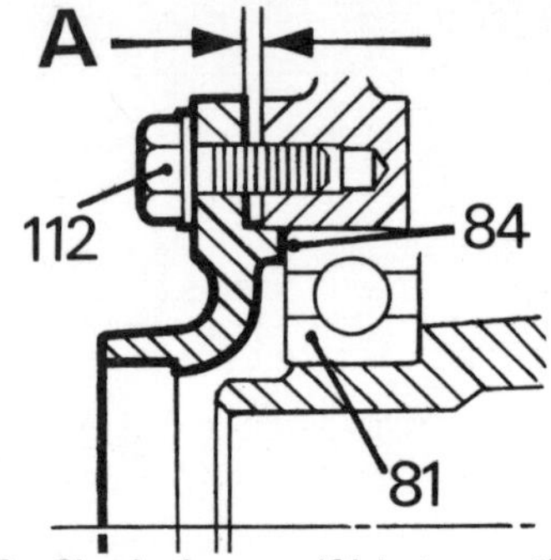

FIG 6:20 Check the gap 'A' between the end cover and the final drive housing, with feeler gauges to calculate the bearing preload

Key to Fig 6:20 81 Bearing 84 End cover 112 Setbolt **A** = measured gap

7 Smear the shims with grease and stick them to the thrust face of the bearing. Fit the new joint washers, followed by the cover and tighten the bolts evenly to 18 lb ft (2.5 kg m).

8 Refit the exhaust mounting and tie rod brackets and tighten $\frac{5}{16}$ inch nuts to 18 lb ft (2.5 kg m). Tighten $\frac{3}{8}$ inch nuts to 25 lb ft (3.4 kg m) and studs to 6 lb ft (.8 kg m).

9 The actual bearing preload required is between .003 and .005 inch (.08 to .13 mm), the figure .004 inch (.102 mm) being taken as the mean.

6:12 Fault diagnosis

(a) Jumping out of gear

1 Broken spring behind selector rod ball
2 Worn groove in selector rod
3 Worn synchromesh coupling dogs
4 Worn selector fork
5 Excessive backlash in gearchange mechanism
6 Worn synchromesh sleeve

(b) Noisy transmission

1 Insufficient oil
2 Excessive end float of laygear
3 Incorrect end float of idler and mainshaft gears
4 Incorrect preload on differential bearings
5 Worn or damaged bearings
6 Worn bushes on third motion shaft
7 Worn or damaged gear teeth
8 Worn splines on drive shafts and gears

(c) Difficulty in engaging gear

1 Faulty clutch or clutch withdrawal mechanism
2 Worn synchromesh cones
3 Backlash or incorrect adjustment of gearchange mechanism
4 Worn selector forks and couplings

(d) Oil leaks

1 Faulty joint washers or joint faces
2 Worn or damaged oil seals or running surfaces

(e) Steering pulls to one side

1 Check for stiffness of one differential shaft

CHAPTER 7

AUTOMATIC TRANSMISSION

7:1 General description

This Borg Warner transmission incorporates a fluid torque converter coupled by chain and sprockets to a hydraulically operated gearbox wnich gives three forward ratios and reverse. The forward ratios are automatically engaged according to accelerator position and the speed of the vehicle. By selecting '1' it is possible to override the automatic control in first and second ratios and this will give engine braking.

The layout of the system is shown diagrammatically in **FIG 7:1**. The hydraulic torque converter is a casing filled with fluid and carrying impeller vanes 5. The casing is bolted to the crankshaft 1. As the casing revolves, fluid is impelled against the vanes of stator 3 and turbine 4. As the stator is virtually stationary at starting, the effect is of torque multiplication. At first this multiplication is about 2 to 1 but as the stator picks up speed this gradually falls to 1 to 1 when it is turning at the same speed as the impeller and turbine. The converter is then turning as a unit and transmitting engine torque to input shaft 8 by way of chain 7.

Front clutch 9 connects the converter to the gears for forward ratios. Rear clutch 11 is for reverse. Bands 12 and 14 are operated by hydraulic pressure and hold elements of the gear set stationary for the ratios required in 1 and 2, band 14 holds the pinion carrier stationary for first ratio. Band 12 holds reverse sun gear 15 stationary for second ratio.

One-way clutch 13 operates in the first ratio to stop pinion carrier from turning in opposite direction to engine. This allows the gear set to freewheel and ensures smooth changes from first to second and back.

Power flow:

Refer to diagrams in **FIG 7:2**.

'1' selected (low ratio):

Front clutch applied, converter connected to forward sun gear (diagram 'A'). Rear band is applied. Pinion carrier gives reaction on drive and overrun to provide engine braking. Reverse sun gears turns in opposite direction. Ratio 2.39 to 1.

'D' and '2' selected (low ratio):

Front clutch applied (diagram 'B'). One-way clutch operates to hold carrier stationary. Freewheel on the overrun. Ratio 2.39 to 1.

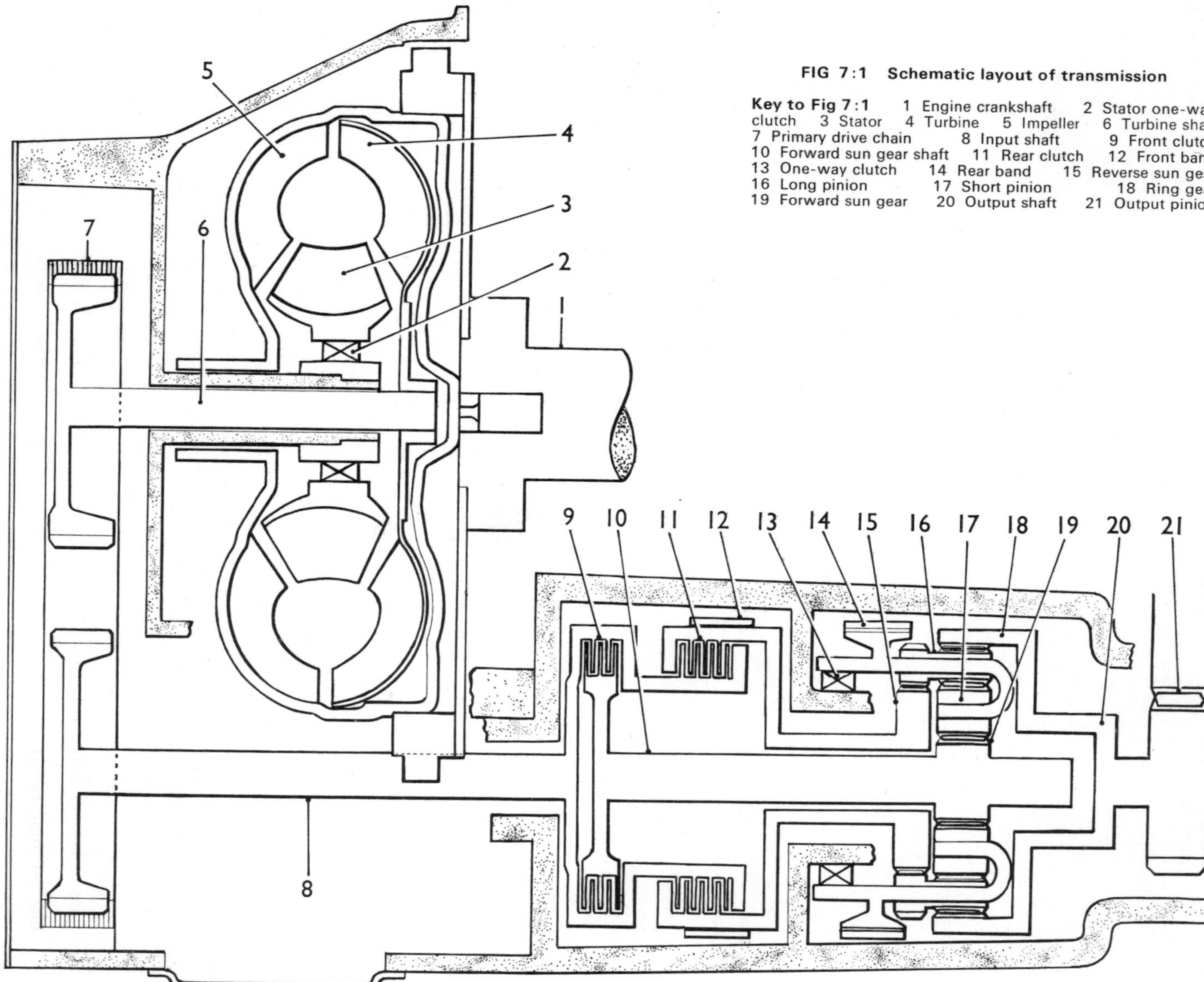

FIG 7:1 Schematic layout of transmission

Key to Fig 7:1 1 Engine crankshaft 2 Stator one-way clutch 3 Stator 4 Turbine 5 Impeller 6 Turbine shaft 7 Primary drive chain 8 Input shaft 9 Front clutch 10 Forward sun gear shaft 11 Rear clutch 12 Front band 13 One-way clutch 14 Rear band 15 Reverse sun gear 16 Long pinion 17 Short pinion 18 Ring gear 19 Forward sun gear 20 Output shaft 21 Output pinion

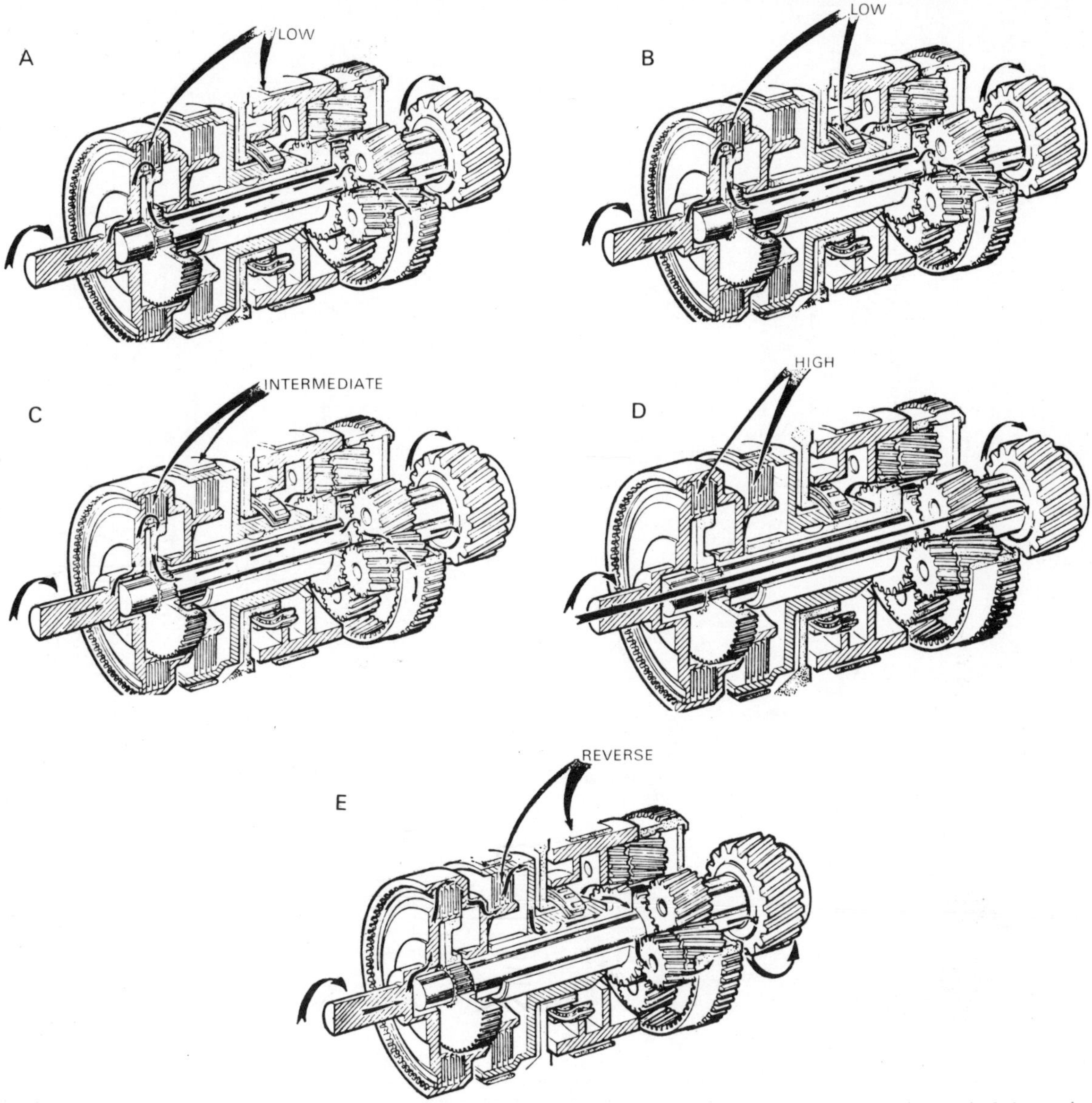

FIG 7:2 Diagrams showing the power flow through the transmission in the various ratios. The input shaft is on the left

Key to Fig 7:2 **A** Low ratio—'1' selected **B** Low ratio—'D' or '2' selected **C** Intermediate ratio—'D', '1' or '2' selected **D** High ratio—'D' selected **E** Reverse ratio

'1', '2' or 'D' selected (intermediate ratio):

Front clutch and front band applied (diagram 'C'). Reverse sun gear provides reaction on drive and overrun, giving engine braking. Ratio 1.45 to 1.

'D' selected (high ratio):

Front and rear clutches applied (diagram 'D'). Both sun gears are locked together, the gear set turning as a unit. This provides drive and engine braking. Ratio 1 to 1.

Reverse:

Rear clutch and rear band applied (diagram 'E'). Pinion carrier provides reaction on drive and overrun, giving engine braking. Ratio 2.09 to 1.

Hydraulic control:

This is shown diagrammatically in **FIG 7:3**. Hydraulic control is achieved by directing hydraulic fluid pressure through valves that are under the combined influences of

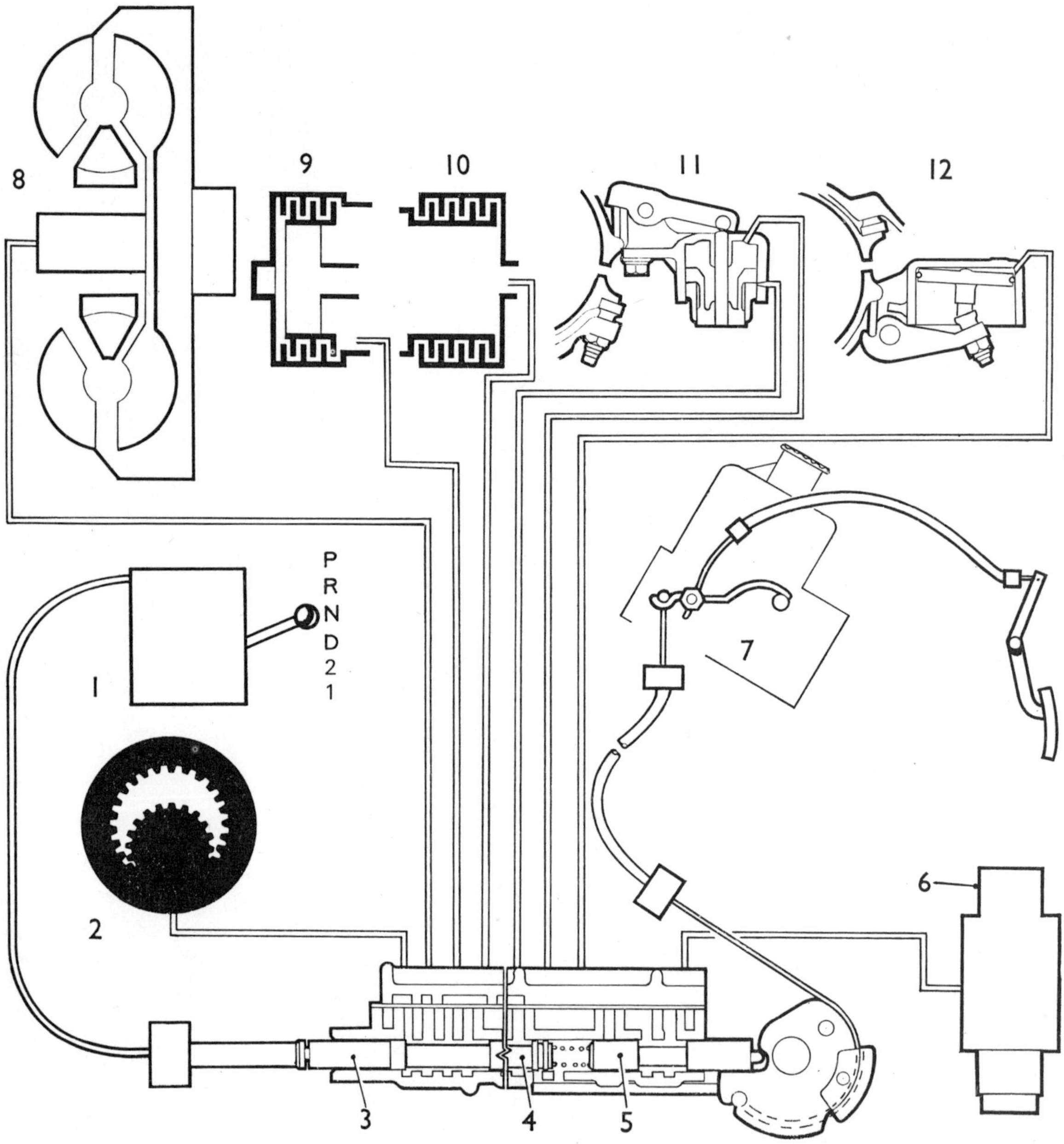

FIG 7:3 How the automatic transmission system is hydraulically controlled

Key to Fig 7:3 1 Selector lever 2 Pump 3 Manual valve 4 Downshift valve 5 Throttle valve 6 Governor 7 Throttle lever 8 Torque converter 9 Front clutch 10 Rear clutch 11 Front servo 12 Rear servo

selector lever and throttle pedal, and also a governor which is sensitive to road speed. Pump 2 supplies the hydraulic and lubrication needs of the converter and transmission.

Moving selector lever 1 to 'D', '1', '2' or 'R' moves valve 3 which then directs fluid to, or exhausts it from, the appropriate valves, clutches or bands.

The downshift cam is connected by cable to carburetter throttle lever 7. Movement of downshift valve 4 modifies pressure from throttle valve 5 to produce a pressure that is related to engine torque and road speed. Full movement of the downshift valve by pressing the throttle pedal through the 'kickdown' position produces up-changes at preset maximum road speeds, or gives a down-change at speeds just below the maximum according to governor pressure.

The governor 6 regulates pressure according to road speed. This pressure decides the points at which ratio changes occur.

7:2 Routine maintenance

Refer to **FIG 7:4**. Keep stoneguards 'A' free from dirt. Clean converter and transmission casings to encourage natural cooling.

Every 3000 miles (5000 km) or 3 months, check fluid level. Have vehicle parked on level ground, with engine and transmission at normal running temperature. Select 'P' (3) and let engine idle for 2 minutes. Wipe dipstick (4), and with engine still idling, insert it and withdraw again immediately. If necessary add correct automatic transmission fluid to bring level to 'high' mark (5). Difference between marks is one pint (.6 litre).

If draining is necessary, take great care if transmission is at running temperature. **The fluid will be extremely hot and may scald.** Do not refill with used fluid if contaminated. Amount needed will depend on fluid that is trapped in the converter and this may be up to 5 pints (2.8 litres). Total capacity of system is 14.8 pints (8.5 litres).

The selector linkage must be checked every 6000 miles (10,000 km) or 6 months.

7:3 Selector lever positions

To prevent direct selection from 'N' the lever must be moved to the right against spring pressure, before engaging '1', '2' or 'R'. Move lever fully to right before engaging 'P'.

'P' (Park): No engine power to wheels. Transmission locked. Use for parking or for running engine for tuning or adjustment. **Do not select when vehicle is moving.**

'R' (Reverse): Gives reverse with full engine braking. Do not select while vehicle is moving forward.

'N' (Neutral): No power to wheels. Apply handbrake when vehicle is at rest.

'D' (Drive): For all normal driving. Fully automatic gear-changes according to speed and to position of accelerator pedal.

'2': Only first and second ratios available; automatic depending on road speed and position of throttle pedal. Must not be selected at speeds above 55 miles/hr (88 km/hr).

'1': First ratio held, full engine braking. Must not be selected at speeds above 55 miles/hr (88 km/hr).

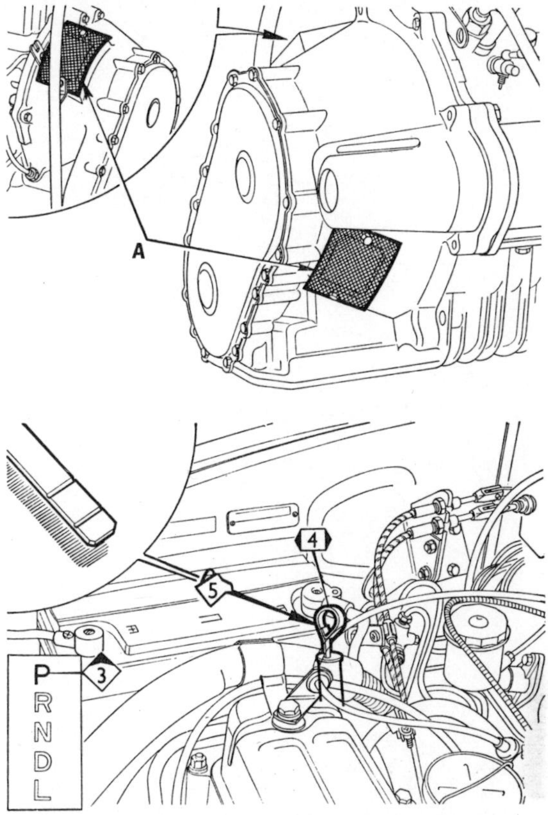

FIG 7:4 Keep the stoneguards (A) free of dirt and mud and study the procedure for checking the oil level

Key to Fig 7:4 3 'Park' position with engine running 4 Dipstick 5 High and Low marks

7:4 Towing

When vehicle is used for towing, always select '2' or '1' before going up or down steep hills.

To tow the vehicle, add an extra 3 pints ($3\frac{1}{2}$ US pints or 1.7 litres) of fluid to the transmission. Do not tow at speeds higher than 30 miles/hr (50 km/hr) or for more than 40 miles (65 km).

Do not tow with front wheels on road if transmission is excessively noisy. The vehicles cannot be tow-started.

7:5 Stationary tests

These tests are essential to determine the nature of defects. **In most cases, rectification is work for a properly equipped service station.** However, the tests may help an owner to check what is wrong. The engine and transmission must be at normal running temperature.

Idling speed:

Correct engine idling speed is essential to avoid stalling or excessive engagement thump. Using an electric tachometer and set to 550 rev/min (see also **Chapter 2**).

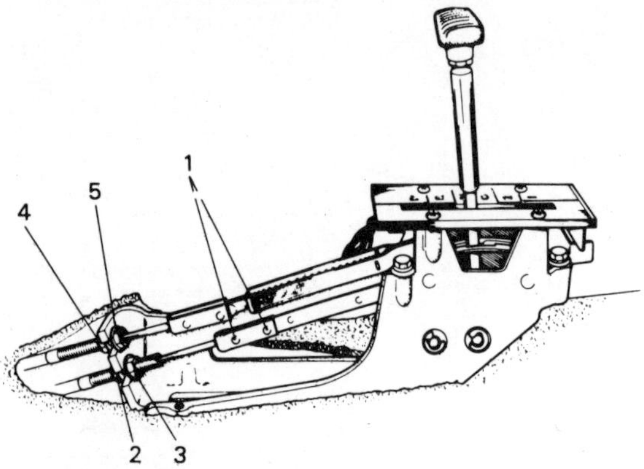

FIG 7:5 Adjusting the selector and park cables

Key to Fig 7:5 1 Clevis pins 2 and 3 Selector cable adjustment nuts 4 and 5 Park cable adjustment nuts

Starter:

Check that starter operates only in 'P' and 'N'.

Reverse light (if fitted):

Should operate in 'R' only.

With brakes applied:

Select 'N' to 'D', 'N' to '2', 'N' to '1', and 'N' to 'R' with engine idling. Transmission engagement should be felt with each selection.

'Creep':

Select 'N' and release brakes. Check that 'creep' does not occur with engine idling and with it revving.

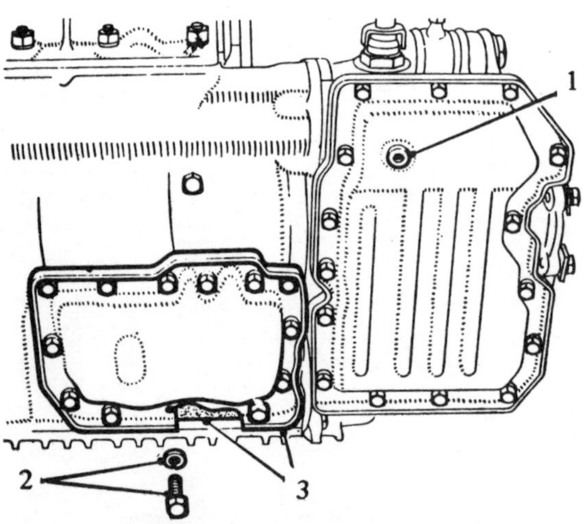

FIG 7:6 **Removal of servo cover**

Key to Fig 7:6 1 Transmission drain plug 2 Cover setscrew and washer 3 Servo cover and gasket

Stall test:

The duration of this test must not exceed 10 seconds. The test is made only when transmission slip or poor acceleration is suspected.

Stall speed is the maximum engine speed obtained at forced throttle opening ('kickdown') with the converter turbine held stationary.

1 Drive for 5 miles (8 km) so that engine and transmission are at running temperature. Set handbrake and chock the wheels.
2 Connect up a tachometer (revolution indicator) so that it can be seen from the driver's seat. Select 'P'. Check that fluid level is correct (see **Section 7:2**). Apply footbrake.
3 Select either '1' or 'R' (whichever is required for the process of elimination). Force throttle through 'kickdown' position for not more than ten seconds. Note highest rev/min reading. If under 1200, a slipping stator is indicated. If over 2200, there is transmission slip. If between 1500 and 1900, the condition is normal, but between 1200 and 1400 the engine power is suspect.

Converter condition is anlayzed by road testing, engine condition and transmission performance together with a stall test.

A slipping stator is due to its freewheel not holding (see 2 in **FIG 7:1**). Condition is confirmed by inability to pull away on a steep hill or poor acceleration from rest.

If stall test shows a normal condition, the converter is probably satisfactory but there is a rare condition of a seized stator freewheel that may still be present. This will show by reduced maximum speed in all gears (more pronounced in top ratio) with severe overheating of converter and transmission.

Transmission slip indicates slip in components employed in the selected gear ('1', '2' or 'R'). Slip in all three positions may be due to low pressure. In one position only, it suggests a faulty component.

As pointed out at the beginning of this section, rectification of defects is a matter for a service station equipped to deal with automatic transmission.

7:6 Adjustments

Selector cable:

1 Check the operation of the selector lever in 'R', 'N', 'D', '1' and '2'. In each position there must be a positive hold in the selector gate with no overriding of the control valve detent (item 3 in **FIG 7:3**).
2 If unsatisfactory, remove the console and refer to **FIG 7:5**. Select 'N' and remove the clevis pins 1, now ensure the lever is fully against the 'N' stop.
3 Push the selector cable in as far as possible then pull it out two stops only, to give a true 'N' position in the control valve detent.
4 Without using any force on the cable or selector, check that the clevis pin holes align through the cable fork and selector rod. If not, slacken either one of the adjusting nuts 2 or 3 and turn the appropriate one to bring the holes into perfect alignment.
5 Tighten the nuts and recheck the selection as described in operation 1.

Park cable:

1 Select 'P' and check for positive engagement by releasing the handbrake and attempting to rock the car backwards and forwards. If the parking pawl ratchets over the ring gear adjust as follows:
2 Remove the console cover and refer to **FIG 7:5**. Select 'R' and slacken either one of the adjusting nuts 4 or 5. Hold the selector lever forward against the 'R' stop and turn the appropriate adjusting nut 4 or 5 to either (a), increase the effective length of the outer cable to engage more fully or (b), decrease the effective length to disengage if fouling in 'R'. Tighten the nuts.
3 Select 'P' and recheck the engagement.

Brake bands:

Adjustment of the brake bands is not a normal service procedure and the adjustment should not be tampered with unnecessarily. However, they do require some adjustment, possibly after a considerable mileage, when the brake bands begin to show signs of wear.

The following malfunctions may indicate that the front brake band requires adjustment:

(a) No second ratio in 'D', '1' or '2'.

(b) Drag in low, high or reverse but not in intermediate.

(c) Bumpy and possibly delayed shifts.

(d) Slip which may cause the engine to 'flare' up when shifting into and out of second ratio.

The following malfunctions may indicate that the rear brake band requires adjustment:

(a) Drag in intermediate and high ratios.

(b) Reduced engine braking in '1' and a high degree of slip in reverse.

Front brake band:

1 Refer to **FIG 7:6** and remove the drain plug 1 but take care against the danger of scalding if the engine is hot. Note also that some oil will remain in the torque converter.
2 Take out the screws and washers 2 (round the servo cover). Lower the cover and gasket 3. Scrap the gasket and obtain a new one.
3 Refer to **FIG 7:7** and note that a special tool BWA 548-2 and a torque wrench are required for the adjustment. A local or home manufacture may solve the acquisition of the special tool but a torque wrench is essential.
4 Slacken the backnut 1 and with the special tool and torque wrench tighten the adjusting screw 2 to a torque of 8 lbf ft (1.1 kgf m). Now back off one complete turn. Tighten the backnut.
5 Replace the dismantled parts, fill up with the correct grade of oil to the procedure described in **Section 7:2**.

Rear brake band:

1 Complete operations 1 to 3 in the previous sub-section but note that a lb inch torque wrench is required for this adjustment.
2 Slacken the locknut 3 and uncouple the return spring.

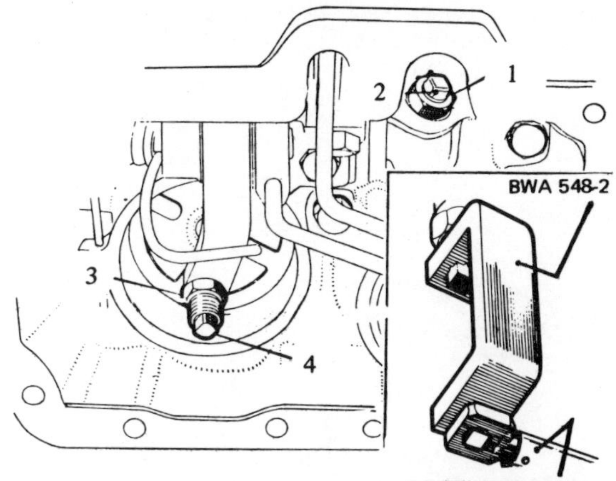

Fig 7:7 Brake band adjustment screws and the special tool required

Key to Fig 7:7 1 Front band locknut 2 Front band adjuster 3 Rear band locknut 4 Rear band adjuster

3 Tighten the adjusting screw 4 to 15 lbf inch or 73 gmf m. Now back off three complete turns. Tighten the backnut and refit the return spring.

If it is discovered during the rear brake band adjustment that the adjusting screw is not long enough to obtain the correct setting, refer to **FIG 7:8** and note that the strut 3 can be exchanged for one marked 255 (Part No. 37H 4407); providing the cause of the problem is not due to excess wear or stretching of the band.

If the adjustment is so restricted that the screw cannot be unscrewed three complete turns, the strut 3 can be exchanged for a shorter type marked 175 (Part No. 37H 4406).
4 Complete operation 5 from the previous sub-section.

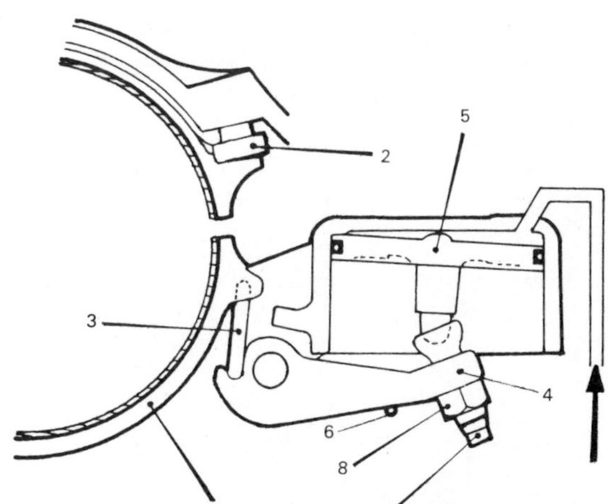

FIG 7:8 The rear band and servo

Key to Fig 7:8 1 Rear band 2 Fixed abutment 3 Strut 4 Actuating lever 5 Piston 6 Hairpin spring 7 Adjuster 8 Locknut (arrow indicates oil pressure direction)

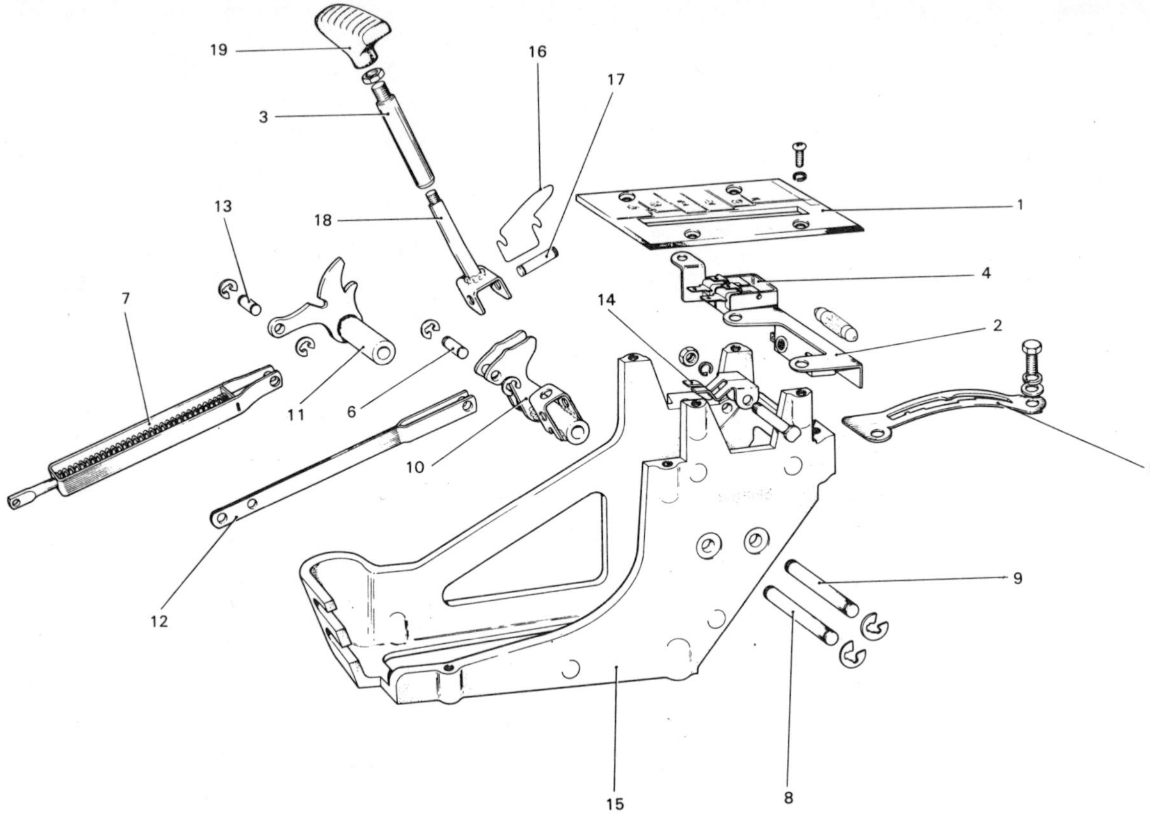

FIG 7:9 Components of selector mechanism

Key to Fig 7:9 1 Indicator panel 2 Panel illumination bulb holder 3 Selector lever extension 4 Starter inhibitor/reverse light switch assembly 5 Selector quadrant 6 Pin-selector cable link 7 Park cable spring box 8 Pin-park cable lever 9 Pin-selector lever 10 Selector lever and cam 11 Park cable lever 12 Link-selector cable 13 Pin-park cable springbox 14 Micro-switch actuating lever assembly 15 Mounting bracket casting 16 Selector lever spring 17 Pivot pin—selector lever 18 Selector lever 19 Selector lever knob

7:7 Micro switches

The reverse light and starter inhibitor micro switches are non-adjustable. Referring to **FIG 7:9**, high spots on the selector cams 10 operate the starter inhibitor switch 4 in 'P' and 'N' positions. A second high spot on the control cam operates the reverse light switch (if fitted) when the lever is in the 'R' position.

To check a faulty switch, remove the lead connectors and short circuit them. If the circuit operates, renew the switch.

Removing switches:

1 Remove the console assembly.

2 Refer to **FIG 7:9** and take off the selector panel 1. Disconnect the four wiring connections from the micro switches 4 (see also **FIG 7:10**).

3 To check the circuit, short-circuit the white/red tracer wires together (starter inhibitor) or the green wires together (reverse light switch). The red/white tracer wire is for the panel illumination.

4 Remove two screws from the micro-switch assembly and release the two spring clips and pins that secure the switches to the mounting bracket.

Refitting:

5 Refit new switches in the reverse order of dismantling.

7:8 Servicing the primary drive

1 Drain the transmission oil and replace the plug.

2 Refer to **Chapter 1, Section 1:10** and remove the power unit.

3 Refer to **FIG 7:11**. Unscrew and remove seventeen set screws and washers and take off the chain cover 1 and gasket 2. Scrap the gasket and obtain a new one.

4 Knock back the locking tabs on washers 3 and 4. Using a wood wedge between the sprocket and pump housing remove the output shaft nut 5. Unscrew and remove the input shaft nut 6.

5 Gently lever the sprockets off their splines complete with chain.

6 Inspect the chain and sprockets for wear, loose links and broken sprocket teeth.

7 Reassemble in the reverse order using new tab washers and gasket.

7:9 Servicing speedometer drive

1 Refer to **FIG 7:12** and disconnect the drive cable 3 from the screwed bush. Unscrew and remove the bolt 7 and washer, lift off the spring plate 8 and withdraw the screwed bush and gasket 3 and the pinion 14, bush 13 and seal 10.

2 Drain the transmission oil, unscrew and remove the seven set screws and washers 2 and lift off the extension housing 1 and gasket.

3 Inspect the drive gear 11 and if it must be removed use a nut splitter, but take care not to side load or damage the shaft.

4 Renew the pinion oil seal 10 and the pinion if the teeth are chipped or worn.

5 Renew the O-ring 6 what ever the condition. Any failure of this seal will permit oil pressure to enter the governor circuit, causing the 1-2 shift valve to blank off the pressure feed to the rear band and causing loss of drive in reverse.

6 Ensure that the governor oil sealing rings 12 are undamaged and free in their grooves.

7 Reassemble the parts in the reverse order noting the following points:

Fit the speedometer gear 11 on to the shaft shoulder end first and tap it into position with a copper mallet.

Ensure the governor pressure tube is correctly located in its O-ring 6.

After completing the assembly fill the transmission with oil as described in **Section 7:2**.

7:10 Driving tests

These are carried out on the road. The speeds are true and may not be those recorded by the speedometer.

Do not select '2' or '1' from 'D' at speeds above 55 mile/hr (88 km/hr) or the engine may be over-revved.

'Kick-down' is obtained by depressing accelerator pedal fully until it touches the carpet. A slight resistance will be felt as the pedal passes through the point of normal full travel. Use delicate pressure on the pedal to determine minimum upward shifts or the shift speeds may seem too high.

1 Select 'D', use 'kick-down' acceleration and check that 1 to 2 shift occurs between 31 and 39 mile/hr (50 to 62 km/hr). 2 to 3 shift should occur between 59 and 65 mile/hr (95 to 104 km/hr). If no drive in 'D' **(1st ratio not operating), select '1', accelerate to** 20 mile/hr (30 km/hr) and select 'D' to verify drive in 2nd and 3rd ratios.

2 Between 53 and 56 mile/hr (85 to 90 km/hr) in 3rd ratio 'kick-down' and check downshift to 2nd ratio.

3 Between 25 and 30 mile/hr (40 to 48 km/hr) in 3rd ratio 'kick-down' and check downshift to 1st ratio.

4 Using minimum throttle, check for 1 to 2 shift between 7 and 14 mile/hr (11 to 22 km/hr). Check for 2 to 3 shift between 14 and 21 mile/hr (22 to 33 km/hr).

5 At 30 mile/hr (50 km/hr) in 3rd ratio (D3), release accelerator and select '1'. Check for 3 to 2 engagement and a subsequent 2 to 1 downshift occurring at approximately 5 mile/hr (8 km/hr) and come to rest.

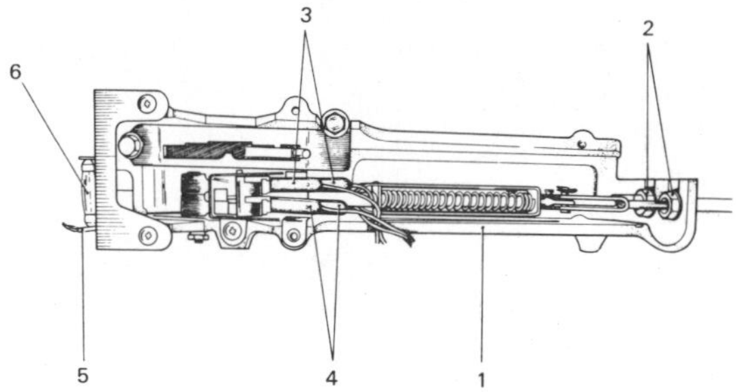

FIG 7:10 Electrical connections to the selector mechanism

Key to Fig 7:10 1 Selector mechanism frame 2 Slector and park cable locknuts 3 Starter inhibitor switch connections (white, red tracer) 4 Reversing light switch connections (green) 5 Selector illumination bulb connection (red, white tracer) 6 Selector illumination bulb

6 Leave '1' selected. Accelerate to about 20 mile/hr (30 km/hr), release accelerator and check that upshift does not occur and engine braking can be felt.

7 Select 'D'. Accelerate to 30 mile/hr (50 km/hr), release accelerator to ensure 3rd ratio and select '1' to get intermediate 'kick-down' between 16 and 27 mile/hr (25 to 43 km/hr) and check for '2' to '1' downshift.

8 Accelerate to 30 mile/hr (50 km/hr), release accelerator to ensure 3rd ratio and select '2', check for '3' to '2' downshift.

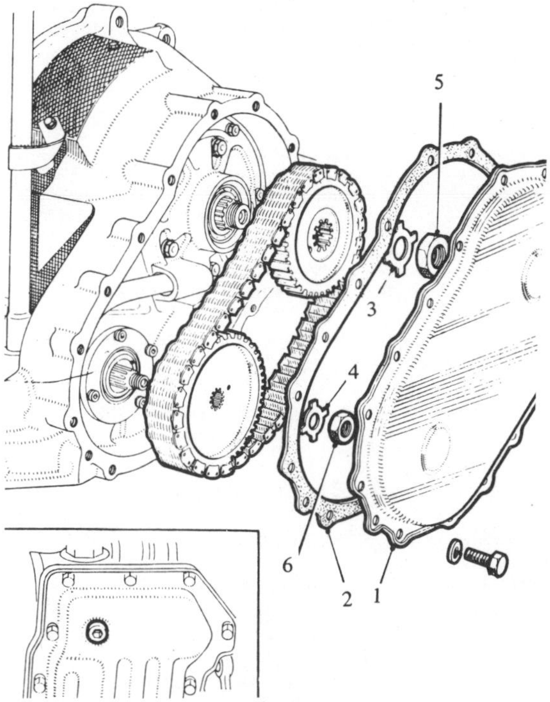

FIG 7:11 The primary drive chain

Key to Fig 7:11 1 Chain cover 2 Gasket 3 and 4 Tab washers 5 Output shaft nut 6 Input shaft nut (inset shows drain plug position)

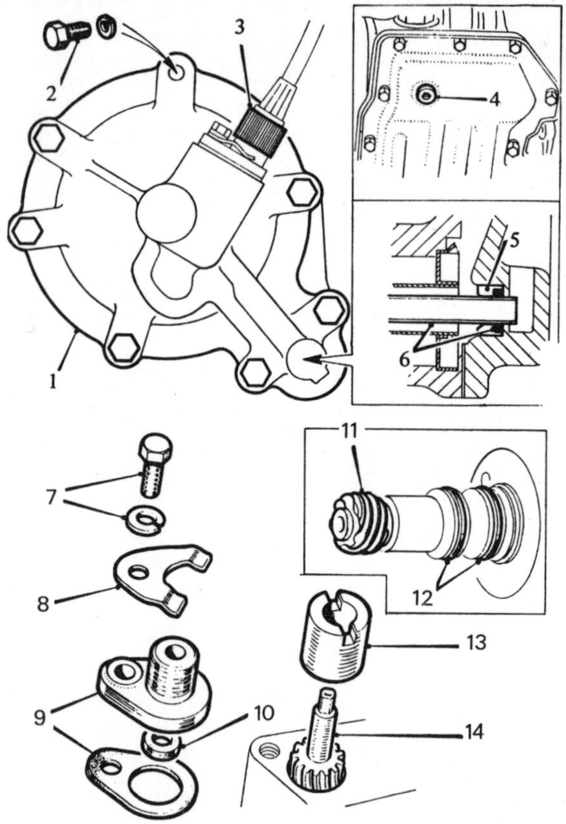

FIG 7:12 Servicing the speedometer gear

Key to Fig 7:12 1 Extension housing 2 Extension housing screw 3 Speedometer cable nut 4 Transmission drain plug 5 Collar 6 Governor pressure feed tube and O-ring 7 Screw and spring washer 8 Spring plate 9 Pinion bush and gasket 10 Pinion oil seal 11 Speedometer gear 12 Governor oil sealing rings 13 Pinion bush 14 Pinion

9 At rest select 'R'. Reverse with full throttle (if possible). Release throttle and confirm engine braking.
10 Stop on steep hill, select 'P'. Check that vehicle is held and selector is trapped by gate. Repeat when facing the other way.

7:11 Separating transmission from engine

1 Refer to **Chapter 1, Section 1:10** and remove the power unit.
2 Refer to **Chapter 11** and remove the starter motor.
3 Working through the starter motor aperture unscrew and remove the four bolts securing the converter to the drive plate.
4 Disconnect the 'kick-down' cable from the carburetter linkage. Remove the engine front mounting plate.
5 Refer to **Chapter 2** and take off the fuel pump, adaptor plate and pushrod.
6 Withdraw the distributor and the quill shaft (see **FIG 1:23**).
7 Manoeuvre the engine into a position whereby the transmission can be removed. Remove all the bolts which secure the transmission and the oil pump, extension housing, to the engine adaptor plate (item 116 in **FIG 1:1**).
8 Separate the transmission from the engine.

Refitting:

9 Refit the transmission unit in the reverse order of dismantling noting the following:
Ensure the engine oil sealing ring is correctly located.
Smear both sides of the engine:transmission gasket with jointing compound.
Engage the converter spigot into the crankshaft before finally mating the units.
Do not tighten the engine:transmission securing bolts until the converter housing drive plate screws (four) have been tightened. Ensure the drive plate and torque converter are aligned and tighten the four screws in a 180 deg. sequence.

7:12 Fault diagnosis

It is impossible to give a detailed fault analysis because most of the innumerable tests for faults and their cure are a matter for a service station. Those that are given may be rectified with the help of instructions in this chapter.

(a) Starter will not operate in 'P' or 'N' or operates in all positions

1 Test inhibitor switch(es), circuit(s) and check cam action

(b) Faulty operation of reversing light (when fitted)

1 See 1 in (a)

(c) Excessive bump on engagement of 'D', '1', '2' or 'R'

1 Reduce idling speed of engine (see **Chapter 2**)
2 If no cure, consult experts

(d) Stall test speed less than 1200 rev/min (slipping stator)

1 Renew torque converter (see experts)

(e) Parking pawl does not hold vehicle

1 Adjust/examine parking cable
2 If no cure, consult experts

(f) 'P' operates, but no drive in 'D', '1', '2' or 'R'

1 Check fluid level
2 Check manual cable selector cable/adjustment
3 If no cure, consult experts

(g) Reduced maximum speed in all ratios, converter overheats

1 Fit new torque converter (see experts)

CHAPTER 8

DRIVE SHAFTS AND SUSPENSION

8:1 Description of drive shafts

The output gears of the transmission are connected to the front wheels by Hardy Spicer drive shafts fitted with constant velocity universal joints at the outer ends and plunge joints at the inner end (see **FIG 8:1**). The outer member of each plunge joint has a mounting face that bolts to the flanged shaft and engages with the final drive gears in the transmission. The splined shaft of each constant velocity joint runs in bearings in the front hub and swivel axle assembly and carries the brake disc and front wheel. The sliding action of the plunge joints accommodates changes in the distance between the transmission and the front hubs due to suspension movements.

8:2 Routine maintenance

The rubber boots enclosing the joints are packed with grease and no routine maintenance is necessary. It is, however, advisable to make an occasional visual check of the condition of the boots. Cracking through damage or deterioration may allow dirt to enter the joint, leading to rapid wear.

8:3 Drive shafts

Removing (see also **Section 8:8**):

1 Fit a $\frac{1}{2}$ inch (13 mm) block between the upper arm of suspension and the rebound rubber.
2 Jack up the front of the car and support with safety stands. Remove the road wheel.
3 Extract the hub nut splitpin, unscrew the nut and remove the outer cone (see **FIG 8:16**).
4 Refer to **FIG 8:1**, first mark the inner flange joint and take out the six setscrews securing the outer race to the differential drive shafts. Tap the edge of the outer race to release the backplate.
5 To drive the shaft from the hub, refit the hub nut with the castellations facing inwards and wind it onto the shaft until it is flush with the end thread. Tap the shaft out of the hub as far as the nut will allow then remove the nut and drift the shaft clear. The inner roller bearing and spacer will come away with the shaft.

Refitting:

6 Refit in the reverse order of dismantling.

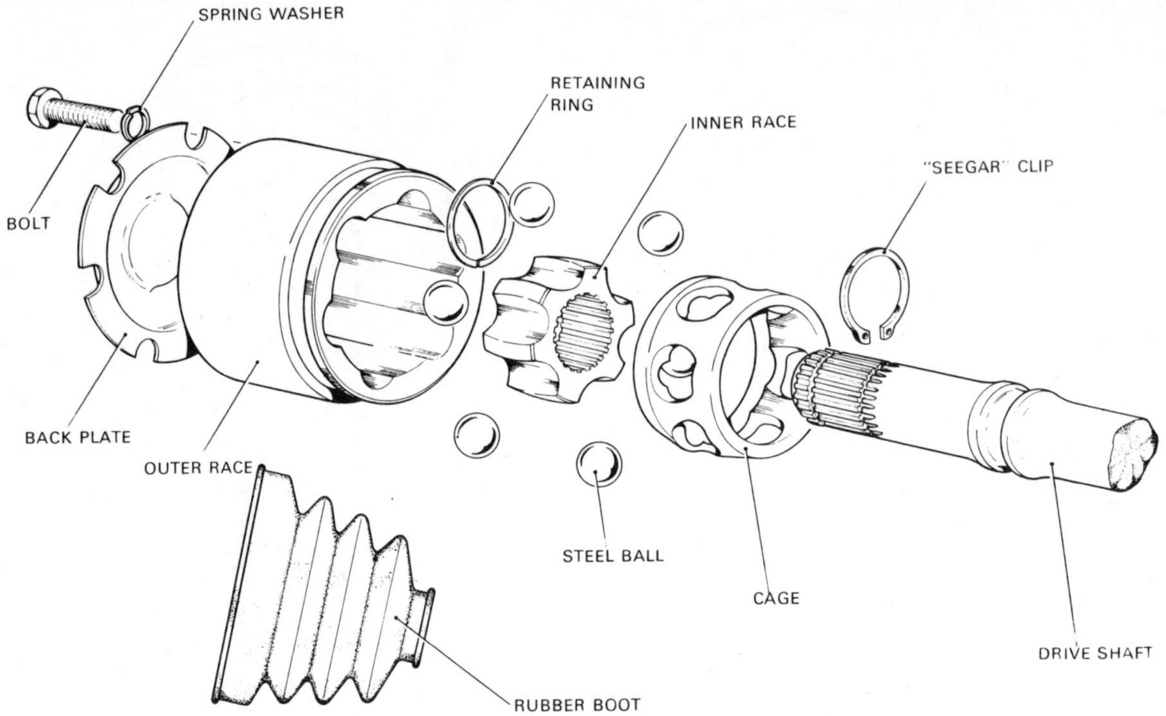

FIG 8:1 Exploded view of the drive shaft inner joint

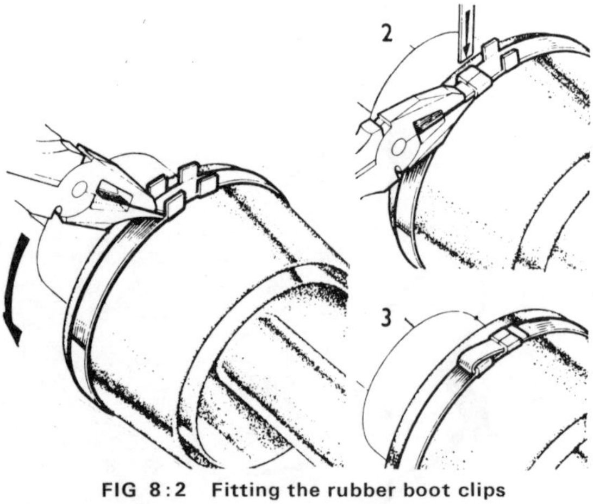

FIG 8:2 Fitting the rubber boot clips

Key to Fig 8:2 1 Pull clip as tight as possible. Pull the free end, hold and take a further grip, and pull downwards again 2 Hold in position, fold over and secure front tabs 3 Bend free end over and secure clip end with rear tabs

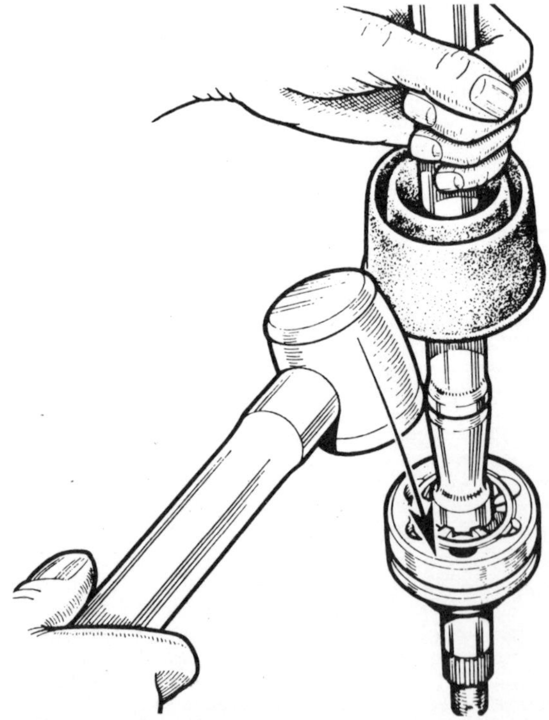

FIG 8:3 Use a soft-faced hammer to strike the edge of the joint to remove it from the shaft

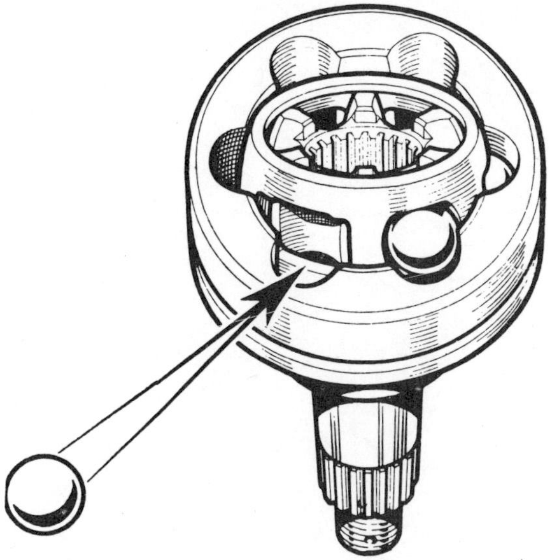

FIG 8:4 Tilt the inner race to release the balls

8:4 Overhauling the constant velocity joint

Removing:

With drive shaft removed, take off and discard the clip securing the boot (see **FIG 8:2**). Holding shaft as in **FIG 8:3**, use a soft-faced hammer to strike the edge of the joint at the point indicated by the arrow. This will contract the circlip to release the joint from the shaft.

Overhauling:

Withdraw the rubber boot. Mark the relative positions of the inner and outer races. Tilt ball cage and prise out balls (see **FIG 8:4**). Turn inner member and ball cage into line with axis of joint. Turn cage until the two large windows coincide with two of the lands in the outer ring of the joint (see **FIG 8:5**). Withdraw the inner race assembly.

Line up inner member with axis of ball cage (see **FIG 8:6**). Two lands of the inner member must coincide with the two large windows in the ball cage. Withdraw inner member. Clean all parts and examine for damage and wear. Check rubber boots for splits and deterioration. The outer edge of the cage windows may show signs of wear which could cause knocking on the extreme lock. If detected renew the cage.

Reassembling:

The majority of production line assemblies use a standard size ball cage, but a .010 inch (.25 mm) oversize cage and bell housing may have been fitted during the original assembly. As a joint will only accept a cage the same size as the original it is essential to know the correct size for renewal.

To check this, a gauge, service tool 18G 1064, is available and this should be used on the dismantled cage before renewing. If possible get the Service Stores to use this gauge to confirm. A standard cage will pass through the gauge but an oversize cage will not. The standard size service kit is colour coded white and numbered 18G 8194. An oversize kit is colour coded red and numbered 18G 8195.

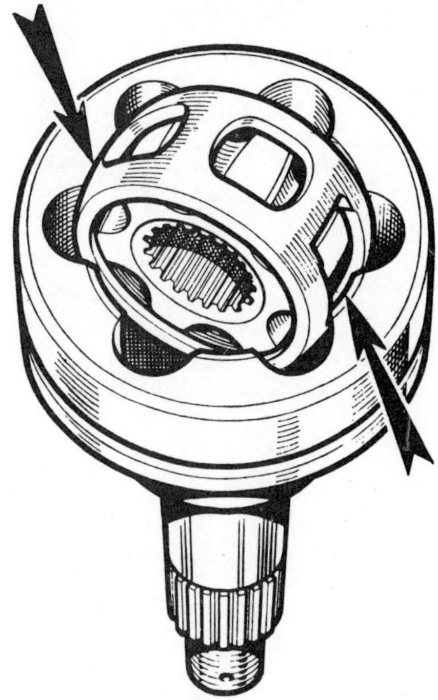

FIG 8:5 Turn cage until two large windows coincide with two of outer ring lands

Lightly lubricate all components with special grease HYL 3434 during assembly and note that they should assemble without undue force.

Refer to **FIGS 8:6, 8:5** and **8:4**. Fit the inner member and ball cage into the outer member of the joint with the chamfered bore side of the cage at the blind end of the outer member, and the lugs on the inner member at the open end (see **FIG 8:4**).

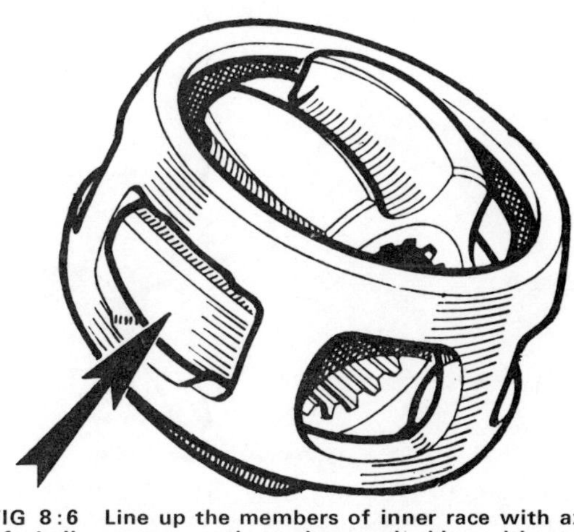

FIG 8:6 Line up the members of inner race with axis of ball cage so that they coincide with two large windows

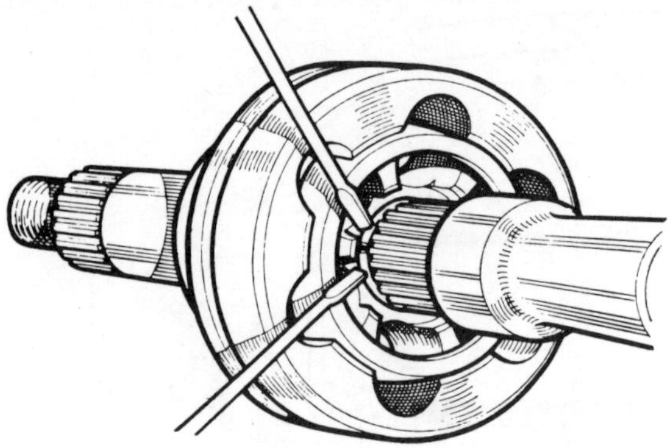

FIG 8:7 Centralize the circlip with screwdrivers before tapping the shaft on to the splines

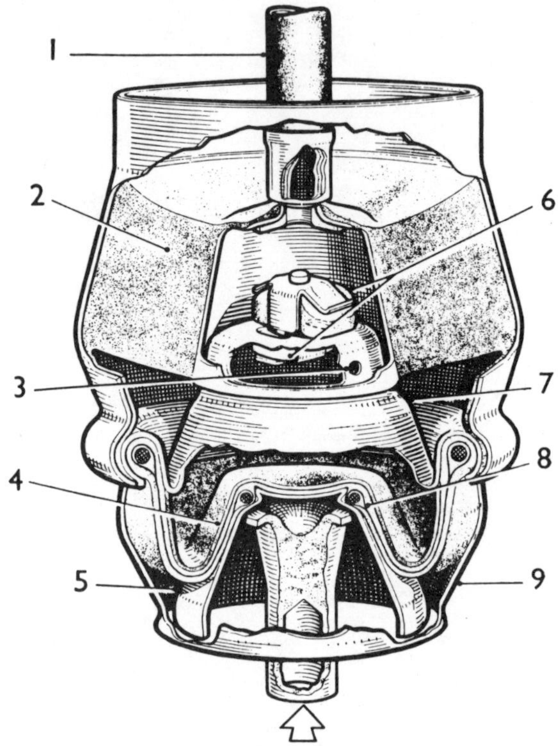

FIG 8:10 Section through a hydraulic displacer

Key to Fig 8:10 1 Interconnecting pipe 2 Rubber spring 3 Damper bleed 4 Butyl liner 5 Tapered piston 7 Fluid-separating member 8 Rubber diaphragm (nylon-reinforced) 9 Tapered cylinder

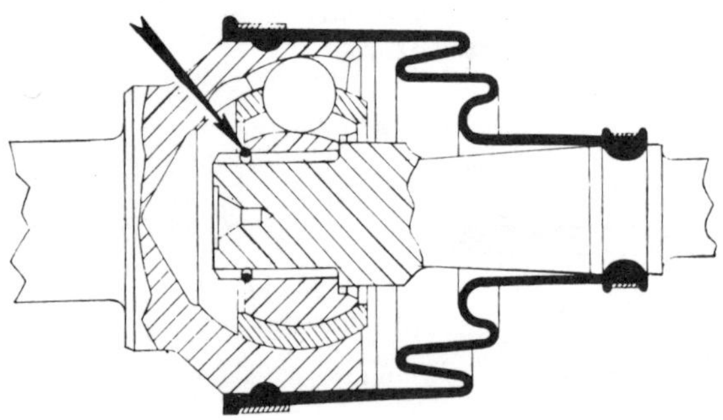

FIG 8:8 Make sure the circlip is fully engaged on the shaft and locked against the inner race

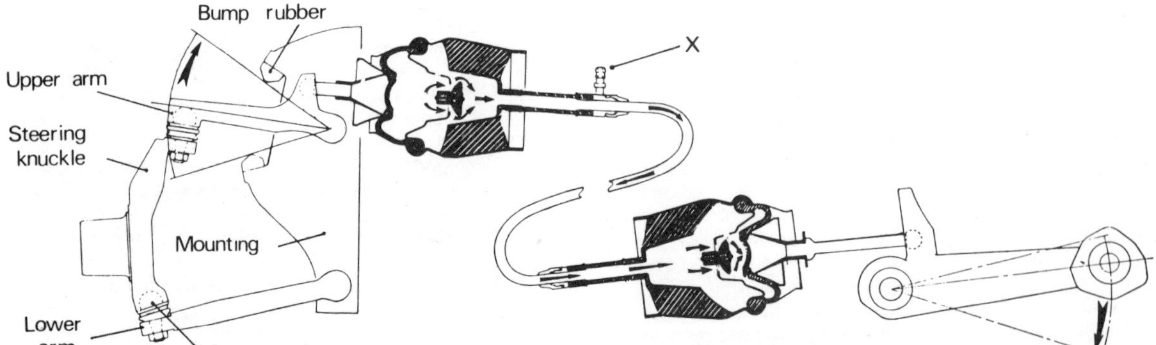

FIG 8:9 Schematic illustration showing a front to rear fluid displacement

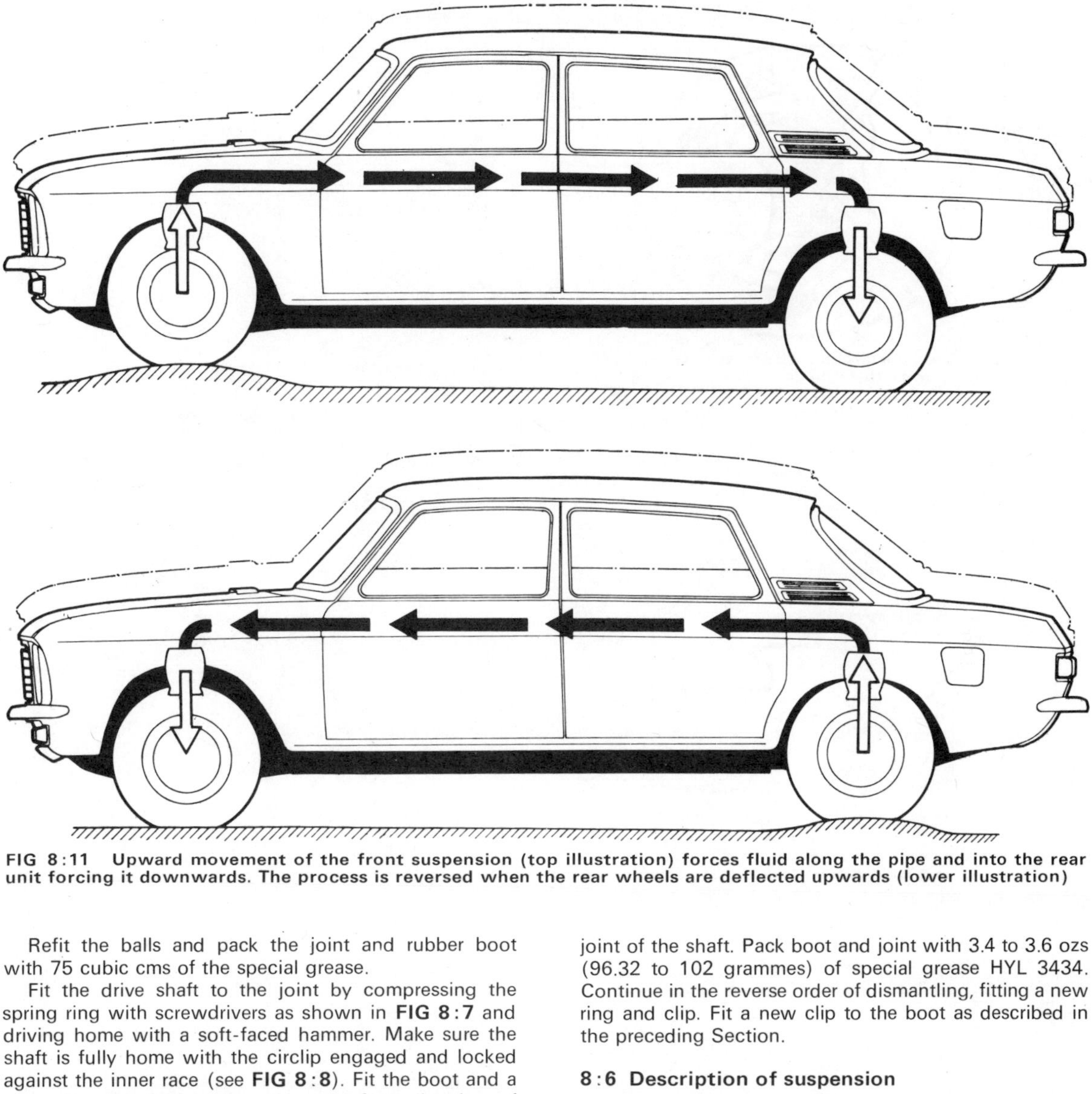

FIG 8:11 Upward movement of the front suspension (top illustration) forces fluid along the pipe and into the rear unit forcing it downwards. The process is reversed when the rear wheels are deflected upwards (lower illustration)

Refit the balls and pack the joint and rubber boot with 75 cubic cms of the special grease.

Fit the drive shaft to the joint by compressing the spring ring with screwdrivers as shown in **FIG 8:7** and driving home with a soft-faced hammer. Make sure the shaft is fully home with the circlip engaged and locked against the inner race (see **FIG 8:8**). Fit the boot and a new clip. The fold in the clip must face direction of rotation (see **FIG 8:2**). Pull free end of clip tight. Close front tabs over free end and fold end back over front tabs and secure with rear tabs.

8:5 Overhauling the plunge joint

With drive shaft removed refer to **FIG 8:1** and withdraw the rubber boot. Remove the retaining ring. Withdraw drive shaft. Remove the Seegar clip from the shaft. Prise out balls and turn inner member until its lands coincide with grooves inside ball cage and withdraw it. Clean the parts and examine for damage or wear. Check boot for splits or deterioration.

Reassemble by fitting the inner member and ball cage assembly to the shaft with the long tapered end of the cage facing towards the constant velocity (outer) joint of the shaft. Pack boot and joint with 3.4 to 3.6 ozs (96.32 to 102 grammes) of special grease HYL 3434. Continue in the reverse order of dismantling, fitting a new ring and clip. Fit a new clip to the boot as described in the preceding Section.

8:6 Description of suspension

The Hydrolastic system has front and rear displacer units connected on the same side by a pipe (see **FIG 8:9**). The units incorporate a rubber spring and a diaphragm as shown in **FIG 8:10**. Upward movement of the front suspension forces fluid along the pipe and into the rear unit, forcing it downwards, thus raising the rear of the car and keeping the body on an even keel. The same process is reversed when the rear wheels are deflected upwards (see **FIG 8:11**). Note the valve marked 'X' in **FIG 8:9**. As the fluid system is pressurized through these valves it is vital not to interfere with them. Any work on pressurizing or de-pressurizing must be carried out by agents with the correct equipment. Because many operations on the suspension system call for de-pressurizing we propose to deal only with those that do not need it.

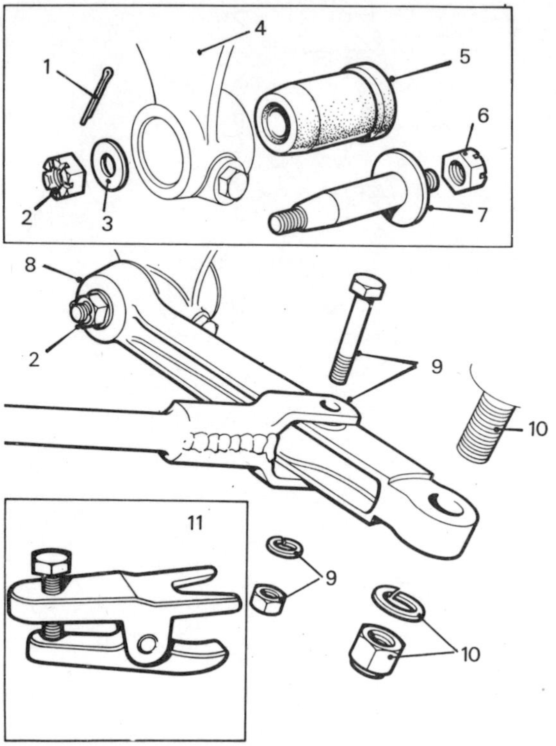

FIG 8:12 Removing the lower pivot arm and bearing

Key to Fig 8:12 1 Splitpin 2 Forward nut 3 Washer 4 Suspension mounting bracket 5 Pivot pin bush 6 Rear nut 7 Pivot pin 8 Pivot arm 9 Tie rod securing bolt 10 Upper ballpin and nut 11 Typical expander tool for separating ballpin tapers

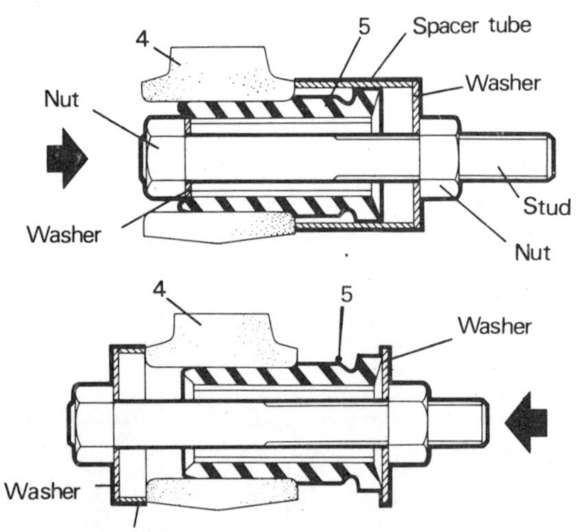

FIG 8:13 Using a 5 inch (12.7 cm) bolt length, spacer and washer to extract the rubber bush (or bushes) from the mounting bracket. (Upper illustration). The lower view illustrates the method of fitting a new 'Silentbloc' bush

8:7 Servicing front pivot bearings and ball joints

Lower arm pivot bearing:

1 Hold upper arm in its laden position by inserting a block of wood $\frac{1}{2}$ x 1.5 inch (13 x 40 mm) between the arm and its rebound rubber.

2 Jack up and support the car and remove the road wheel. Refer to **FIG 8:12**. Disconnect lower ball pin 10 from the arm using an expander tool. Do not hammer on the pin. Remove the tie rod bolt 9.

3 Remove nut 2 (splitpin). Drive the arm free of the pivot pin 7, using a copper hammer adjacent to the pivot. Ease the pin back, remove nut and washer 6 and extract arm. Remove pin and extract bush 5 (or bushes) with stud or bolt with long thread as shown in **FIG 8:13**. The spacer should be 1.3 inch (33 mm) long with a bore of 1.5 inch (38 mm), the washer OD should be .87 inch (22 mm) in diameter.

4 Fit a new one-piece rubber and metal bush 10, drawing it in as shown in **FIG 8:13**. The spacer on the left should be .31 inch (8 mm) long with a bore of 1.37 inch (35 mm). First smear the outside of the bush with genuine rubber grease. **Do not use ordinary grease**. Press bush in from rear until its flange contacts the bracket.

5 Fit plain washer and nut to pivot pin, and holding the lower arm in its normal unladen position, tighten the nut and fit a new splitpin. Now check clearance between arm and bracket at 'A' (see **FIG 8:14**). It should be $.14 \pm .01$ inch ($3.56 \pm .25$ mm). If necessary, adjust by altering the location of the bearing.

6 Reverse the rest of the dismantling procedure, tightening the tie rod bolt to 40 to 50 lbf ft (5.5 to 6.9 kgf m), the swivel axle joint nut to 45 lbf ft (6.2 kgf m) and the wheel nuts to 60 lbf ft (8.3 kgf m).

Upper arm bushes:

As the sleeve is swaged over at each end it is advisable to have the bushes renewed at a Service Station.

Upper ball joint:

1 Repeat preceding operations 1 and 2 but this time remove the top ball pin and do not remove the tie rod bolt. Refer to **FIG 8:15**. Knock back tab of lockwasher 6. Remove dust cover 4 and unscrew the ball pin housing.

2 Clean all parts and examine for wear. Renew as necessary. Make sure that the boot is sound or dirt may enter the joint.

3 Press ball pin into socket and locate in housing. Screw housing into arm until the ball pin has no end play but can still be moved in all directions. Measure the gap between the housing flange and the upper arm with feelers. Remove housing and lubricate ball pin and socket liberally with molybdenized grease (HYL 3434).

4 Fit a new tab washer and shims. From the measured gap subtract .036 inch (.91 mm) for the tab washer and .009 to .013 inch (.23 to .33 mm) for preloading the bearing. Select shims from thickness of .002, .003, .005, .01 and .03 inch (.05, .08, .13, .25 and .76 mm).

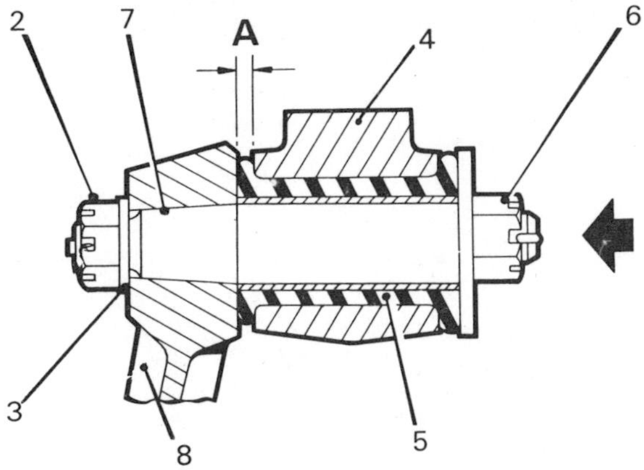

FIG 8:14 The clearance 'A' should be terminated at .14 inch ±.01 inch (3.56 ±.25 mm). Adjust the position of the bearing if necessary. Consult Fig 8:12 for key reference

5 Fit housing with shims and washer and tighten to 70 lbf ft (9.6 kgf m). Turn up one locking tab over the end of the arm nearest the brake disc and two over the housing. Fill space between ball and housing with the same grease and fit dust cover.

6 Reverse rest of dismantling procedure, tightening the ball pin nut to 45 lbf ft (6.2 kgf m) and wheel nuts to 60 lbf ft (8.3 kgf m).

Lower ball joint:

1 Remove the front hub assembly (see **Section 8:8**). Remove the brake disc dust shield. Knock back the tab washer, unscrew the ball pin housing and remove the pin assembly.

2 Carry out operations 2 to 5 for the upper ball joint. When refitting the dust shield, tighten the bolt to 20 lbf ft (2.8 kgf m). Refit the front hub (see **Section 8:8**).

8:8 Servicing the front hubs

Removing:

1 Repeat operation 1 in **Section 8:7**. Slacken hub nut and wheel nuts before jacking up and supporting car. Remove road wheel. It is not necessary to disconnect the brake hose but support the caliper securely when it is removed.

2 Remove brake caliper. Disconnect tie rod ball joint, using an expander tool. Refer to **FIG 8:16** and remove hub nut 3, tap the end of the hub with a mallet and extract the outer cone 5. Pull off disc and flange 1 with a suitable tool or use tool 18GA 146 with adaptor base plate 18GA 146Z. The bolts screw on the wheel studs.

3 Disconnect the drive shaft at the differential coupling (see **Section 8:3**) and disconnect the ball pin tapers as described in **Section 8:7.** Withdraw hub and shaft assembly. Do not pull on the drive shaft to do this or the plunge or inner joint will be separated. Press the shaft out of the hub.

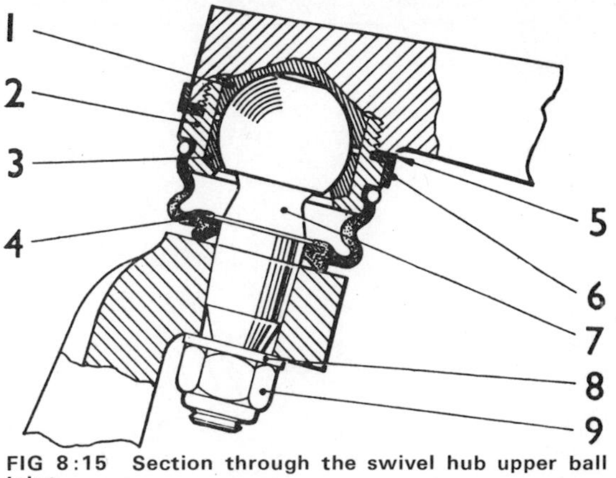

FIG 8:15 Section through the swivel hub upper ball joint

Key to Fig 8:15 1 Bottom socket 2 Housing (hexagon) 3 Top socket 4 Dust cover 5 Shim 6 Lock washer 7 Ball pin 8 Flat washer (special) 9 Locknut

Renewing hub bearings and oil seals:

Refer to **FIG 8:16** and remove oil seals 6 and 10. These will be damaged during removal and must be renewed. Use a soft metal drift in the grooves behind them to drive out the bearing cones. Press the bearings from the shaft.

Clean the parts and check the bearings unlubricated for roughness. Remove all burrs from hub bore and shoulders and assemble parts in perfectly clean state.

Drive bearing cones hard against hub shoulders with a copper drift and drive the bearings onto shaft. Pack bearings with recommended lubricant and smear the spacer. Soak inner seal 3 in oil for one hour and dip outer seal 2 in oil. Press in outer seal until flush, using tool 18GA 134BN. Fit inner seal using tool 18GA 134BP.

Pack space between bearings and oil seals with grease. Do not pack grease in space in hub between the bearings.

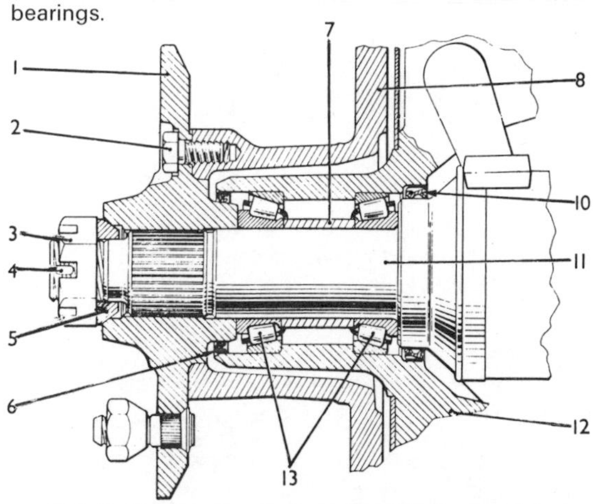

FIG 8:16 Section through front hub assembly

Key to Fig 8:16 1 Driving flange assembly 2 Bolt—flange to disc 3 Nut—hub 4 Splitpin 5 Cone—outer 6 Oil seal—outer 7 Distance tube (spacer) 8 Disc 10 Oil seal—inner (single lip) 11 Drive shaft 12 Swivel hub 13 Taper roller bearings

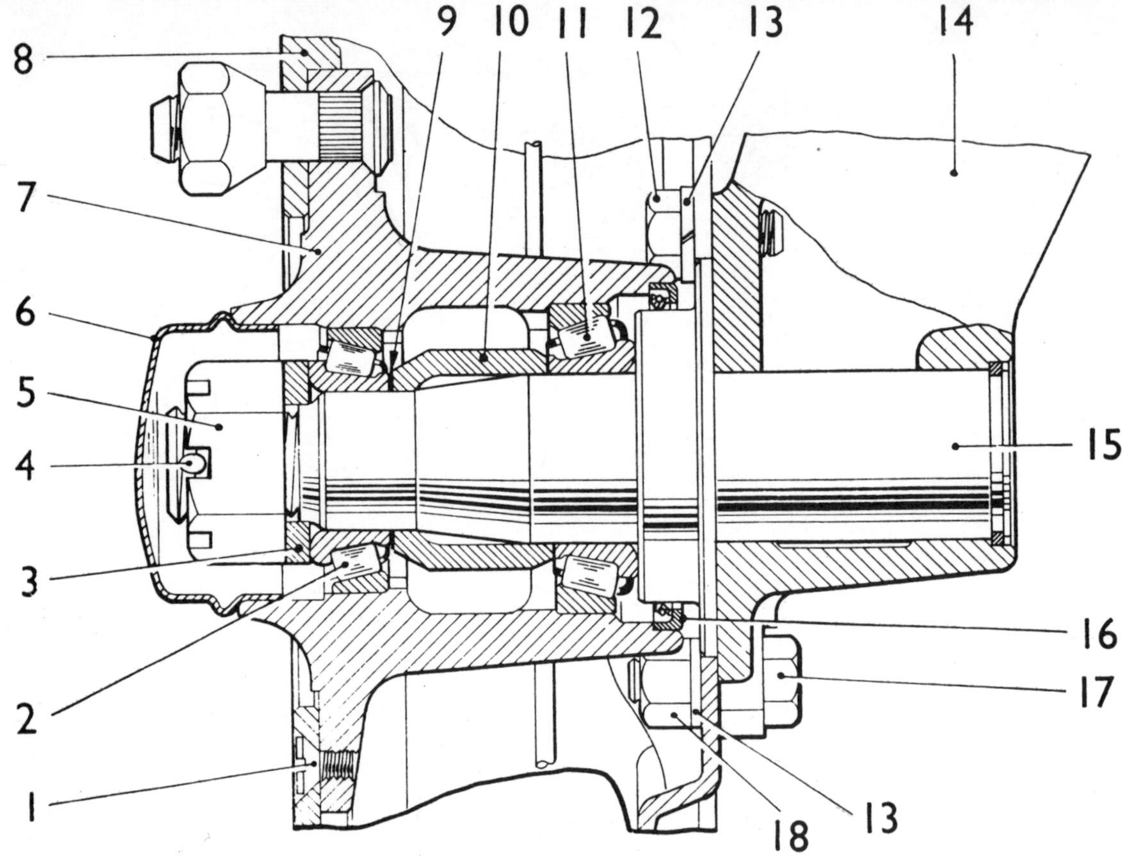

FIG 8:17 Section through rear hub assembly

Key to Fig 8:17 1 Screw-drum to hub 2 Taper bearing—outer 3 Washer 4 Splitpin 5 Nut—R.H. or L.H. thread 6 Grease retaining cap 7 Hub assembly 8 Brake drum 9 Shims (when fitted) 10 Distance piece or spacer bearing 11 Taper bearing—inner 12 Set screw back plate to radius arm 13 Spring washer 14 Radius arm 15 Stub shaft 16 Oil seal 17 Bolt—back plate to radius arm 18 Nut

Renewing outer oil seal only:

This can be done by removing the brake disc and flange. Refer to **FIG 8:16** and remove nut 3 and split cone 5. Remove the brake caliper and then withdraw the hub with a suitable puller (see operation 2 under 'Removing').

Prise out the old seal and clean out old grease in front of the bearing. Dip new seal in oil and drive in flush. Pack space between seal and bearing with grease and refit the hub.

Refitting:

Make sure space between bearings is not packed with grease. Fit shaft and bearings in hub and draw shaft into place. Fit shaft as described in **Section 8:3**. Reverse the rest of the dismantling procedure, tightening swivel axle ball joint nuts to 45 lbf ft (6.2 kgf m), steering ball joint nut to 35 lbf ft (4.8 kgf m), dust shield bolt to 20 lbf ft (2.8 kgf m), caliper bolts to 45 to 50 lbf ft (6.2 to 6.9 kgf m), hub nut (tightening further to next hole) 150 lbf ft (20.7 kgf m) and road wheel nuts to 60 lbf ft (8.3 kgf m).

8:9 Servicing the rear hubs

Removing:

Take the weight of the car on a jack. Slacken wheel nuts, remove cup 6 and slacken nut 5 (see **FIG 8:17**). **The lefthand hub has a lefthand thread and the righthand hub a righthand thread.** Jack up car and support on a stand. Remove the wheel.

Slacken off brake adjustment (see **Chapter 10**). Remove drum (two screws). Remove nut 5 and special washer 3. Withdraw hub using a puller or tools 18GA 146 and adaptor plate 18GA 146Z.

Renewing bearings and oil seal:

Prise out seal 16. It will be damaged so make sure that a new seal is available. Remove distance piece 10 and shims 9 (if fitted). Pull off inner bearing 11. Use a soft metal drift to drive out the bearing cones, placing drift in grooves provided.

Clean the parts and check the unlubricated bearings for roughness. Remove burrs or high spots from bores and shoulders. Check bearing lands on axle stub.

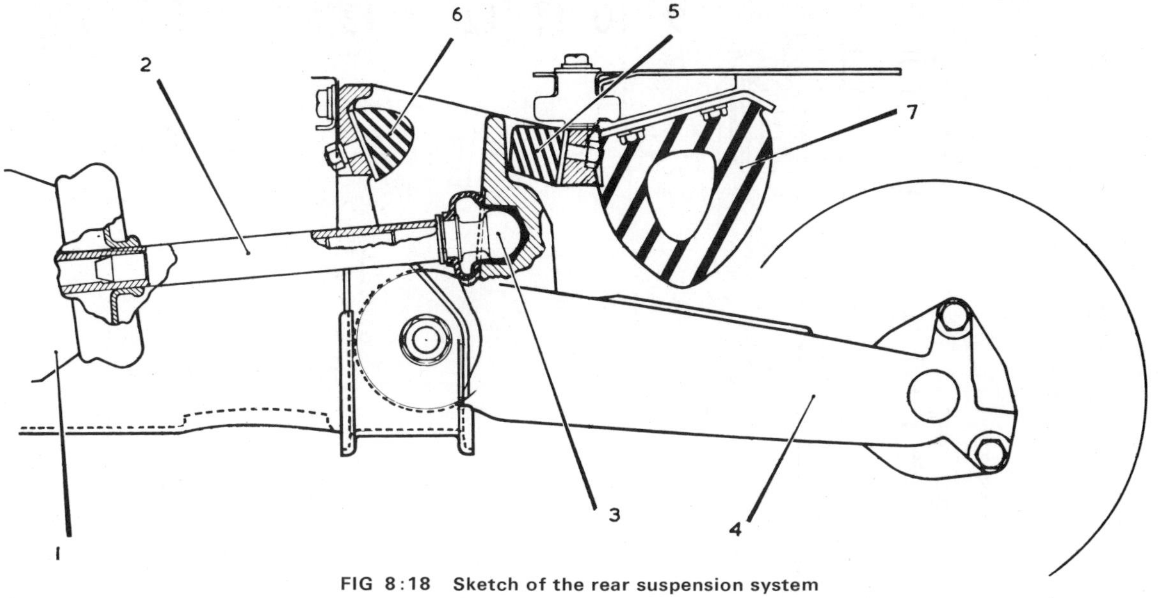

FIG 8:18 Sketch of the rear suspension system

Key to Fig 8:18 1 Hydrolastic displacer 2 Strut 3 Ball joint assembly 4 Rear trailing arm 5 Rebound rubber 6 Bump rubber 7 Auxiliary rubber spring

Press in new bearing cones hard up to shoulders. Drift inner bearing onto shaft. Fit standard spacer and enough shims to produce excessive end float. Fit hub with chamfer on washer 3 to bearing. Tighten nut to 40 lbf ft (5.5 kgf m). **Note that original bearing assemblies are made using a specially selected spacer. When renewing the bearings, use a standard spacer and select the necessary shims.**

Use a dial gauge to check the hub end float by pushing the hub in and out. Remove the hub and calculate the shims required to give an end float of zero to .002 inch (.05 mm). Shims have thicknesses of .003 inch (.08 mm), .005 inch (.23 mm) and .01 inch (.25 mm).

Dip a new seal in oil and fit it, using tool 18G.134BN. Pack bearings with Lithium based grease and also recess between inner bearing and seal. Smear spacer with grease. **Do not pack grease into the hub space between the bearings and do not put grease in cup 6.**

Fit spacer and correct shims, fit hub and put chamfer of washer against the bearing. Tighten nut to 40 lbf ft (5.5 kgf m), tightening still more when aligning splitpin hole. Fit new pin. Fit drum and wheel, tightening nuts to 60 lbf ft (8.3 kgf m). Adjust brake (see **Chapter 10**).

When fitting a new seal only, clean out old grease from recess, dip seal in oil and refit as just described and pack recess between seal and bearing with grease.

8:10 Servicing tie rods, wheel studs and bump rubbers

Tie rods:

When removing the tie rods, support the car and take the weight off the suspension. **Do not let the suspension take the weight of the car while a rod is detached.** Renew perished rubbers and check rod for straightness. Tighten Nyloc nut at bracket end to 27 to 33 lbf ft (3.7 to 4.6 kgf m) and bolt at fork end to 40 to 50 lbf ft (5.5 to 6.9 kgf m).

Wheel studs:

The front drive flange studs are renewable. **If one has failed, always renew all five studs.** To remove the flange, slacken hub nut and wheel nuts, jack up and support car and remove wheel. Remove hub nut and coned washer (see 3 and 5 in **FIG 8:16**). Use a puller to withdraw the flange or use tool 18GA 146 and adaptor plate 18GA 146Z. Press the studs out.

Check that countersinks are free from burrs. Press in new studs hard up to the heads. Mating faces of flange and disc must be clean. Refit flange and tighten bolts to 40 to 54 lbf ft (5.5 to 6.2 kgf m). Fit coned washer and hub nut, fit wheel, lower car and tighten wheel nuts to 60 lbf ft (8.3 kgf m). Tighten hub nut to 150 lbf ft (20.7 kgf m). If necessary, tighten still more to align splitpin holes. Fit new pin.

Bump rubbers:

Front rubbers are shown in **FIG 8:9**. When fitting new rubbers, tighten the bolts to 5 lbf ft (.7 kgf m).

Rear bump rubber is shown in **FIG 8:18**. After removing the wheel and lifting out the rear seat, remove nut and washer from rear of seat pan. Extract the rubber from inside the suspension mounting member.

Rear rebound rubbers are part 5 in **FIG 8:18**. As it is necessary to depressurize the Hydrolastic system renewal of these rubbers is a job for a properly-equipped service station.

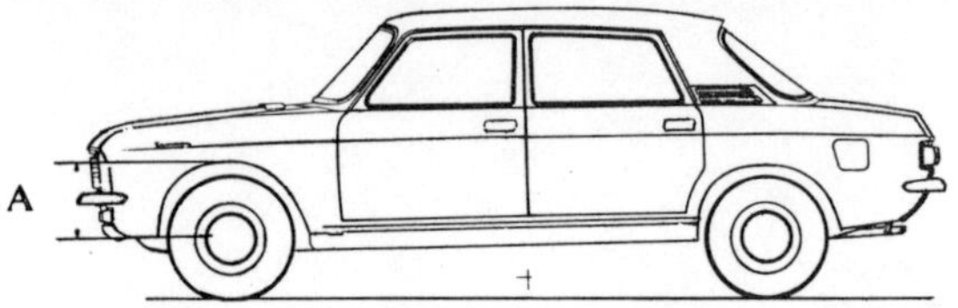

FIG 8:19 Checking the suspension trim height

Key to Fig 8:19 Dimension 'A', centre of hub cap to top curve of wheel arch=$15\pm\frac{1}{4}$ inch (381 ± 6 mm)

Auxiliary rubber spring:

This is item 7 in **FIG 8:18** which is mounted on the body above the rear radius arm. Its purpose is to apply a shock absorbing action to the radius arm. To remove, raise the rear end and support on stands; remove the two bolts holding the rubber in position.

8:11 Suspension geometry and trim height

With the exception of front wheel alignment (toe-in), the various angles of the suspension system are not adjustable. If the car is damaged or the suspension badly worn, the effect on steering and general handling may be serious. The only cure is a thorough check of the angles and alignment and replacement of defective parts.

Dimensions and angles are given in Technical Data. The method of checking and adjusting wheel alignment is given in **Chapter 9.**

Trim height:

Although errors in trim must be rectified by a garage equipped to modify pressure in the Hydrolastic system, the actual checking is a simple job.

Car must be filled with oil, water and 5 galls of fuel with all wheels standing on a level surface. The spare wheel and tool kit should be included. With tyres at correct pressure, roll car to and fro and bounce the suspension. Measure from the centre of each front wheel cap to the body arch immediately above as shown in **FIG 8:19.** The correct figure at 'A' should be 15 inch$\pm\frac{1}{4}$ inch (381 mm$\pm$6 mm).

Damaged suspension:

If fluid in the system is lost through accidental damage, it is permissible to drive the car on metalled roads at speeds not exceeding 30 mile/hr (50 km/hr). The suspension on the damaged side will contact the bump rubbers.

8:12 Fault diagnosis

(a) Wheel wobble

1 Incorrect tracking
2 Worn hub bearings
3 Defective suspension units
4 Worn swivel hub joints
5 Loose wheel fixings

(b) 'Bottoming' of suspension

1 Check 3 in (a)
2 Incorrect pressurizing
3 Rebound rubbers worn or missing

(c) Heavy steering

1 Defective swivel hub joints
2 Wrong suspension geometry
3 Tight differential assembly on one side

(d) Excessive tyre wear

1 Check 1 in (a) and 2 in (c)

(e) Rattles

1 Check 1 in (c)
2 Suspension mountings defective
3 Tie-rod mountings loose

(f) Excessive rolling

1 Check 3 in (a) and 2 in (b)

CHAPTER 9

THE STEERING

9:1 Description

The components parts are shown in **FIG 9:1**. The steering inner column is connected to pinion 18 or 19 by a flexible coupling and splined coupling 21 (see also **FIG 9:2**). The pinion meshes with rack 9 or 10 which slides in a housing, the housing being secured to the underside of the body. The ends of the rack are connected by jointed tie rods 31 to the steering arms that are bolted to the front wheel swivel hubs.

9:2 Routine maintenance

No lubrication service is needed on the steering gear. Every 6000 miles (10,000 km or 6 months) jack up the front wheels and check all steering joints for security and for backlash. Check the rubber gaiters 36 for splits and deterioration. Check security of bolt for coupling flange 21. Tighten to 12 to 15 lbf ft (1.7 to 2.1 kgf m). Do not overtighten.

9:3 Servicing the steering column assembly

Removing and refitting steering wheel:

Press and turn anticlockwise the padded horn push. Remove the assembly. Unscrew the nut and use a puller to draw off the wheel. Mark the relative position before parting.

When refitting, set the front wheels in the straight-ahead position with steering wheel spokes at the 4 and 8 o'clock position and aligned to the previously made marks. Tighten nut to 50 lbf ft (6.9 kgf m). Refit the horn push.

Removing and refitting steering column:

1 Disconnect battery. Remove steering wheel. Remove cowl from around steering column by taking out two lower screws first, then single one from upper part. Lift off upper half first.
2 Release combination switch (2 screws). Disconnect multi-plug from below facia. Disconnect the leads from the horn and trafficator terminals. Move floor covering and release clamp plates and bush (4, 5 and 6 in **FIG 9:2**).
3 Remove bolts 3 from coupling. Remove the two bolts securing the column to the parcel shelf. Withdraw the assembly and disengage the inner column from the splines on the rack pinion.
4 When refitting, reverse the procedure, setting the road wheels straight-ahead before connecting the inner column. Note that direction indicator stud must be midway between the arms on the switch. Lug in bore of switch must locate in slot in outer column. Ensure

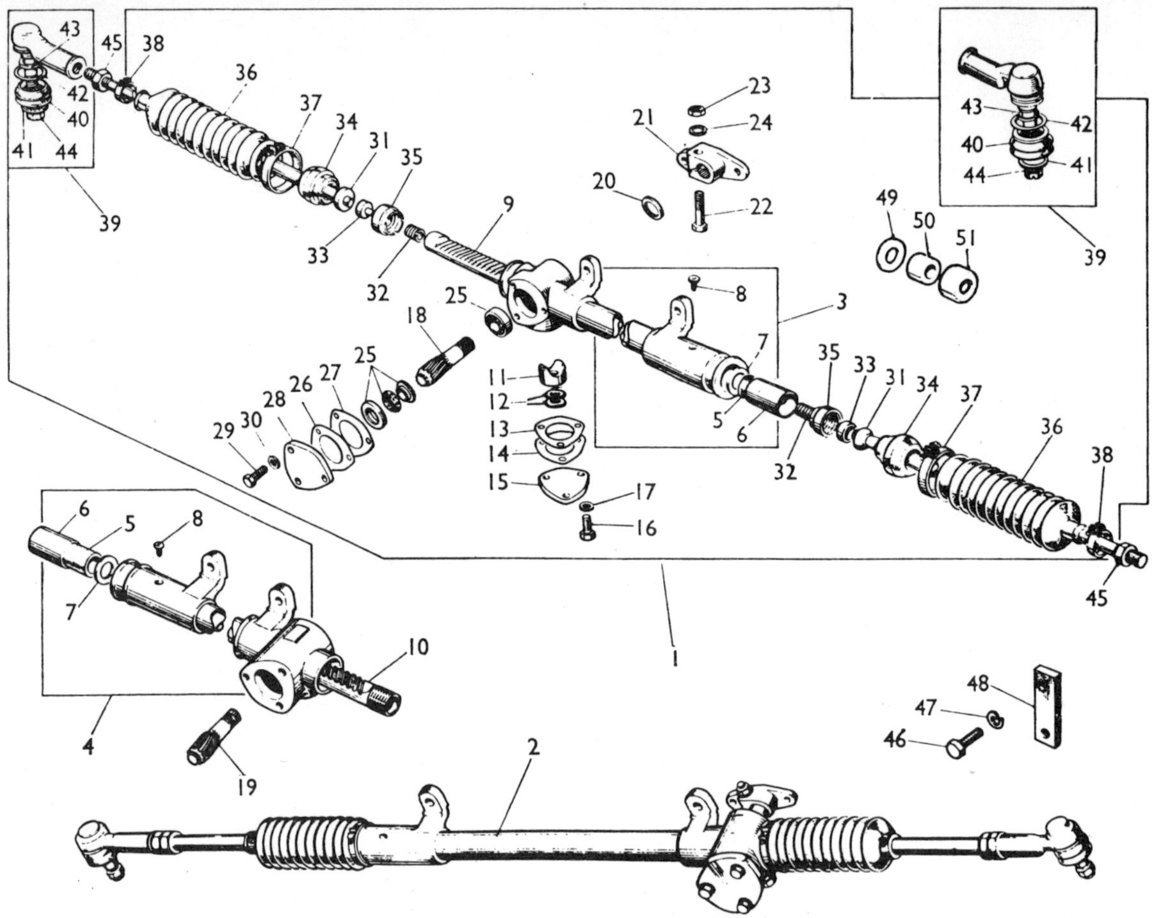

FIG 9:1 Component parts of steering rack system

Key to Fig 9:1 1 Steering rack assembly—R.H.D. 2 Steering rack assembly—L.H.D. 3 Steering assembly—R.H.D. 4 Housing assembly—L.H.D. 5 Felt bush (deleted) 6 Bush housing (deleted) 7 Backing disc (deleted) 8 Retaining screw 9 Rack—R.H.D. 10 Rack—L.H.D. 11 Rack support yoke 12 Spring disc (2 off) 13 Yoke cover joint washer 14 Yoke cover shim(s) 15 Cover-plate yoke 16 Cover-plate bolt 17 Spring washer 18 Pinion—R.H.D. 19 Pinion—L.H.D. 20 Oil seal 21 Pinion coupling 22 Bolt—coupling 23 Nut—coupling 24 Spring washer—coupling 25 Ball cage 26 End cover shim(s) 27 Joint washer 28 End cover 29 Bolt—end cover 30 Spring washer 31 Tie rod 32 Thrust spring 33 Ball seat 34 Ball housing 35 Locknut—ball housing 36 Rack seal (Gaiter) 37 Clip—inner seal 38 Clip—outer ring 39 Ball socket assembly 40 Boot 41 Ring—boot 42 Spring garter—boot 43 Retainer—boot 44 Slotted nut 45 Ball socket locknut 46 Screw-rack to body 47 Spring washer 48 Tapped block-rack to body 49 Retainer 50 Bush-Polyvon 1st production 51 Housing

that peg and slot in the parcel tray packing are properly engaged. Ensure that the earthing strip at the base of the column is clean before replacing.

Overhauling steering column:

To remove inner column, remove trip stud. Straighten tongue and extract bush with tool 18G.1191. Withdraw inner column downwards.

Check bushes, shaft splines and locking bolt and groove for wear. Note that top bush may be renewed without stripping the columns. Repeat operation 1 and remove the combination switch. Remove the trip stud and extract bush as just described. Drive bush into place with drift making sure slot in lower edge engages with key pressed into bore of outer column. Smear bore with graphited grease.

Reassemble column in reverse order of dismantling. Adjust height of trip stud if necessary.

Flexible coupling:

Refer to the parts in **FIG 9:2**. Do operations 1 and 2 for removing the column, also disconnecting the three multi-plugs from under the facia. Remove bolts 3 and 8.

Before fitting bolts 3 when reassembling, set road wheels straight-ahead with spokes of steering wheel at the 4 and 8 o'clock position and the coupling plates 10 set as shown. Tighten these bolts to 15 lbf ft (2.1 kgf m).

9:4 Servicing gaiters and ball joints

Steering rack gaiters:

These are parts 36 in **FIG 9:1**. A damaged and leaking seal may allow dirt to enter the rack housing and lubricant will be lost. Renew at once and check condition of rack (see **Section 9:5**).

To renew seals, remove ball joints 39 (see later). Remove clips 37 and 38 and pull off seals. When reassembling, leave off small clip on steering side of car and inject into the seal $\frac{1}{3}$ pint (.18 litre) of E.P. 140 oil.

Ball joints:

With road wheel removed, unlock and slacken nut 44. Break ball pin out of steering arm using an expander tool (see **FIG 8:12** in preceding chapter). **Do not try to hammer pin out of arm.** Unscrew ball joint after releasing locknut 45. Note number of turns.

Reverse procedure to refit. If joint is rough in action and has backlash, or if rubber boot is damaged, renewal is indicated. Check that tie rod assemblies on each side of car are equal in length and then check alignment (toe-in) as described in **Section 9:7**).

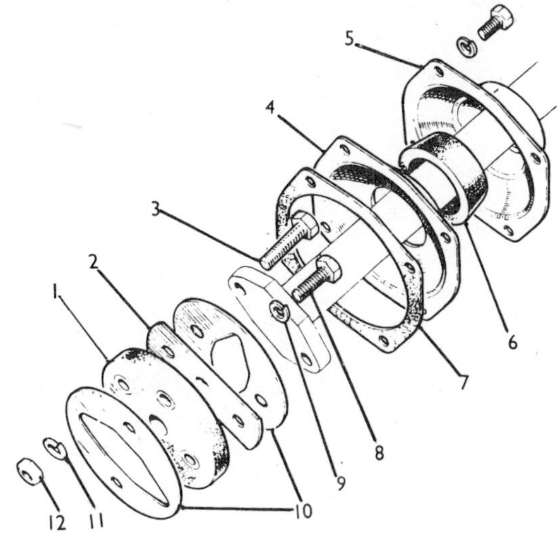

FIG 9:2 Components of steering column coupling

Key to Fig 9:2 1 Coupling-steering column to rack 2 Earthing strip-dimple to column 3 Screw-coupling to column 4 Clamp plate—lower 5 Clamp plate—upper 6 Bush 7 Seal 8 Screw-coupling to rack 9 Spring washer 10 Coupling plates 11 Spring washer 12 Nut

9:5 Removing and refitting steering rack

Removing:

Disconnect column from pinion flange (see preceding Section). Remove both front wheels. Remove splitpins and nuts 44 from outer ball joints (see **FIG 9:1**). Press ball joint pins out of steering levers with an expander tool or any suitable extractor. Do not try to drive the pins out with a hammer or the threads will be ruined. The tapered fitting is exceedingly tight.

Release rack housing from toeboard (4 bolts). Withdraw assembly through valance, turning to clear the pinion flange.

Refitting:

Reverse the removal procedure. Check that steering wheel and rack are centralized before connecting the coupling flange. Check wheel alignment as in **Section 9:7**.

9:6 Servicing steering rack

Having removed rack assembly as described in preceding Section, do the following:

1 Hold rack housing in a vice. Unlock and unscrew ball joints from outer ends of tie rods after noting amount of tie rod thread exposed.

2 Remove gaiters (clips 37 and 38 in **FIG 9:1**), having a container handy to catch the oil. Set rack in central position. Total rack travel is 6.56 inch (166.6 mm) so that half this from either end will give the central position. Half the travel is 3.28 inch (83.3 mm) (see **FIG 9:3**). Mark pinion coupling pinion shaft and rack housing to ensure correct refitting.

3 Remove coverplate 14, shims and washer 13 and 14, spring(s) 12 and yoke 11. Remove pinion cover 28, shims 26, washer 27, lower bearing 25 and pinion 18. Top bearing 25 cannot be removed until the rack is withdrawn.

4 Remove oil seal 20 if it has been leaking. Using spanners 18G.1030 (see **FIG 9:4**), unlock and unscrew the rack ball joints after clearing the indentations in the locking ring 35 out of the slots in housing 34.

5 Withdraw rack 9 from pinion end of housing. Withdrawal from the other end may damage bush 5 or 50. Remove screw 8 and withdraw bush and housing. If first-type with felt bush 5, loosen screw two turns, prise up felt at joint and extract.

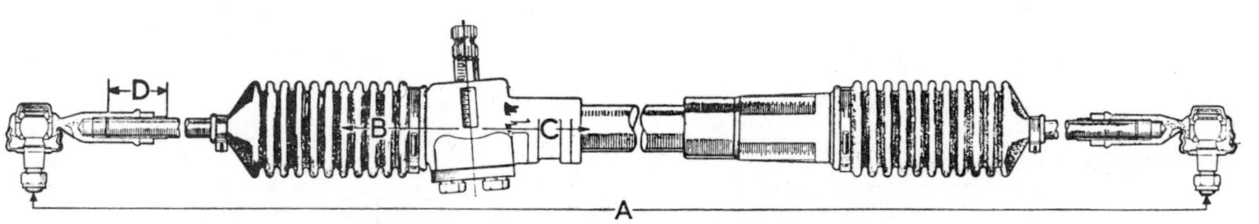

FIG 9:3 Steering rack assembly dimensions

Key to Fig 9:3 **A** The assembled length between the ball pins: 49.62-06 in (1246.63-1.52 mm) **B** Rack travels from the central position: 3.28 in (83.3 mm) **C** Rack travels from the central position: 3.28 in (83.3 mm) **D** The threaded length of the tie rod

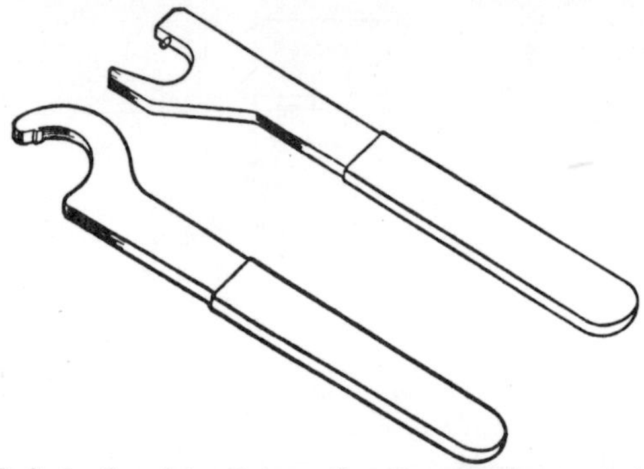

FIG 9:4 Special spanners for the steering rack ball joints (18GA 1030). Designed to adjust the steering rack ball joints to the correct torque figure

Inspection:

After cleaning, examine rack and pinion teeth for roughness, chipping or cracks. Renew gaiters on slightest signs of deterioration. Check fit of bush in rack housing and renew to prevent rattling. Check ball seats at inner end of tie rods. Slackness or rough action of the outer ball joints can be cured only but fitting new assemblies. Check condition of ball joint boots 40 as joints will wear rapidly if dirt enters through cracks.

Reassembling:

Insert bush and housing in rack housing so that hole for the screw is between flats in bush (see inset in **FIG 9:5**). Support bush on a mandrel and drill a $\frac{7}{64}$ inch (2.8 mm) hole through from the existing one. If originally fitted with a felt bush, assembly should be modified by fitting Polyvon bush 50 and housing 51 with retainer 49. If the felt bush is retained, the rack housing must be lubricated with SAE.140.EP oil. Secure bush and housing in place with screw 8, putting sealing compound under the head.

Refit pinion bearing 25 into housing, insert rack and refit pinion, aligning the marks made prior to dismantling. Fit lower bearing and prepare to adjust pinion bearing preload.

Pinion bearing preload:

Refer to **FIG 9:6**. Fit cover without shims or washer. Tighten bolts lightly. Measure gap 'A'. Subtract .007 inch (.178 mm)—gasket thickness—from feeler gauge measurement. Result in thickness of shims required. Shims are available in thicknesses of .0024 inch (.06 mm), .005 inch (.13 mm) and .010 inch (.25 mm). Treat joint faces with sealing compound and reassemble using a new joint washer. Pinion bearings will now be preloaded.

Reassembling (continued):

If necessary, renew pinion oil seal by pressing in a new one until it is flush with top of housing.

Screw a new locking ring onto the rack to the limit of the thread. Refit spring 32, seat 33, tie rod 31 and ball housing 34. Tighten housing until tie rod is nipped. Run locking ring up to ball housing, keeping tie rod still nipped. Slacken ball housing by $\frac{1}{8}$ of a turn so that tie rod can be moved. Relock by tightening locking ring to a torque of 33 to 37 lb ft (4.6 to 5.7 kg m) using tool 18GA1030. Make sure ball housing does not turn. If adjustment is correct, preload on rack ball joint will be such that a torque of 32 to 52 lb in (.37 to .6 kg m) will be needed to move tie rod sideways. This is equivalent to a side pull of 3.2 to 5.2 lb (1.45 to 2.35 kg) at a distance of 10 inches from the tie rod ball. Check this by hooking a spring balance on the tie rod at that

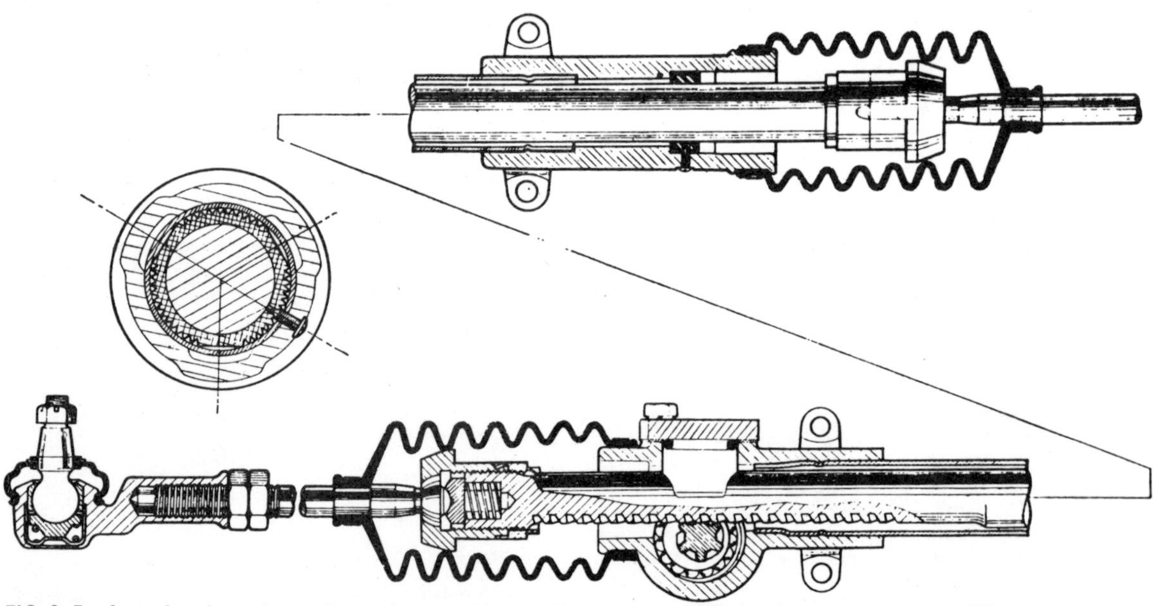

FIG 9:5 A section through steering rack and ball joints. The inset shows the correct position of the flats on the Polyvon rack bush in relation to the securing screw and oilways

distance from the ball and pulling at right-angles to the rod. Take the reading the moment the tie rod starts to move.

When satisfied, lock the ball housing to the rack by punching the lips of the locking ring into the slots in the housing and the rack (see **FIG 9:7**).

Damper adjustment:

The damper is on the left in **FIG 9:6** and the parts are 11 to 17 in **FIG 9:1**. For this operation it is necessary to check the torque required to turn the pinion shaft. This may be done using preload gauge 18G.207 and adaptor 18G.207A. As the torque is measured in lb inches it may be possible to attach a lever ten inches long (measured from centre of pinion shaft) to the pinion coupling and use a spring balance pulling at right angles to the lever in the direction of pinion rotation. With a lever of that length, the required torque must be divided by ten to give the reading on the spring balance. Make similar calculations when working in kg m.

1 Check torque needed to turn pinion shaft and add the reading to the preload figure of 15 lb in (.18 kg m).
2 Fit yoke 11 and spring washers 12. Do not fit shims. Tighten bolts in damper cover with rack in central position until it is just possible to turn the pinion shaft with the preload gauge set to the combined figure obtained in the preceding operation.
3 Use feelers to measure the gap at 'B' and select shims and a new joint washer with a total thickness of the width of the gap. Shims are available in thicknesses of .0025 inch (.06 mm), .005 inch (.13 mm) and .010 inch (.25 mm).
4 Apply sealing compound and refit the cover, shims and joint washer. Check torque load needed to turn pinion shaft. **Figure must not exceed 25 lb in (.3 kg m).**

Final assembling:

Refit gaiters and clips. Leave clip off gaiters at pinion end, stand assembly upright and pour in about $\frac{1}{3}$ pint (.2 litre) of Extreme Pressure (EP) oil. Refit gaiter and clip.

Centralize the rack (see **FIG 9:3**). If pinion shaft is not marked, make a mark so that the central position can be checked after fitting assembly to vehicle. Note that full travel of the rack gives 3.8 turns of the pinion. Keeping rack centralized, fit flange coupling 21 in original position as marked. If new parts have been fitted, correct position for flange can be found by fitting it to the pinion shaft so that centre line through flange bolt holes is in line with the centre line of the rack and housing. Rack must be central. Now withdraw the flange and refit it by turning it anti-clockwise by two splines to give an angle of 20 deg. to the centre line of the rack. The position should then be as shown in **FIG 9:6**. Tighten the clamp bolt to 12 to 15 lb ft (1.7 to 2.1 kg m).

Refit outer ball joints, screwing them up to the original position if possible. This helps in tracking adjustments. Check that distance between ballpins is 49.62$\pm$.06 inch (1246.63$\pm$1.52 mm) as shown in **FIG 9:3**. Tighten locknuts just enough to prevent movement. **If two locknuts are fitted, remove one of them.** Later assemblies have one locknut only.

Refit the assembly to the vehicle as explained in **Section 9:5**.

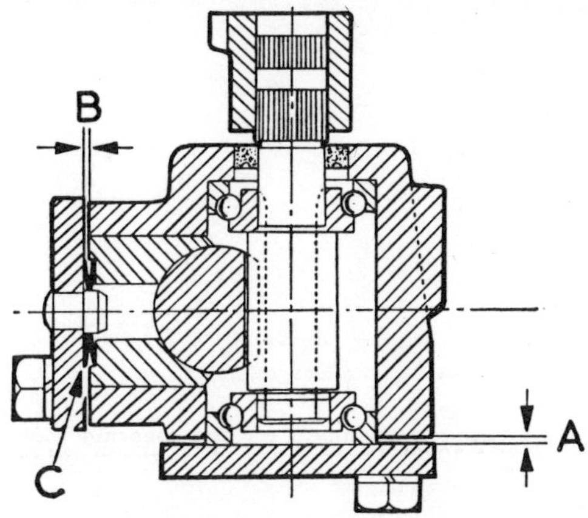

FIG 9:6 Section through rack damper. For bearing preload shims, measure gap at 'A'. Measure gap at 'B' for damper shimming. 'C' indicates spring washers for damper

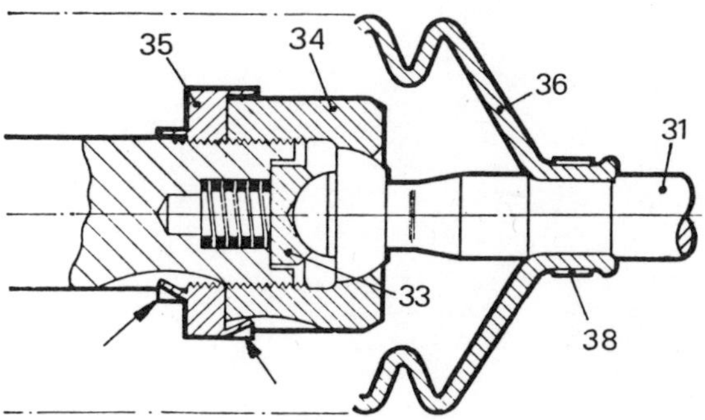

FIG 9:7 The rack ball joint assembly showing how the lips of the locking ring are pushed into the recesses of the housing and rack. Refer to Fig 9:1 for key

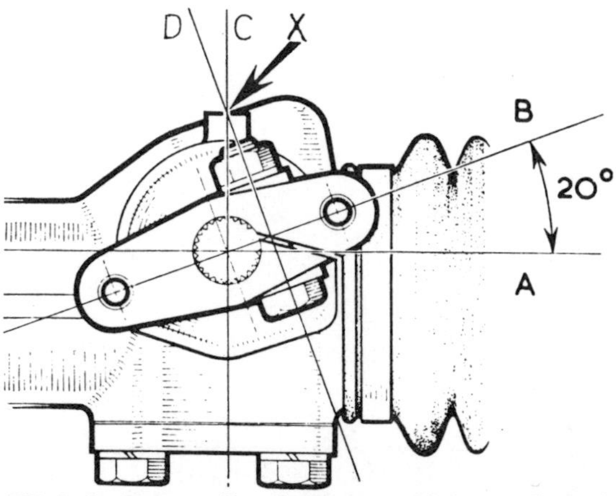

FIG 9:8 The coupling flange set at 20 deg. to the rack centre line when rack is centralized

Key to Fig 9:8 **A** Centre-line of pinion parallel to rack axis **B** Centre-line of coupling flange **C** Centre-line of casting lug **D** Centre-line of pinch-bolt **X** Point of intersection

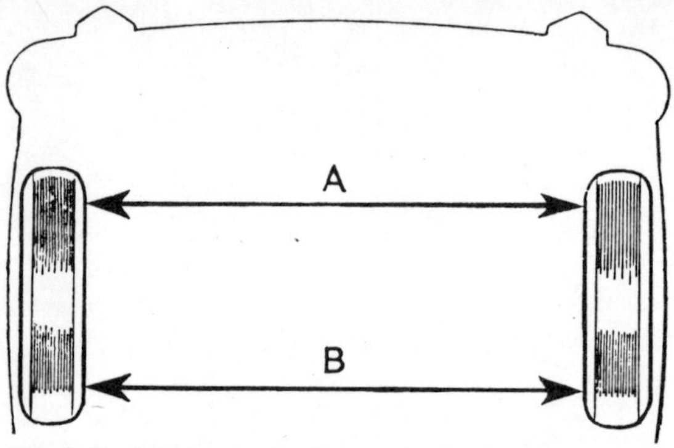

FIG 9:9 Front wheel alignment check taken at the wheel hub centre height. Wheels in straightahead position. Dimension A must be $\frac{1}{8}$ inch (3.2 mm) less than B

9:7 Wheel alignment

Check this every 6000 miles (10,000 km) or 6 months. Radial ply tyres: Inflate front tyres to 28 lb/sq in (1.97 kg/sq cm) and rear to 22 lb/sq in (1.55 kg/sq cm). Crossply tyres: Front tyre pressure should be 26 lb/sq in (1.8 kg/sq cm) and rear 22 lb/sq in (1.55 kg/sq cm).

Correct alignment is with wheels toeing-in by $\frac{1}{8}$ inch (3.2 mm) unladen. The wheels are not parallel by the angular amount of 22 minutes (see **FIG 9:9**).

With vehicle on level ground and wheels straightahead, measure distance between tyres at wheel centre height, in front and behind. Mark positions on tyres with chalk. Roll vehicle forward by half a turn of the wheels. Take a second set of readings. Dimension across vehicle between inner walls of tyres must be an average of $\frac{1}{8}$ inch (3.2 mm) less at the front than the back.

This is a rough check only. For real accuracy it is best to entrust the checking to a service station.

To adjust for correct alignment, slacken gaiter clips 38 and tie rod locknuts 45. Turn tie rods an equal amount, noting that they both have righthand threads. The amount of thread visible behind each locknut must be the same on both sides. If it is not, screw one tie rod in, and the other one out by equal amounts until satisfied. **This is essential if the rack is to be central and the steering geometry correct.**

After adjustment, hold outer ball joints square with their ballpins and tighten the locknuts to 35 lb ft (4.8 kg m). Tighten the gaiter clips.

9:8 Fault diagnosis

(a) Wheel wobble

1 Unbalanced wheels and tyres
2 Slack steering ball joints
3 Incorrect steering geometry
4 Excessive play in steering gear
5 Faulty suspension
6 Worn hub bearings

(b) Wander

1 Check 2, 3 and 4 in (a) and check (d)
2 Uneven tyre pressure
3 Uneven tyre wear

(c) Heavy steering

1 Check 3 in (a)
2 Very low tyre pressures
3 Neglected lubrication (damaged dust covers)
4 Wheels out of track
5 Rack damper too tight
6 Excessive pinion bearing preload
7 Steering column bent or misaligned
8 Column bushes tight

(d) Lost motion

1 Loose steering wheel, worn splines
2 Defective column coupling
3 Worn rack and pinion teeth
4 Worn ball joints
5 Worn swivel hub joints
6 Slack pinion bearings

CHAPTER 10

THE BRAKING SYSTEM

10:1 Description

Hydraulically operated, self-adjusting brakes are fitted to all four wheels. The front wheels incorporate the disc and pad system and the rear wheels the 'leading' and 'trailing' expanding shoe and drum system. The brake pedal is coupled to a tandem master cylinder that operates separate hydraulic circuits to the front and rear brakes, ensuring a braking system, albeit reduced, in the event of a failure in either the front or rear system. There is no pressure reducing valve in the system but a residual line pressure valve is incorporated in the master cylinder rear brake outlet port, to reduce pressure to the rear wheels and prevent locking during heavy braking.

Self-adjustment of the rear brakes is effected only when the vehicle is reversing and sufficient lining has been worn away to bring the adjuster into operation. The self-adjustment of the front brakes is effected in either direction when pad wear permits.

The front wheel disc brakes are power assisted by a vacuum-hydraulic type servo unit. The rear brake shoe linings are bonded to the shoes and the mechanically operated handbrake applies the rear brakes only.

10:2 Routine maintenance

Topping-up:

Every 3000 miles (5000 km or 3 months) check the fluid level in the master cylinder reservoir (see **FIG 10:1**), the master cylinders have the level marked on the outside.

Clean area round cap before unscrewing. Check that the cap vent hole is clear. If necessary, top-up with BLMC HBF-6 brake fluid. **Do not use any other type of fluid. Take great care to keep out dirt and do not let the fluid contact paintwork as it is a solvent.** If there is a marked drop in level at any time, check the whole system for leaks as it may eventually lead to brake failure.

Inspecting rear brake drums:

Every 12,000 miles (20,000 km or 12 months) jack up and remove the rear wheels. With front wheels chocked, remove rear wheels, turn adjusters to release brake (see **FIG 10:2**) and remove drums (2 screws). Clean out dust, examine cylinder for leaks and check thickness of

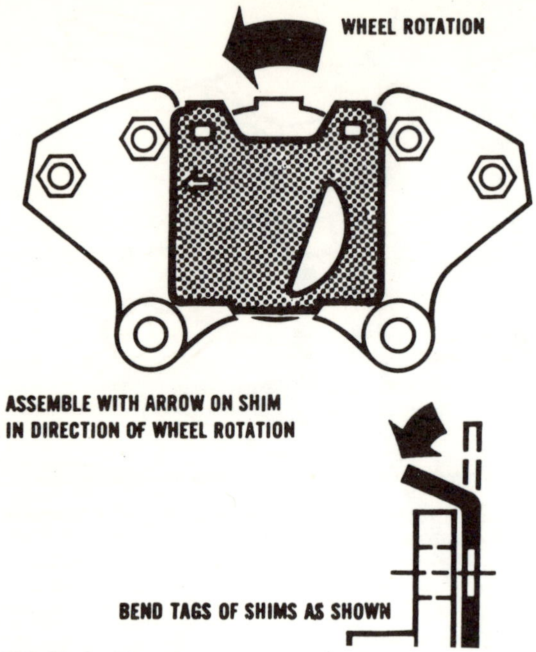

FIG 10:6 The arrow on the shims must point forward. Bend the tag on the shims as shown

Renewing seals:

4 It is not necessary nor advisable to separate the caliper halves therefore do not disturb the retaining bolts 13 and 14. Clean the outside of the caliper unit with brake fluid or methylated spirits.

5 Remove and scrap the retainer clips 9 and the dust seals 8. To remove the pistons from their bores apply air pressure to the hydraulic inlet port 'A', ensuring that no water or oil in the air line will enter the bores. Keep the fingers away from the inside of caliper when injecting air pressure and retain the piston in the bore of the mounting half, by tying a suitable piece of cloth or wire around the piston and caliper. After the first piston has been ejected remove the restriction and eject the second piston.

6 Use a blunt tool to extract the bore seals 12 from their grooves. Do not scratch or damage the bores or grooves.

7 Examine pistons and bores for score marks or corrosion. To clean surface corrosion use 400 grit 'wet and dry' rubbing paper wetted with brake fluid. Parts showing pitted or deep corrosion must be renewed. Clean all parts with methylated spirits.

8 Smear the new seals with clean, unused brake fluid and fit them into their grooves using the fingers only. Replace the pistons using thumb pressure to push them down the bores.

9 Fit the dust seals 8 and retainers 9.

Refitting:

10 Check the brake disc before refitting the caliper unit (see **Section 10:4**).

11 Refit the shims to their original locations, refit the caliper unit and, if necessary, adjust with other shims to ensure the caliper is central to the disc. A measurement each side of the disc must be equal to within .005 inch (.127 mm).

12 Tighten the mounting bolts to a torque of 40 to 50 lbf ft (5.5 to 6.9 kgf m). Complete the assembly, bleed the system and adjust the brake pads as described previously.

10:4 Removing and refitting front disc

With handbrake on and wheel removed, unlock and unscrew the drive shaft nut and prise the split inner cone off the shaft (see **FIG 8:16**). Remove the caliper (see preceding Section). Fit puller 18GA146 and adaptor 18GA1462 and withdraw disc assembly. Remove tool and hold disc in a vice with soft jaws and separate the disc from the flange (5 bolts).

Check disc for wear, cracks and excessive scoring. Some slight scoring is normal if it is concentric. A worn disc may be reground to restore the surface but a variation in machining of the two surfaces parallel to one another must not exceed .0012 inch.

Refit the disc and tighten the bolts to 40 to 45 lbf ft (5.5 to 6.2 kgf m). Fit to drive shaft and tighten nut to 150 lbf ft (20.7 kgf m). Lock with a new splitpin. Check disc for runout. If excessive try moving disc to another location or flange and check for burrs (see Technical Data). Finish reassembly and bleed the system (see **Section 10:7**).

10:5 Servicing rear brakes

Removing rear brake shoes:

1 Jack up the rear of the car, support with safety stands and remove the road wheel and brake drum. If the drum is difficult to remove, back off the brake adjustment by inserting a screwdriver through the access hole in the backplate and push the adjuster lever off the ratchet wheel, then use a shaped tool to turn the wheel and contract the shoes (see **FIG 10:2**).

2 Take note of the type and location of all springs and levers, observe how the automatic adjusters are located. To remove the two steady springs and pins on the shoe webs, depress the spring and turn the pin washer through 90 deg. to release the spring and pin.

3 If necessary, slacken the handbrake cable adjusting nuts to disconnect the cable from the parking brake lever. Disconnect the adjuster cable from the anchor pin and release the springs from the shoe webs. Remove the shoes.

Brake shoe linings:

4 Renew the shoes and linings in complete sets if worn down to rivets. It is best to exchange old parts for shoes already lined. Do not let oil, grease or paint contact the linings and do not handle with oily fingers. It is useless to try to clean old linings that are soaked in oil or brake fluid. Make sure linings are of correct grade and all the same.

Refitting:

5 Before installing the shoes fit the parking brake lever to the secondary shoe and secure the lever with the spring washer and retaining clip (see **FIG 10:7**).

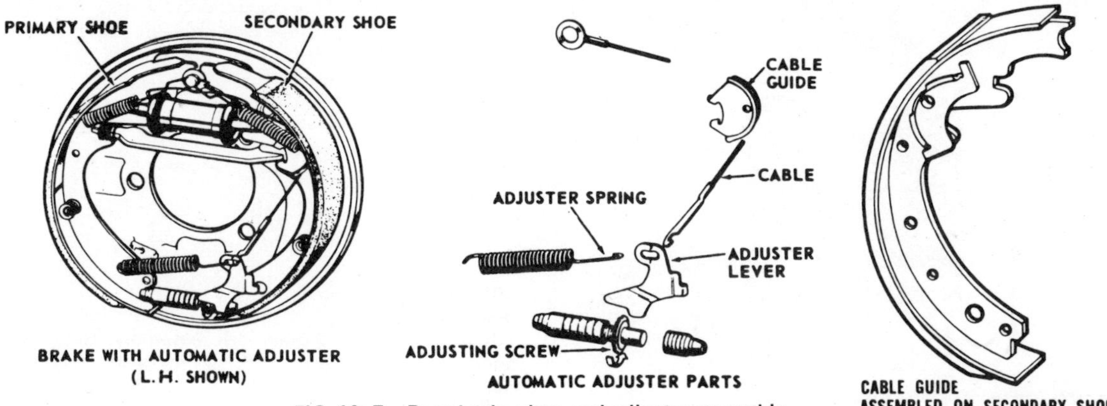

FIG 10:7 Rear brake shoe and adjuster assembly

Apply a thin smear of Bentone Base grease where the shoes contact the backing plate and grease all the anchor pins.

6 Position the shoes on the backing plate, refit the steady springs and pins and the parking brake link and spring. Reconnect the handbrake cable to the operating lever.

7 Fit the cable guide to the web of the secondary shoe ensuring that the flanged hole in the guide is properly located in the web of the shoe. Fit the secondary shoe anchor spring.

8 Thread the adjuster cable around the cable guide groove and make periodic checks during the cable assembly to ensure the cable does not come out of the groove and slip between the guide and the shoe web. Fit the cable eye over the anchor pin and check that it is not cocked or binding on the pin when it is installed.

9 Apply grease to the adjusting screw threads and the socket end. Wind the screw into the adjusting pivot nut as far as it will go—to the limit of the threads—and then unscrew it a half turn. The socket end of the screw is stamped with a letter L or R to identify it for fitment to a lefthand or righthand wheel. A similar identification on the adjusting pivot nuts can be recognized by the number of grooves machined around the body of the nut. Two grooves identify a righthand fitment and a single groove indicates a lefthand fitment. It is very important that these parts are not interchanged otherwise the adjuster will retract rather than expand.

10 Place the adjusting socket on the screw and install the assembly between the shoe ends, with the toothed wheel nearest the secondary shoe. Engage the adjuster cable hook in the slot of the adjuster lever and note that the adjuster levers are also stamped with a letter L or R. Engage the adjuster spring hook into the large hole in the primary shoe web and note that the last coil of the spring should be positioned at the edge of the anchor hole. Engage the other end to the hole in the adjuster lever.

11 The pivot hook on the adjuster lever must now be engaged in the large hole in the secondary shoe web. To do this, pull the lever, cable and the spring downwards and towards the rear to insert the pivot hook into the anchor hole.

12 Check the action of the adjuster by pulling a section of the adjuster cable—the section between the cable guide and the adjuster lever—towards the secondary shoe and far enough to lift the lever over a tooth on the screw wheel. The lever should snap into position behind the next tooth and when the cable is released the return action should cause the lever to turn the screw one tooth.

13 If this test does not produce the desired effect or if the lever action is sluggish rather than positive and sharp, check the position of the lever in relation to the toothed wheel. The lever should contact the wheel at a point $\frac{3}{16}$ inch (4.76 mm) above the centreline of the adjuster axis. If the lever contact point is below the centreline the lever will not lock in the teeth and turn the wheel. The following are possible causes of a malfunction of the lever.

(a) Incorrect cable length

The cable should measure $8\frac{3}{4}$ inch (213 mm) overall. Check the crimped section of the cable fittings and note that the cable should completely fill or extend slightly beyond the crimped portions.

(b) Damaged cable guide

The groove should be parallel to the shoe web and the guide body should be flat against the web.

(c) Damaged cable hook

The cable hook should be square with the lever to ensure correct pivoting.

(d) Screw socket malaligned

Make sure the adjusting screw socket is seated properly in the notch in the shoe web.

Adjusting:

14 Having rectified any possible faults and the adjuster is working correctly, refit the brake drum and turn the screw wheel through the access hold to expand the shoes to the drum. Continue unwinding the wheel from the adjuster body until the wheel can just be turned by hand. At this point, refer to **FIG 10:2**, insert a screwdriver through the access hole to push the lever away from the wheel and wind the wheel back into the body one complete turn. Refit the wheel, repeat on the other side and make several brake applications in reverse to complete the adjustment.

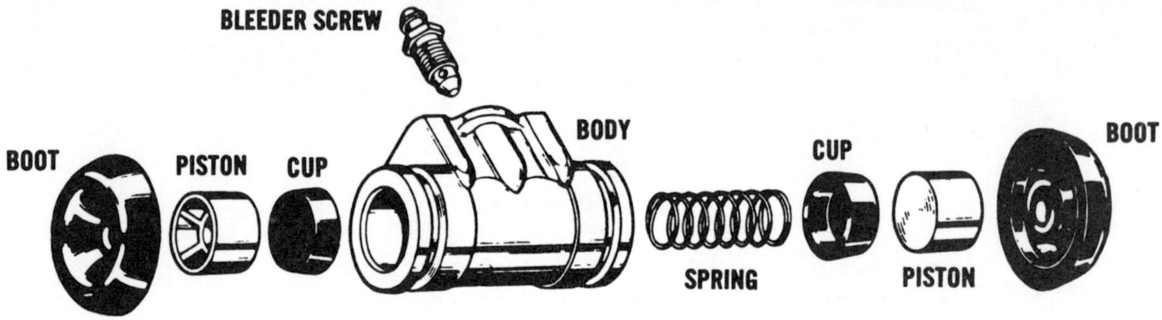

FIG 10:8 Rear wheel cylinder components

Wheel cylinder overhaul:

Removal:

1 Refer to the previous sub-section and remove the brake shoes.
2 Unscrew the hydraulic brake line connector from the wheel cylinder and plug the pipe to prevent the ingress of dirt.
3 Remove the wheel cylinder securing bolts.

Dismantling:

4 Refer to **FIG 10:8**, remove the rubber boots, pistons, and the cups and spring with expanders.
5 Scrap all rubber parts and remove the bleed screw.

Inspection:

6 Wash all the metal parts in clean methylated spirits. Inspect the cylinder bores for scores, deep scratches or corrosion. Light scratches and surface corrosion may be polished out using No. 400 'Wet and Dry' wetted with brake fluid. Do not use emery cloth or sandpaper.
7 Check the piston for wear or damage and check its clearance in the cylinder bore (see **FIG 10:9**). It should be between .002 and .005 inch (.051 to .13 mm).
8 Ensure the bleed screw is not blocked.

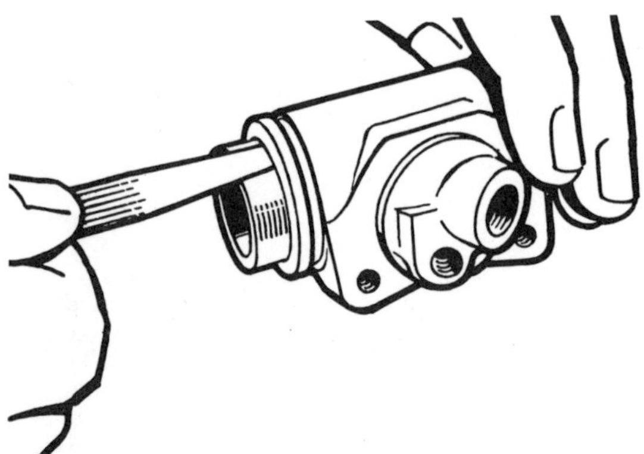

FIG 10:9 Checking piston to bore clearance with feeler gauges

Assembling:

9 Assemble the cylinders with all the parts wetted in clean brake fluid. Take care not to turn the lips of the seals as they enter the bores.

Refitting:

10 Clean the backplate mounting and reassemble the parts in the reverse order of dismantling, referring to the previous sub-section to assemble the brake shoes.
11 Bleed the brakes as described in **Section 10:7**.

10:6 The master cylinder

The tandem master cylinder provides a separate hydraulic circuit to the front disc brakes and the rear drum brakes. The idea being that if any one system fails the car can be brought to a controlled standstill, albeit with a very much reduced braking efficiency and particularly so if it is the front circuit that has failed. However, it is definitely preferable to having no brakes at all. The chances of such a situation arising are considerably reduced if the car is serviced regularly and to the instructions given in this Chapter.

Referring to **FIG 10:10**, separate fluid reservoirs are provided for each hydraulic circuit and the fluid level can be easily seen through the transparent plastic containers, making a visual check a simple procedure as often as the bonnet is opened.

Operation:

When the brake pedal is applied a build up of pressure accumulates in the fluid between the primary and secondary pistons, and progressively through the outlet port to the front brake circuit, which commences to apply the front brakes. As the pressure increases in the front brake circuit the secondary piston is forced down the bore to build up the pressure in the rear brake circuit and apply the rear brakes. As the pistons pass down the bores they operate valves to shut off the supply ports from the reservoirs to prevent the re-entry of the fluid. When the pedal is released the pistons are returned to their neutral position by the return springs and some back-pressure by the fluid. The reservoir inlet ports are re-opened and the excess fluid passes into the containers.

A pressure differential is necessary between the two circuits to compensate for the uneven weight distribution between the front and the rear of the car under heavy

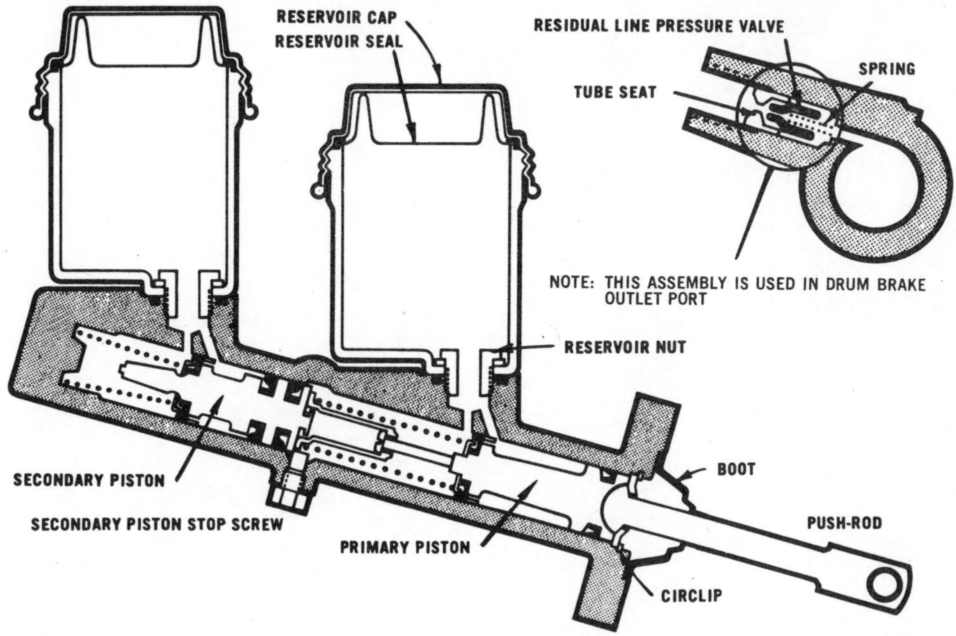

FIG 10:10 Section through master cylinder and residual line pressure valve

braking, the weight being most prevalent on the front wheels; therefore more pressure is required on the front wheels and a reduction in pressure on the rear wheels. A vacuum-hydraulic servo assists with extra power to the front brakes and pressure to the rear brakes is reduced by the embodiment of a spring loaded reduction valve in the rear brake hydraulic circuit, at the master cylinder outlet port.

Removal:

1 Disconnect one of the supply lines and drain the reservoir of fluid. Drain the other reservoir.

2 At the footbrake pedal lever, remove the splitpin, washer and clevis pin to detach the pushrod from the pedal.

3 Unscrew the fixing bolts and nuts that secure the master cylinder to the bulkhead.

Refitting:

4 Refit in the reverse order of dismantling but connect the hydraulic pipes to the master cylinder before connecting the pushrod to the pedal arm. Bleed the system as described in **Section 10:7** and recheck the fluid lever in the reservoirs. Check all fluid connections for leaks.

Overhauling:

1 If it is necessary to remove the residual line pressure valve, extract the tube seat, which is an interference fit in the casting, by means of a self-tapping puller or extractor. The pressure valve will come out with the tube seat. Note that the operation will render the valve unserviceable and a new assembly should be obtained with other spares supplied in kit form.

2 Press the pushrod very slightly into the bore and remove the retaining circlip. Remove the pushrod and the primary piston assembly. Remove the stop screw.

3 To extract the secondary piston carefully force it out with a compressed air line introduced to the outlet port.

Cleaning and inspection:

4 Scrap all rubber parts as these are supplied in the service kits. Ensure that the parts in the kit are correct by comparing them with the removed items. Note also that the parts supplied should be for a master cylinder bore of .80 inch (20.32 mm) diameter.

5 Clean all the metal parts with methylated spirits and examine the pistons and bore for wear, corrosion and score marks. In this instance do not attempt to polish them but obtain new parts.

Reassembly:

6 Refer to the figure and note the location of the seals on the pistons. Wet the seals in clean, unused brake fluid before assembling and fit them using the fingers only. Wet the bore with fluid before inserting the piston assemblies. Take care not to damage the seals as they pass over the circlip groove.

7 After fitting the secondary piston return spring—note the shape and location—and the piston assembly, hold them in position down the bore with a wooden rod whilst the stop screw is replaced and tightened.

8 Press the new residual line pressure valve assembly into the **rear** brake outlet port.

9 Fill both reservoirs with clean, unused BLMC HBF-6 brake fluid and work the pushrod to bleed the assembly. Check the compensating port clearance in

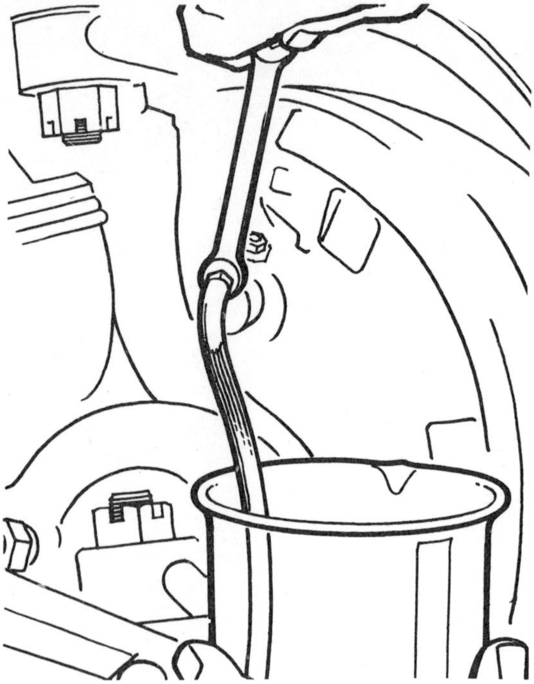

FIG 10:11 Bleeding the hydraulic system

the front (secondary) reservoir by watching for a spurt of fluid when the pistons are slightly depressed.

10 After bleeding block the outlet ports to prevent the entry of dirt and the brake fluid from escaping.

11 Refit the assembly as previously described taking care not to spill brake fluid over the paint work. Wipe it off immediately if it does spill otherwise it will lift the cellulose off the metal.

10:7 Bleeding the system

Fill the reservoir with fluid as instructed, and make frequent checks on the fluid levels as the operation is in progress. The grade of fluid must be as specified. Be careful not to spill fluid on the paintwork as it is a solvent.

Start with the rear brakes. Attach rubber or plastic bleed tubes to the rear bleed screws and immerse the free ends in some brake fluid in clean glass containers (see **FIG 10:11**).

Open both screws half a turn and instruct your assistant working the pedal to start with very light strokes of the brake pedal. Do not make complete strokes and let the pedal return unaided. Go on pumping with a slight pause after each stroke. Watch the fluid that emerges from the immersed ends of the tubes and when air bubbles cease, give four more pedal strokes, hold the pedal down and tighten both bleed screws to 4 to 6 lbf ft (.5 to .8 kgf m).

Repeat the procedure on the two front brakes. Keep an eye on the fluid level in the reservoir, topping-up if necessary.

10:8 Handbrake servicing

Adjusting:

If the handbrake is not effective and it is known that the rear brakes are in perfect order and do not need new linings, it is possible to adjust the cable operation.

Refer to **FIG 10:12.** Set handbrake lever on third ratchet tooth, jack up rear wheels clear of the ground with front wheels chocked and check that heavy hand pressure will just turn them. Resistance should be equal on both sides.

If the wheels are quite free release the handbrake and remove the inner edge of the front and rear tread plates on the drivers side. Ease away the floor covering.

Turn adjusting nut at the rear of the handbrake lever. After adjustment, pull on handbrake lever by three notches and check both rear wheels again. Release handbrake and check that wheels are free. Ensure that the cable is not twisted and the balance sector lever is at right angles to the centre line of the car.

Look for trouble in the rear brakes if this adjustment fails.

Renewing cables:

1 Release the handbrake and remove the front bench seat or the driver's seat.

2 Loosen the inside edge of the front and rear tread plates and withdraw the covering from under them, pass the covering over the handbrake lever.

3 Remove the two bolts which secure the handbrake assembly to the body panel. Detach the assembly then remove the brackets that secure the front cable to the internal body panels.

4 Loosen the wheel nuts on both rear wheels. Jack up the rear of the car and support with safety stands. Chock the front wheels before jacking.

5 Release the centre and rear exhaust pipe mounting's and disconnect the front cable from the balance sector assembly (see **FIG 10:12**). Disconnect the front cable assembly from the body brackets and withdraw it, with its tube, from the floor pan.

6 Unscrew the rear cable adjusting nuts and withdraw the rear cable assembly from the retaining brackets.

7 Refer to **Section 10:5** and remove the brake shoes. To remove the cable from the backplate, depress the retaining spring unit and use removing tool, PBR cable remover No. 982170.

Refitting:

8 Refit in the reverse order of dismantling noting the following:
Adjust the rear cables until the inner side cable retaining slots in the balance sector are angled approximately 45 deg. from the full on position (see angle in figure).

9 Check with the handbrake applied that the balance sector link assembly 14 or 19 is parallel to the centre line of the car and the cable retaining slots in the sector 12 or 17 are at right angles to the link.

10 Tighten the locking nuts and adjust the front cable.

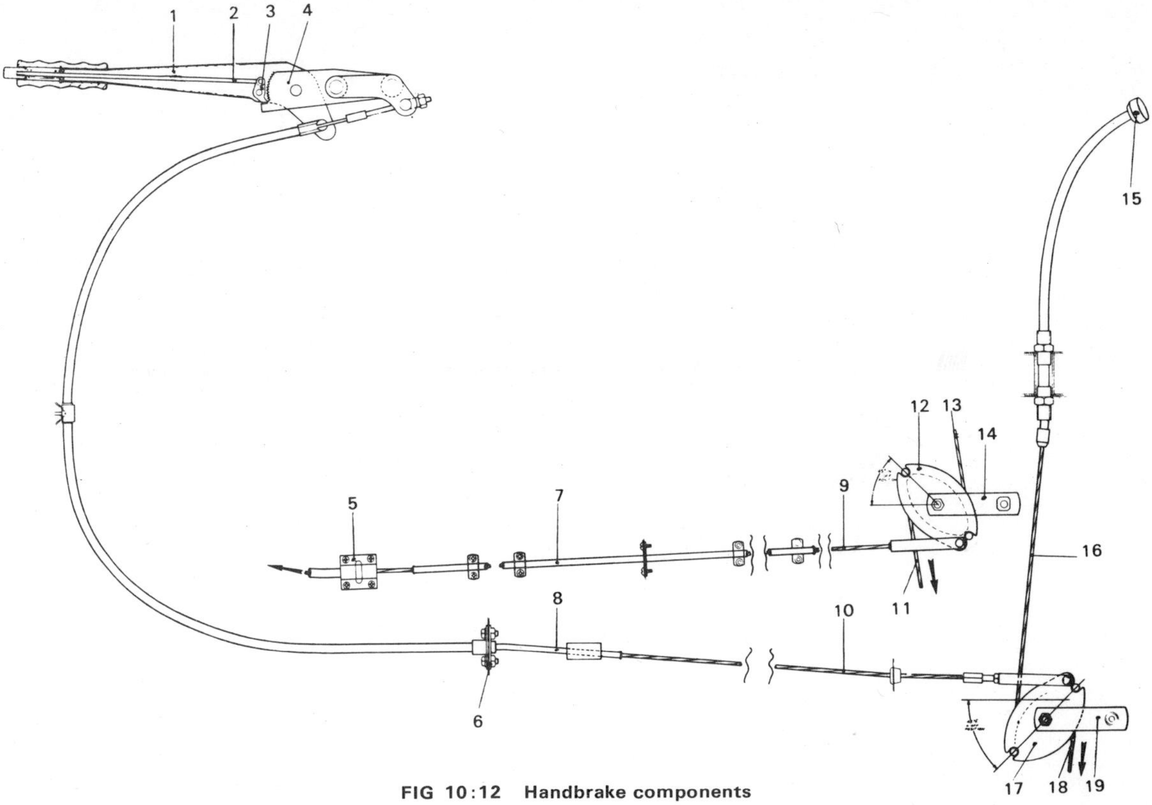

FIG 10:12 Handbrake components

Key to Fig 10:12 1 Lever—handbrake 2 Ratchet release pushrod 3 Pawl 4 Ratchet lever 5 Body fixing 6 Body fixing 7 Cable tube 8 Cable tube 9 Front cable 10 Front cable 11 Rear cable—L.H. 12 Compensator 13 Rear cable—R.H. 14 Compensator mounting plates 15 Brake backplate attachment 16 Rear cable—R.H. 17 Compensator 18 Rear cable—L.H. 19 Compensator mounting plates

10:9 Removing a flexible hose

1 Do not attempt to release a flexible hose by just trying to unscrew either one of its connecting ends. First, unscrew the metal pipe union nut from its connection to the hose.

2 Now hold the hexagon on the hose at the disconnected end and unscrew the locknut securing it to the support bracket.

3 Unscrew the hose at the wheel end.

4 Refit a new hose in the reverse order of removal.

10:10 Stop light switch

The stop light switch is positioned under the dash panel and is operated by depressing the brake pedal. With the pedal in the rest position the stop light operating rod on the pedal shaft must be between $\frac{11}{64}$ and $\frac{7}{32}$ inch (4.37 and 5.56 mm). Adjust by resetting the attachment bracket.

10:11 The servo unit

Referring to **FIG 10:13** the Hydropower servo unit comprises two steel pressings held together at their rims by a clamping ring 1. The rear half 2 is separated from the front half 3 by a diaphragm 4 and pushrod assembly 5. The diaphragm perimeter is clamped between the two half rims. The spring 6 holds the diaphragm and pushrod in the released position.

A check valve 7 is fitted through the wall of the vacuum half 3 and attached to the vacuum half is an aluminium cast hydraulic slave cylinder 8. A bleed screw 9 is incorporated in the slave cylinder and the components consist of a bush 10 fitted with vacuum and hydraulic seals and a spacer 11. The pushrod 5 passes through the seals and spacer to actuate the slave cylinder piston 12 and cup assembly 13.

The control valve 14 is actuated hydraulically to control atmospheric pressure into the chamber 2 when the brake pedal is applied and to prevent the entry of air in the released position so that manifold vacuum is transmitted to both sides of the diaphragm 4.

Operating principle:

Brake fluid from the master cylinder enters at the inlet post 15 and passes through port 16 into the slave cylinder and to the upper side of the control valve piston 17 through the port 18.

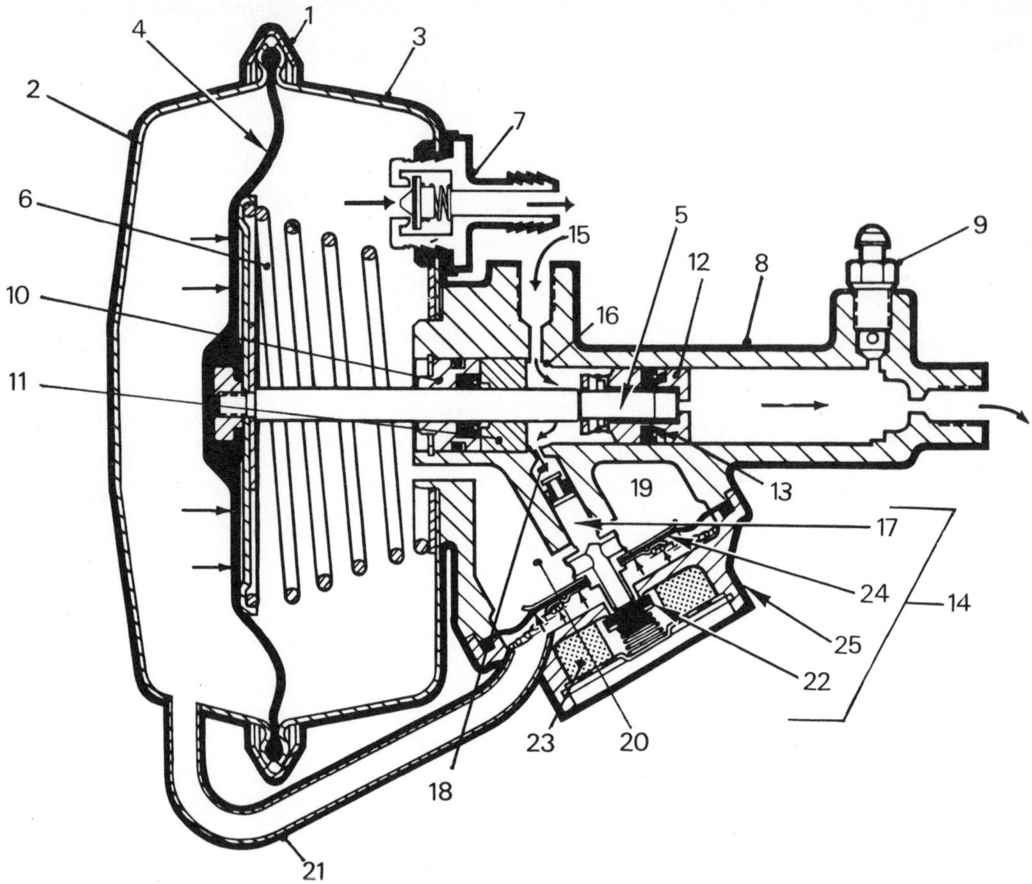

FIG 10:13 Section through servo unit

Key to Fig 10:13 1 Clamp ring 2 Rear chamber 3 Front chamber 4 Diaphragm 5 Pushrod assembly 6 Diaphragm spring 7 Check valve 8 Slave cylinder 9 Bleed screw 10 Bush 11 Spacer 12 Slave cylinder piston 13 Cup assembly 14 Control valve 15 Fluid inlet port 16 Fluid port 17 Control valve piston 18 Fluid port 19 Valve chamber 20 Valve chamber 21 Interconnecting tube 22 Poppet valve 23 Filter 24 Valve diaphragm 25 Valve body

Air is drawn from the unit by the intake manifold through the check valve 7, the vacuum being transmitted to the chamber 3 and through ports and passages to the chambers 19 and 20, and through the interconnecting tube 21 to the rear half chamber 2. The unit in this condition is described as vacuum suspended.

When the pedal is applied, fluid from the master cylinder enters the slave cylinder and at the same time exerts pressure on top of the piston 17 forcing it downwards to open the valve 22 and allow air to enter through the filter 23.

The incoming air expands rapidly in chamber 2 and pushes the diaphragm 4 and pushrod 5 forward against the tension of spring 6. The pushrod forces the piston 12 down the cylinder bore to exert pressure on the fluid and apply the brakes.

Removing servo:

The servo unit is mounted on brackets attached to the engine bulkhead.

1 Disconnect the vacuum hose from the non-return valve.

2 Disconnect the two hyraulic pipes and remove the bolts securing the servo to the mounting brackets.

Dismantling:

The servo unit can be dismantled but it is a job best left to the experts. Availability of component parts may present a problem even if the operator is capable of stripping the unit. It is far better and quicker to renew the assembly on an exchange basis.

Refitting:

Refit the unit in the reverse order of removal. After fitting the hydraulic system must be bled as described in **Section 10:7**.

10:12 The brake pedal

Removing:

The brake pedal is mounted at a fulcrum point on the toe-board bracket.

1 Remove the splitpin and clevis pin to release the master cylinder pushrod from the brake pedal.

2 Detach the pedal return spring and separate the nut and washer from the fulcrum bolt. The bolt also secures the bracket but it may be withdrawn complete with brake pedal, distance sleeve and spacing washer.

Refitting:

3 Refit in the reverse order locating the head of the fulcrum bolt to the outer side of the assembly.

4 Take note that on automatic models a spacer is fitted between the pedal and bracket, the flat washer is adjacent to the pedal.

10:13 Fault diagnosis

(a) 'Spongy' brake pedal

1 Leak in hydraulic system
2 Worn master cylinder
3 Leaking wheel cylinder
4 Air in brake fluid
5 Gaps between rear brake linings and shoes

(b) Excessive pedal movement

1 Check 1 and 4 in (a)
2 Adjusters faulty
3 Very low fluid level in reservoir

(c) Brakes grab or pull to one side

1 Distorted or badly worn discs or drums
2 Wet or oily pads or linings
3 Disc loose on hub
4 Worn suspension or steering connections
5 Mixed linings, wrong grade or different thicknesses
6 Unequal tyre pressures
7 Broken shoe return springs
8 Seized piston in one brake cylinder
9 Loose caliper or backplate

(d) Excessive pedal pressure needed

1 Check 5 in (c)
2 Leak in vacuum hose to servo unit
3 Defective servo unit
4 Servo filter blocked
5 Brake linings water soaked
6 Linings glazed due to heat
7 Defect in one circuit of dual line system

(e) Loss of pedal pressure

1 Defective master cylinder, worn bore, piston or seals
2 Leaking wheel cylinder or servo unit
3 Leaking brake pipes or connections
4 No fluid in master cylinder reservoir

NOTES

CHAPTER 11

THE ELECTRICAL SYSTEM

11 :1 Description

This is a 12-volt system in which the negative terminal of the battery is earthed. A belt-driven 'Email' alternator provides charging current and an 'Email' VBT vibrating type regulator controls the system voltage. The starter motor is a Lucas M40 of the pre-engaged type. In this the pinion is engaged with the flywheel ring gear before the current is switched on automatically. The standard battery is a 12-volt 9-plate with a capacity of 46 amp/hrs at 20 hours rating.

There are wiring diagrams in Technical Data. Although servicing instructions are given, we recommend that seriously defective parts be replaced by new ones on an exchange basis.

11 :2 Routine maintenance

Every 3000 miles (5000 km or 3 months) check level of electrolyte (acid) in battery. Car must be standing level.

The electrolyte should just cover the perforated guide. Do not top-up unless the liquid is below the perforated guide. Do not use a naked light to examine the cells, as imflammable gas may be present.

Top-up with distilled water until the level is reached, clean the manifold cover and dry the surrounding area. Refit the cover and press firmly into place. If weather is cold enough for icing, run the engine immediately after topping up.

At the same intervals, clean off all corrosion with diluted ammonia, dry thoroughly and paint affected parts with anti-sulphuric paint. Smear terminal posts with petroleum jelly and check tightness of connections. Clean mating surfaces of terminals, particularly if the starter does not turn briskly.

Do not leave a battery in a discharged condition. An unused battery should be given a freshening charge every fortnight.

Checking electrolyte for specific gravity:

Every 60000 miles (10,000 km or 6 months), use an hydrometer to check the specific gravity of the electrolyte. Insert the tube into the liquid, squeeze the bulb and wait until the float is lifted. Read off the level on the scale of the float. At climates below 27°C (80°F) the readings will indicate battery conditions as follows:

Cell fully charged . .	1.270 to 1.290
Cell about half-charged . .	1.190 to 1.210
Cell discharged . .	1.110 to 1.130

These figures are for an electrolyte temperature of 16°C (60°F). For every 3°C (5°F) above this, add

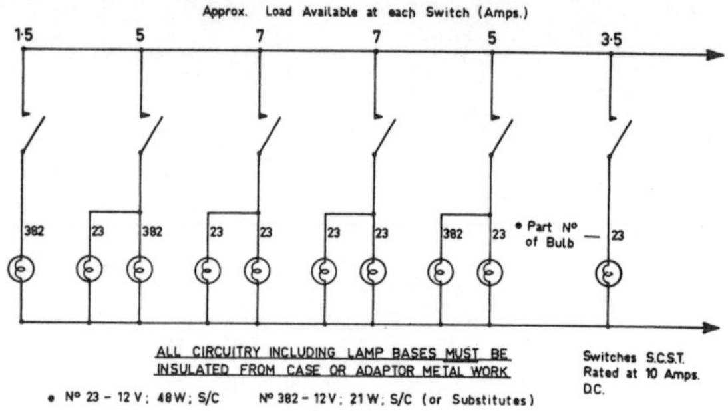

FIG 11 :1 A typical example of a made-up test lamp bank for checking the alternator output

.002 to the specific gravity. Subtract .002 if below. All cells should read about the same. If not, the difference may be due to a defective cell. **Do not try to rectify by adding acid.**

Checking equipment:

Every 3000 miles (5000 km or 3 months), check that all electrical equipment works properly. Check all lights and have the alignment of the head lamps checked. Operating the switches and brake pedal in a darkened garage will verify the action of the direction indicator and stop lamps.

11 :3 The alternator

Adjusting belt:

Refer to **FIG 4:4**. Check tension midway between pulleys on longest run of belt. Total deflection under normal thumb pressure should be $\frac{1}{2}$ inch (13 mm). To adjust, slacken pivot and link bolts 1 and 2. Move alternator by applying pressure at the mounting bracket **at the driving end only.**

Testing alternator:

Moving coil meters will be required, a moving coil voltmeter, reading up to 20 volts, a moving coil ammeter up to 50 amps, and a lamp bank made up as shown in

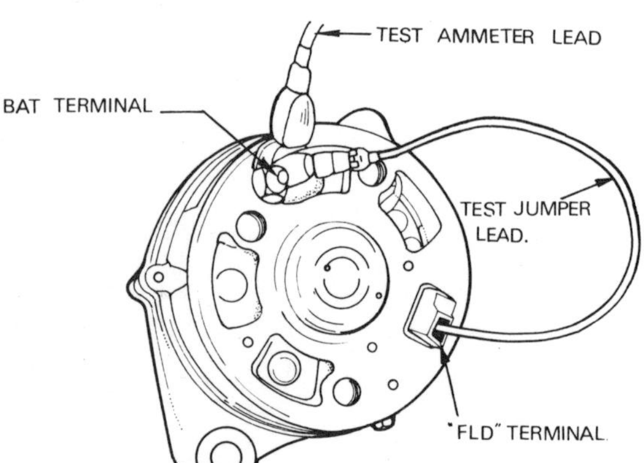

FIG 11 :2 The jump lead connected between the FLD and BAT terminals. Ammeter test lead also to BAT terminal

FIG 11 :1. Before testing ensure that the belt is tensioned correctly, battery is good and connections clean and tight.

First check that battery voltage is reaching the alternator. **Remember that the battery must never be disconnected while the engine is running and the battery must be correctly connected (negative earth).**

Full output test of charging system (regulator in circuit):

1 Disconnect the negative battery terminal and the changing circuit lead from alternator BAT terminal.
2 Connect the test ammeter positive (+) lead to the alternator BAT terminal and the negative (—) lead to the disconnected charging circuit lead.
3 Connect the voltmeter and the lamp bank to the positive (+) and negative (—) terminals of the battery, essentially, positive to positive and negative to negative.
4 Reconnect the battery.
5 Start the engine and run at approximately 2200 rev/min. Adjust the lamp bank to obtain a maximum output at 14.2 volts. The reading must be equal to, or greater than, the rating of alternator.
6 If the results of the test indicate a low system output, carry out a full output test without the regulator or harness connections as described under the next heading.
7 **Stop the engine and disconnect the battery before reconnecting the test equipment.**

Full output test of alternator (regulator out of circuit):

1 Disconnect the battery and the alternator FLD and AUX harness plugs. Keep the plugs clear of the frame whilst testing is in progress.
2 Connect a jump-lead to the alternator, one end connected to the FLD terminal and the other end to the BAT terminal (see **FIG 11 :2**).
3 Reconnect the battery and start the engine. Increase engine speed to 2200 rev/min and maintain a 14.2 voltmeter reading by adjusting the lamp bank load.
4 The output should be equal to, or greater than, the rating of alternator. If the output is considerably below the rated output try a further test, under the same conditions, but transfer the negative test lead from the ammeter to the positive battery terminal. If the output is still low take the test one stage further and connect a second jump-lead (5 mm) between the alternator frame and the negative battery terminal. If the output is still low a new or reconditioned alternator will be necessary.
5 If the output is satisfactory, stop the engine, disconnect the battery and the jump-leads. A further, but last test, can now be carried out to determine the serviceability of the alternator. Connect a jump-lead to the alternator terminals AUX and FLD as shown in **FIG 11 :3**.
6 Reconnect the battery and start the engine. The alternator should now 'excite' as the engine speed is raised to approximately 1700 rev/min as the field current will now be supplied by the excites diodes.

The output, measured by the same method, should be the same value or greater than the rating of the alternator.

7 If the output is lower a new or reconditioned alternator will be necessary.

Removing alternator:

Disconnect the vehicle battery before removing the harness connections from the alternator as the BAT terminal is 'live' at all times.

Manual transmission models:

1 Disconnect the battery.
2 Noting their locations before removing, detach the terminal connections from the alternator.
3 Refer to **FIG 4:4** and remove the adjusting link bolt 2 and slacken the pivot bolts 1. Lower the alternator and remove the drive belt from the pulley.
4 Remove the pivot bolts 1 and lift the alternator away from the engine. Take off the adjusting link if the alternator is to be renewed.

Automatic tranmission models:

1 Complete the necessary operations as for the manual models and also the following:
On the Kimberley models the radiator grille and the lefthand inner headlamp assembly must be removed.
Remove the distributor to gain access to the alternator (see **Chapter 3**).

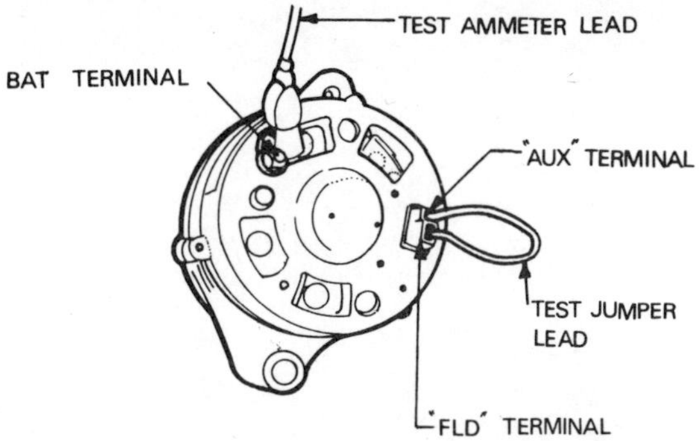

FIG 11:3 The jump lead connected between AUX and FLD terminals with ammeter test lead on BAT terminal

Refitting:

Refit in the reverse order of removal but be sure to position the split bush in the mounting lugs. Do not rely on the fixing bolts to push them back into position otherwise the lugs could be fractured. Tension the drive belt.

On the automatic models recheck the ignition timing (see **Chapter 3**).

11:4 The VBT 'Email' regulator

The regulator assemblies are calibrated during production with precision measuring equipment and it is not

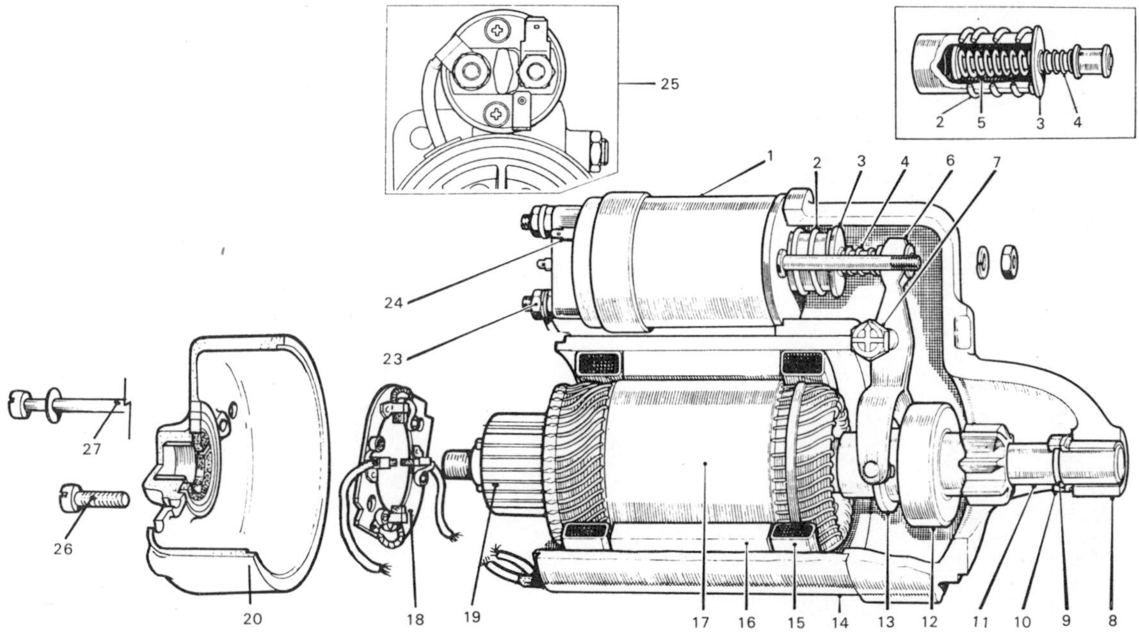

FIG 11:4 The Lucas M40 pre-engaged starter motor

Key to Fig 11:4 1 Solenoid 2 Plunger return spring 3 Plunger 4 Lost motion spring 5 Drive engagement spring 6 Engaging lever 7 Pivot pin 8 Fixing bracket 9 Retaining ring 10 Thrust collar 11 Armature shaft extension 12 Clutch 13 Drive operating plate 14 Yoke 15 Field coils 16 Pole shoes 17 Armature 18 Brush plate assembly 19 Commutator 20 End cover 21 Bush bearing 22 Brushes 23 Solenoid 'STA' terminal 24 Solenoid operating terminal 25 Solenoid 26 Brush plate fixing bolt 27 Through bolt

advisable to tamper with them in an attempt to adjust the output. Consult an authorized British Leyland agent if the regulator is suspect.

11 :5 The starter motor

The Lucas M40 starter motor shown in **FIG 11 :4** is a four-pole, four-brush, earth return unit with the field coils connected in series-parallel. A solenoid 1 mounted on top of the unit is energized when the ignition key is turned and actuates a lever 6 to engage the drive pinion with the teeth on the flywheel on the drive plate. The pre-engaged drive assembly is carried on an extension of the armature shaft 11.

Starter tests (suspect starter):

If the starter fails to turn the engine, first ensure that the battery is fully charged and topped up to the correct electrolyte level.

1 Switch on the headlamps and operate the starter control. If the headlamps go dim but with little or no response from the starter, it would indicate that the current is reaching the starter motor windings. The starter should be removed for examination.
2 If the headlamps retain their brilliance when the control is operated, check that the switch is functioning correctly. Then examine the starter solenoid and battery connections and the interconnecting leads. If the starter still fails after a satisfactory inspection it should be removed for examination.
3 If the starter operates, but sluggishly, it would indicate a defective battery or poor wiring connections.

Removing starter:

1 Disconnect the battery earth cable and the earth cable, at the starter.
2 Disconnect the cables and leads from the solenoid, noting their locations before removing.
3 Remove the two bolts securing the starter to the flywheel housing. On some early automatic models a small plate may be fitted between the starter and the engine backplate.
4 The starter may be removed either upwards or downwards.

Overhauling starter motor:

Refer to **FIG 11 :4** and do the following:

1 Remove solenoid noting that the plunger 3 must be lifted upwards to disengage it from lever. Remove end cover 20 by taking out the through-bolts 27, remove the bolts 26 to release the brush gear.
2 Remove the nut from the pivot pin 7 and withdraw pin. Withdraw armature from drive-end bracket. Drive collar 10 off its jump ring, remove the pinion and drive assembly.

Inspection:

Check the armature shaft bushes for wear. When renewing, immerse bushes in engine for 24 hours or for 2 hours if oil is at 100°C (212°F). Allow oil to cool before removing bush. **Bushes must not be reamed after refitting.** Press into place with a shouldered mandrel having a diameter to fit in a bore or bush.

Check that roller clutch turns freely in one direction and immediately locks when turned in the opposite direction. The drive assembly must move freely on the curved splines on the shaft.

Brushes must be free in their boxes. Renew if down to a thickness of $\frac{3}{16}$ inch (5 mm). Cut off old field coil brushes, leaving $\frac{1}{4}$ inch (6 mm) of the flexible wire still attached to field coil tag. Solder new brush leads to the old ends. Renew the remaining two brushes which are soldered to the terminal plates. Check brush springs and renew them if they are corroded and weak. Using 110 volts A.C. and a 15-watt lamp, check the insulation of the brush springs. Lamp must not light when connected between spring and commutator end bracket.

Overheated field coils 15 will have tape discoloured by burning. Make sure all field coil connections are sound and then check for continuity by connecting a 12-volt battery and test lamp between either field coil brush and the yoke (the body of the starter motor) Failure under test calls for renewal or repair.

Clean the copper commutator segments that contact the brushes with very fine glass paper. If badly worn or burned, the commutator may be skimmed in a lathe by mounting the armature between centres. Do not reduce thickness of copper below .14 inch (3.5 mm). After machining, polish with a flat surface of very fine glass-paper. Check windings for earthing by connecting a 15-watt lamp and 110-volt A.C. supply across each commutator segment and the armature shaft. Further tests must be carried out by experts with the necessary equipment.

Check the solenoid windings using a 12-volt battery and an ohmmeter or a moving coil ammeter connected in series across the starter terminal and the solenoid body. Resistance should be 1.01 to 1.07 ohms and current consumption 11.2 to 11.8 amp. If test is satisfactory, solenoid trouble may then be due to faulty contacts.

Reassembling:

Reverse the dismantling procedure, making sure that the lever is attached to the roller clutch drive in the position shown. Attach solenoid plunger to lever. Lubricate splines on shaft, moving parts of lever, outer surface of roller clutch housing and the lip of seal in drive-end bracket with Shell SB.2628 grease. In very hot climates use Shell Retinax A grease. Before tightening the through bolts make sure that the pin at the end of the armature is aligned with the slot in the brake assembly (see **FIG 11 :5**).

If it is thought advisable to test the motor while it is removed, connect it across a well-charged battery, using thick cables. The motor should run at high speed, taking about 40 amp.

Adjusting the pivot pin:

The pivot is adjusted and locked in a predetermined position so that when the solenoid plunger 3 is fully home (zero air gap) and the drive pinion assembly is gently shunted towards the flywheel the distance between the pinion and the thrust collar 10 should be between .010 and .020 inch (.25 and .50 mm). To adjust carry out the following instructions:

1 Connect a 6-volt battery, with a switch in the circuit, between the small unmarked solenoid terminal and earth. During the test energize the solenoid as briefly as possible to avoid overheating the series winding.
2 Close the switch to engage the starter drive and measure the gap between the pinion and the collar 10. Take up the slack in the engagement linkage with light finger pressure before measuring.
3 To adjust, slacken the locknut on the pin 7 and rotate the pin to obtain the correct setting. The arc of adjustment is 180 deg. but the head of the arrow, marked on the pin head, should be set only between the arrows on the arc that are marked on the drive end bracket.
4 Tighten the locknut.

Checking starter switch contacts:

1 Connect a 10-volt supply, with a switch in circuit, between the small unmarked solenoid terminal and earth.
2 Connect a test lamp across the solenoid main terminals.

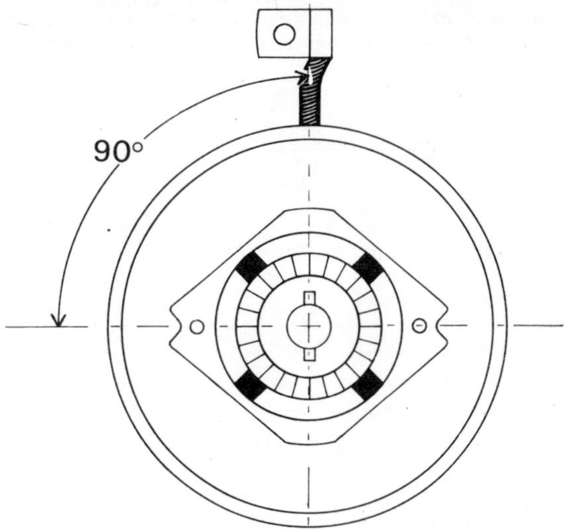

FIG 11:5 Aligning the slot in the starter brake assembly

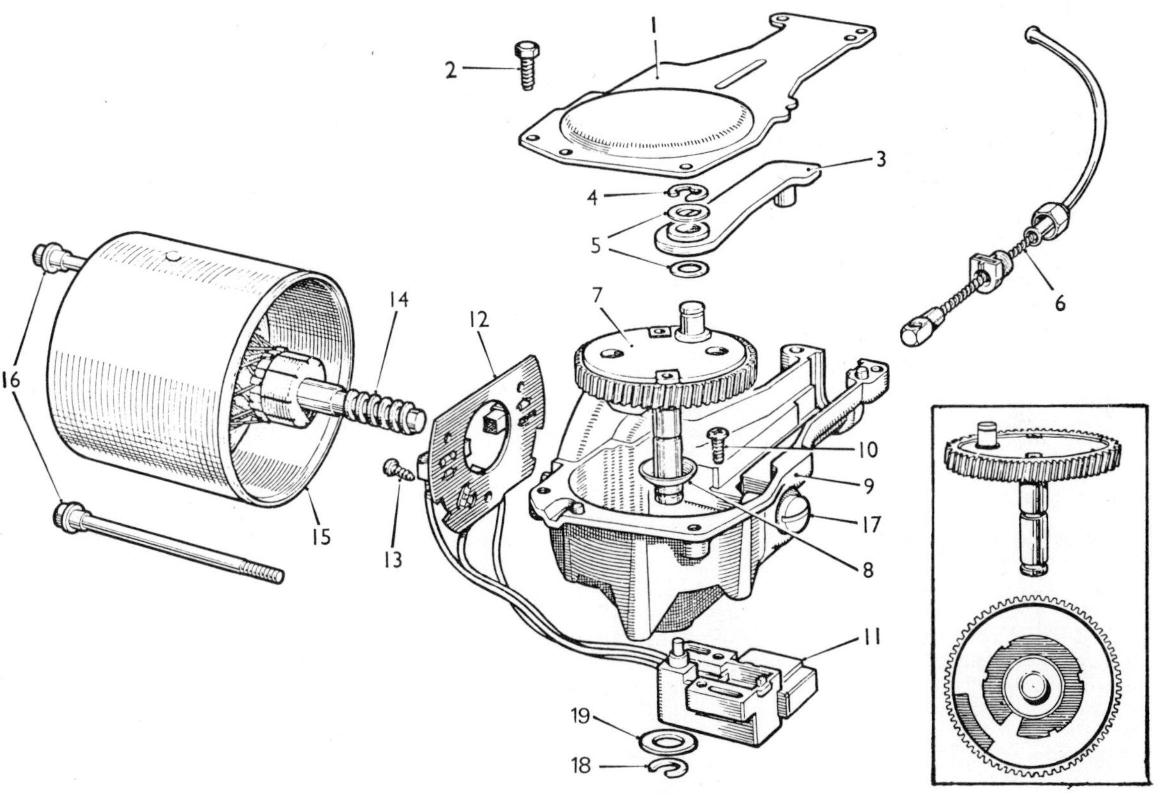

FIG 11:6 The Lucas 12AUW windscreen wiper motor

Key to Fig 11:6 1 Gearbox cover 2 Screw for cover 3 Connecting rod 4 Circlip 5 Plain washer 6 Cable assembly 7 Shaft and gear 8 Dished washer 9 Gearbox 10 Screw for limit switch 11 Limit switch assembly 12 Brush gear 13 Brush gear screw 14 Armature 15 Yoke assembly 16 Yoke bolts 17 Armature adjusting screw 18 Circlip 19 Washer
Inset shows position of crankpin with cable rack extended

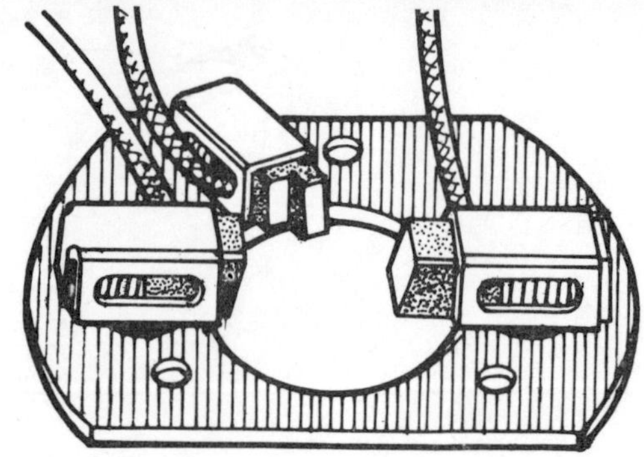

FIG 11:7 The two-speed motor brush assembly

3 Insert a stop in the drive end bracket to hold the pinion in the neutral position. Close the switch. The test lamp should light.
4 Switch off and remove the stop. Switch on and hold the pinion in the fully engaged position then switch off. The lamp should go out.

Refitting:

Reverse the removal sequence. Hold terminal tags of cables while tightening the nuts. Do not overtighten.

11:6 The windscreen wiper

The Lucas 12 AUW windscreen wiper, shown in exploded form in **FIG 11:6**, is of the two-speed type that incorporates a third brush (see **FIG 11:7**), to which the armature positive lead is connected when the fast speed is required.

In association with the terminal assembly a limit switch 11 is provided and a slipring secured to the underside of the gear wheel, on which three fixed contacts run. One of these provides contact for the limit switch and the other two, in conjunction with a control switch, provide regenerative braking of the armature to decelerate, and self park the blades in a predetermined position.

As the motor is of the permanent magnet design, the direction of rotation of the armature depends on the correct polarity supply. If it is found necessary to test-run the motor when it is removed to the bench, refer to **FIG 11:8** and connect the negative supply cable to motor terminal 1 and the positive supply cable to terminal 5 (normal speed) or terminal 3 (high speed).

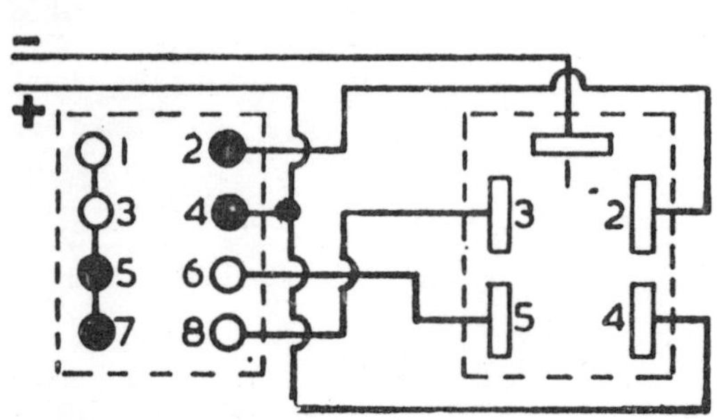

FIG 11:8 Wiper motor wiring diagram illustrating switch to motor terminals

Removing motor:

1 Disconnect the battery.
2 Refer to **FIG 11:6** and remove the four screws 2 and cover 1. Slacken the cable rack clamp, detach the circlip 4 and washer (upper 5) from the crankpin and withdraw the connecting rod 3. Pick up the washer (lower 5).
3 Disconnect the four cables at the switch plate (see **FIG 11:9**).
4 Remove the two self-tapping screws securing the unit to a mounting bracket. Lift out the motor.

Dismantling:

Before dismantling consider the more propitious method of rectification by renewing the unit on an exchange basis. Components parts could be difficult to obtain.

Remove circlip 18 and washer 19, remove burrs from shaft and pull out gear 7. Note dished washer 8. Do not separate the crankpin mounting plate from the moulded gearwheel.

Mark yoke and gearbox, if it is refitted 180 deg. out the motor will run in reverse. Release yoke, storing it away from steel particles, which will adhere to it. Release brush gear 12 and switch 11.

Inspection:

Main brushes (opposite each other) must be not less than $\frac{3}{16}$ inch (4.8 mm) thick. If narrow part of third brush is worn down to full width it needs renewal. In both cases renew complete brush assembly.

Brushes must move freely. Renew assembly if brush base is not level with bottom of slot in brush box under a load of 5 to 7 oz (140 to 200 gm).

Renew armature if open- or short-circuited. Renew gears and link if worn.

Reassembling:

Adopt the reverse order of dismantling. Use zinc oxide grease on gear teeth and cam, armature worm gear, connecting rod, crosshead and rack 6 and gears in wheelboxes.

Use Shell Turbo 41 oil on bearings, shafts and crankpin. Soak felt washer in yoke bearing. Be sparing on armature shaft.

Tighten yoke bolts to 14 lb in (.16 kg m). If armature is renewed, slacken screw 17. Fit washer 8 with concave face to gear. Larger of washers 5 goes under rod 3. If the crankpin mounting plate does detach itself from the gear wheel refer to the inset and position the crankpin above the gap in the slipring outer area.

Adjust armature end float by tightening thrust screw 17 and turning it back one quarter of a turn. Measure gap under head of screw and fit suitable shim to give end float of .002 to .008 inch (.05 to .2 mm) when screw is tightened.

Refitting:

Fit in the reverse order, leaving wheelbox covers slack until cable rack has been inserted and motor secured.

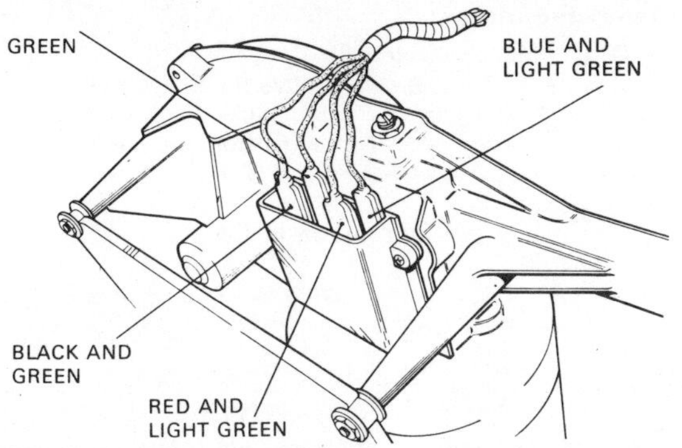

FIG 11:9 Identification and location of the wiring connections

Removing wheelboxes and rack:

1 Disconnect the battery.
2 Refer to **FIG 11:6** and loosen the nut that locks the rack tube to the gearbox.
3 Disconnect the wire terminals and remove the wiper arms and blades.
4 Remove the screws securing the motor mounting bracket to the body and withdraw the assembly and the rack inner cable complete.
5 Remove both wheelbox locknuts and spacer rubbers. Refer to **Chapter 12** and remove the glove box, demister tubes and air ducts.
6 Lift out the wheelboxes and outer tubing complete.

Inspection:

7 Open up the wheelboxes and examine the spindles and gear teeth. Renew worn or chipped parts.
8 Smear the new spindles and gears with a liberal coating of zinc oxide grease.

Reassembling and refitting:

9 Refit all parts in the reverse order of dismantling. Liberally grease the inner cable with zinc oxide grease and do not tighten the wheel box covers until the rack has been inserted.

11:7 Servicing the lights and switches

Headlamp alignments:

The setting is very critical and is best carried out on optical test equipment. The main beams must be $\frac{1}{2}\pm\frac{1}{4}$ deg. below horizontal and parallel with each other in the straight-ahead position, or in accordance with the local regulations. The car must be in normal trim.

Sealed beam unit renewal (FIGS 11:10 and 11:11):

Remove the radiator grilles. Remove the three retaining plate screws and remove rim. Pull light unit and plate forward and disconnect cable adaptor. When fitting the new unit, make sure the three lugs on the unit engage the slots in the seating.

Front side and flasher lamps (FIGS 11:12):

Remove the lenses (4 screws). Press bulbs in and turn them anticlockwise to remove. The side lamp bulb is 4 candle power and the flasher bulb is 32 c.p. or 21 w.

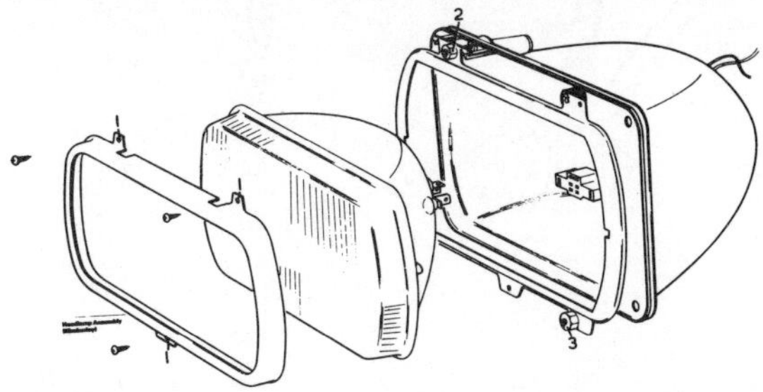

FIG 11:10 The headlamp assembly for the Kimberley four unit system

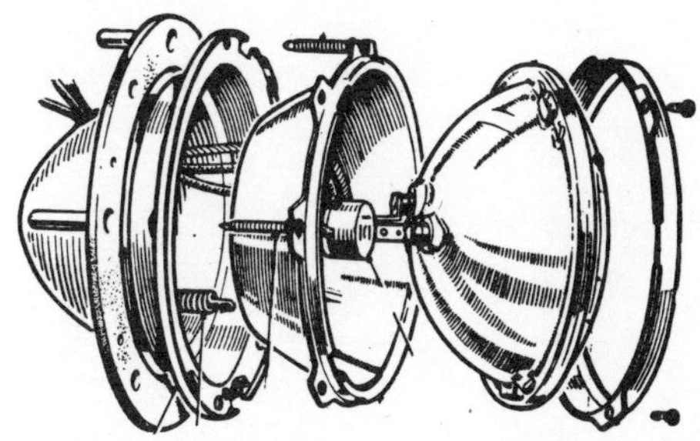
FIG 11:11 The headlamp assembly for the Tasman two-unit system

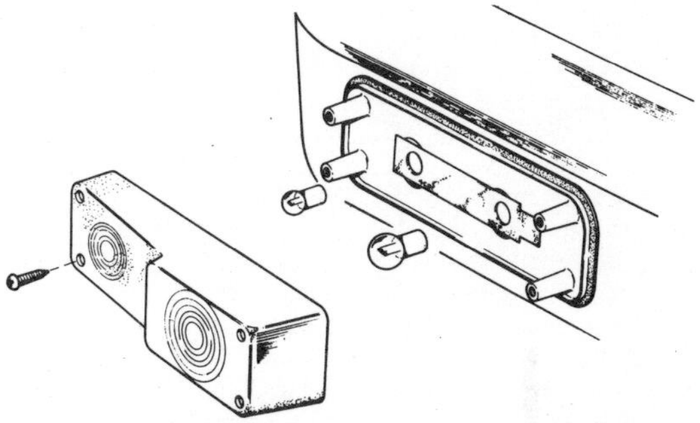
FIG 11:12 Detached lens and bulbs from the front side and flasher lamp combination

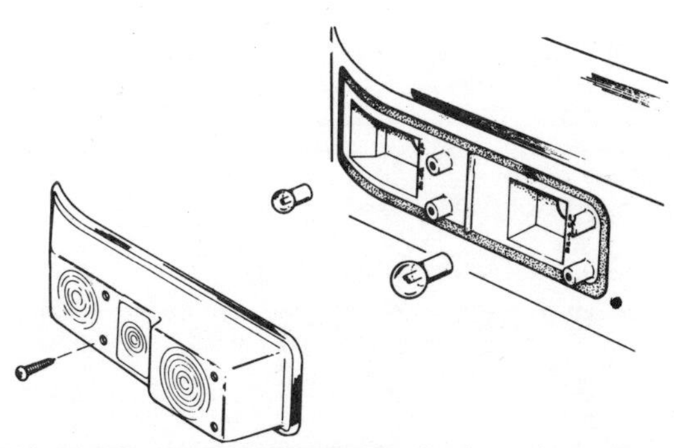
FIG 11:13 Detached lens and bulbs from the rear stop/tail and flasher lamp combination. The Kimberley has a reversing light also incorporated

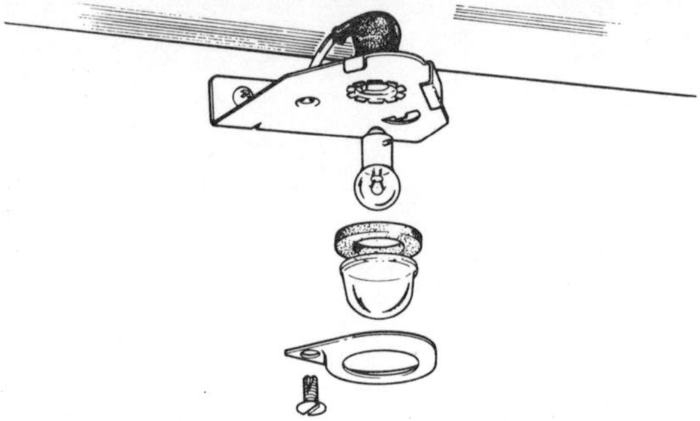

FIG 11:14 Detached components of the rear number plate illumination

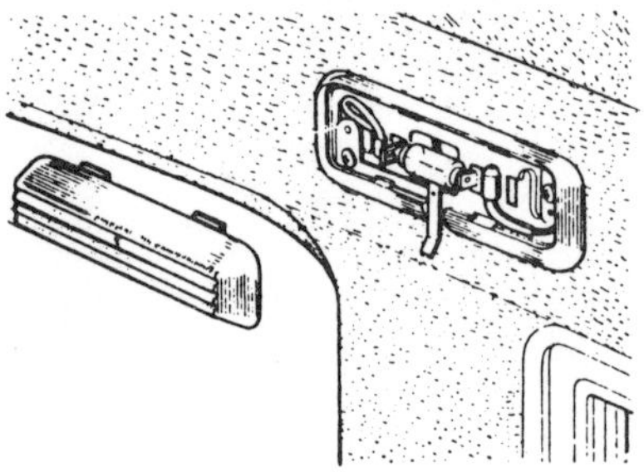

FIG 11:15 Interior lamp with plastic cover removed

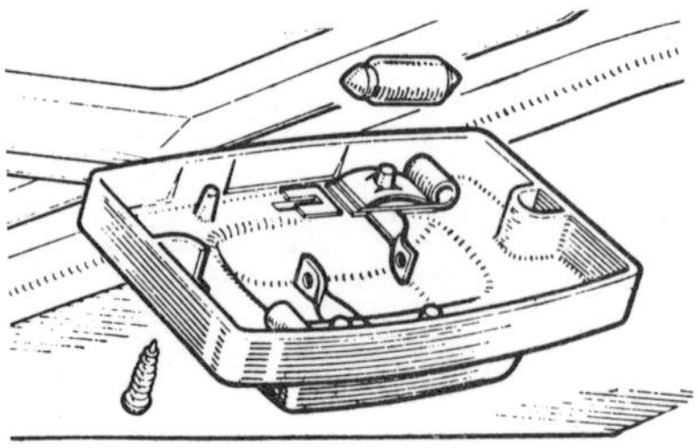

FIG 11:16 Boot and engine compartment lamps (Kimberley only)

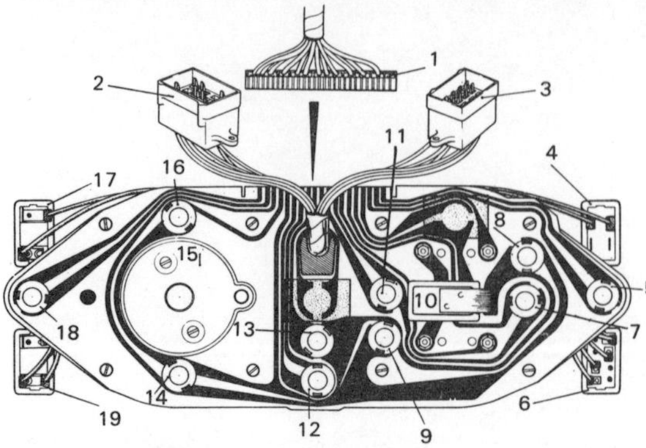

FIG 11:17 The panel warning lamps and connections. The illustration is a viewed position from the drivers seat with the panel inverted

Key to Fig 11:17 1 Main connector 2 Red connector 3 White connector 4 Screen washer switch 5 R.H. trafficator indicator 6 Windscreen wiper switch 7 Ignition warning light 8 Dash illumination 9 Dash illumination 10 Voltage stabilizer 11 Oil warning light 12 Brake light failure indicator 13 Hazard warning light 14 Dash illumination 15 Speedometer 16 Highbeam indicator 17 Heater fan switch 18 L.H. trafficator indicator 19 Light switch

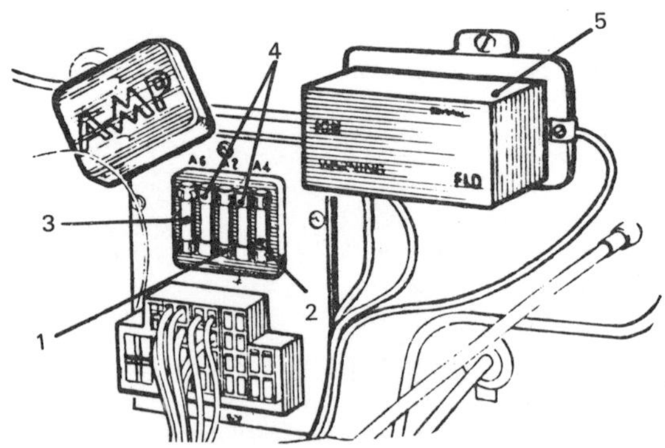

FIG 11:18 The fuses

Key to Fig 11:18 1 Fuse A1-A2 2 Fuse A3-A4 3 Fuse A5-A6 4 Spare fuses 5 Control box

Tail, stop and flasher lamps (FIG 11:13):

Remove the four screws through the lenses, and lift the assembly away. Press bulbs in and turn anticlockwise to remove. When refitting holders, note lugs in apertures for correct positioning.

The stop light/park bulb is 4/32 candle power and the reverse/flasher bulb 32/32 candle power. Reverse lights are fitted to Kimberley models only.

Number plate lamps (FIG 11:14):

Remove the screw securing the lens retaining plate. Remove the plate, domed lens and sealing ring. Push and turn the bulb anticlockwise to remove. The bulbs are 6-watt.

Reverse lamp (Kimberley):

See 'Tail, stop and flasher lamps'.

Interior lamp (see FIG 11:15):

Squeeze the long sides of the lens lightly together to release it. The 6-watt festoon bulb is removed by pulling it out of the contact clips.

Luggage boot and engine compartment lamp (Kimberley):

Release lamp (2 screws). Detach 6-watt festoon bulb from contact clips (see **FIG 11:16**).

Panel lights:

Panel and warning lights are fitted into a printed circuit panel behind the instrument assembly. The trafficator warning light bulbs are 4 watts and the remaining bulbs are 2 c.p. or 2.2 watts.

Removing:

1 Disconnect the battery.
2 Refer to **FIG 11 :17** and very carefully remove the main harness connector 1 from the lower edge of the printed circuit panels. Care over this operation cannot be over emphasized, as the printed circuit panels are easily damaged.
3 Take out the four screws securing the instrument assembly to the fascia panel.
4 Withdraw the red and white wiring connections 2 and 3 and disconnect the speedometer cable.
5 Invert the instrument panel to gain access to the panel and warning lights as shown in the illustration.

The flasher unit:

Checking faulty operation:
1 Check the bulbs for correct type and failure.
2 Check the connections (see wiring diagrams).
3 Check the fuses.
4 Check the voltage between 'B' terminal and earth (ignition switched on) at the flasher unit.
5 Connect the 'B' and 'L' terminal wires of the flasher unit together, switch on the ignition and the indicator switch. If the lamps illuminate the flasher unit is defective.

11 :8 The fuses

The fuse holder shown in **FIG 11 :18** is mounted on the connection panel which is attached to the engine bulkhead. There are three active fuses and two spare. Referring to the illustration, the fuse 1 between terminals A1 and A2 is a 35 amp and protects the accessories and the engine cooling fan. Fuse 2 between terminals A3 and A4 is also a 35 amp that protects those accessories that are energized only when the ignition is switched on. And fuse 3 is a 15 amp that protects the pilot and tail lamps.

It is important that only the fuses of the correct amperage are used.

11 :9 The electric windscreen washer

The washer bottle is attached to the lefthand panel in the engine compartment. When the switch is operated water is forced from the bottle by an electrically driven impeller. If the washer fails to operate carry out the following tests:

Testing:

1 Check that there is a supply of water and the jets and tubes are not blocked.
2 Check that A3-A4 fuse-No. 2 in **FIG 11 :18**.
3 Check that the hold-down switch on the facia panel is operative by bridging the two wires, if the washer operates the switch is defective.
4 Disconnect the leads from the motor (see **FIG 11 :19**) and supply an alternative power or from the battery direct. If it fails to operate the motor is defective.
5 The bottle and motor are supplied only as a complete unit.

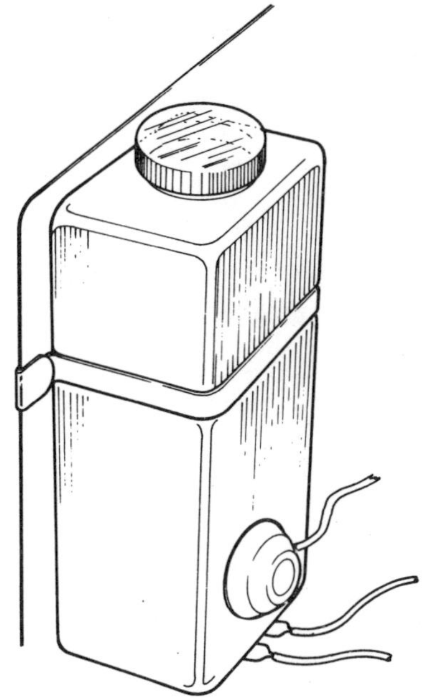

FIG 11 :19 Windscreen washer bottle assembly

11 :10 Electrical instruments

A stabilized voltage is needed for these. The voltage stabilizer is shown as item 10 in **FIG 11 :17**. It is reached by following the instructions under 'Removing', in this section.

A coolant temperature gauge is fitted to the instrument panel and the thermal transmitter is screwed into the thermostat housing on the engine and can be traced by the single cable attached to it. Before removing it, partially drain the cooling system (see **Chapter 4**).

A fuel gauge is similarly placed on the instrument panel. The tank unit is under the floor of the luggage compartment. To remove it, refer to **Chapter 2, Section 2:11**.

Removing:

1 Remove the printed circuit panels as described under 'Panel lights' in **Section 11 :7**.
2 Remove the warning light bulb holders noting their locations.
3 Pull out the voltage stabilizer 10, remove the eight screws around the panel and the four nuts holding the temperature and fuel gauges.
4 Lift the white section of the panel away from the black panel to detach the gauges.
5 If the printed circuit panel is to be removed, remove the connections from the terminals and pull the wires through the panel. No attempt should be made to repair a damaged circuitry panel.

Refitting:

6 Refit the components in the reverse order of removal. Do not overtighten the eight fixing screws.

11:11 Fault diagnosis

(a) Battery discharged

1 Terminals loose or dirty
2 Shorts in lighting circuits
3 Alternator faulty
4 Battery internally defective

(b) Insufficient charging current

1 Check 1 and 3 in (a)
2 Driving belt slipping

(c) Battery will not hold charge

1 Low electrolyte level
2 Battery plates sulphated
3 Electrolyte leaking from cracked case
4 Plate separators defective

(d) Battery overcharged

1 Regulator faulty

(e) Alternator output low or nil

1 Broken or slipping belt
2 Regulator or rectifier faulty
3 Worn bearings, bent shaft
4 Worn, burned or shorted slip rings
5 Brushes sticking, springs weak or broken
6 Battery voltage not reaching alternator

(f) Starter motor lacks power or will not operate

1 Battery discharged, terminals loose or dirty
2 Starter pinion jammed in engagement
3 Starter switch or solenoid faulty
4 Brushes worn or sticking. Leads faulty, springs weak
5 Commutator dirty or worn
6 Armature shaft bent
7 Engine abnormally stiff, perhaps after overhaul
8 Windings faulty

(g) Starter motor runs but will not engage

1 Pinion seized on shaft
2 Defective roller clutch
3 Worn or broken teeth

(h) Starter motor rough or noisy

1 Worn bearings or shaft
2 Worn teeth
3 Mounting bolts loose

(i) Lamps inoperative or erratic

1 Battery low, bulbs burned out
2 Faulty earthing of lamps or battery
3 Switches faulty, connections loose or broken

(j) Wiper motor sluggish

1 Faulty windings
2 Bearings dry
3 Commutator dirty

(k) Fuel or instrument gauges do not work

1 Breaks in wiring
2 Voltage stabilizer faulty
3 Instruments and transmitters at fault

CHAPTER 12

THE BODYWORK

12:1 Bodywork finish

Leave serious body damage to the experts. However, small dents and scratches may be filled and then painted with self-spraying cans of colour in the maker's shades. Remove wax polish with white spirit, but if silicone polish has been used, a very fine abrasive will be needed.

Use primer surfacer or paste stopper according to the amount of filling required. When dry, rub down with 400 grade 'Wet or Dry' paper and plenty of water. Surface must be perfectly smooth and flush to get a good finish. Several light coats of paint are better than a heavy application that may cause runs. When finish is dry, blend it with a cutting compound and then use a liquid polish.

12:2 Fitting seat belts

The two makes are provided with seat belts at the front. Any owner who doubts his ability to make a first-class job of fitting the rear belts to the earlier models should entrust the work to a competent garage. It is dangerous to take chances. 1971 models onwards have rear belts provided.

Renew seat belt assemblies that have been used in a car that has suffered severe impact in an accident.

12:3 Servicing doors

Removing trim pad (front door):

1 Remove the screw from the window winder handle and detach the handle and bezel.
2 Lift the door release handle and take out the screw that holds the escutcheon plate; remove the plate.
3 Refer to **FIG 12:1** and prise off the arm rest trim plate. Remove the two large Phillips-head screws and take off the arm rest.
4 Unscrew the interior lock snipper button. Prise the upper trim pad nylon spring clips out of their locating holes in the door frame, one front and one rear, take off the upper panel.
5 Remove the screws holding the lower trim panel and detach the panel.

Rear door:

Complete operations 1 to 3 as described for the front door, remove the interior lock snipper button and working outwards from the bottom centre of the trim panel, release the nine nylon liner clips (see **FIG 12:2**). Lift the panel upwards to detach it.

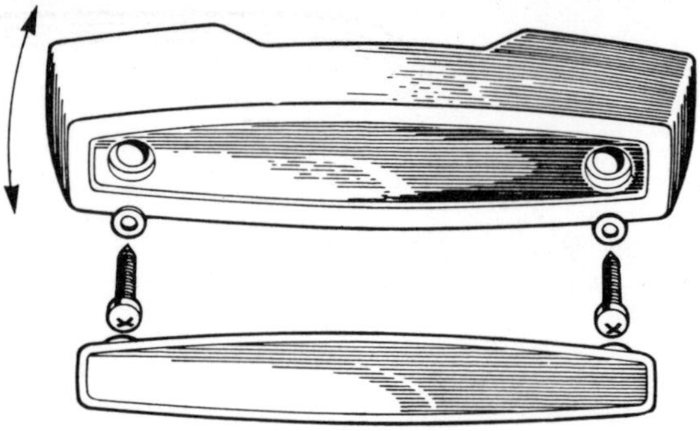

FIG 12:1 Armrest adjustment and support screws

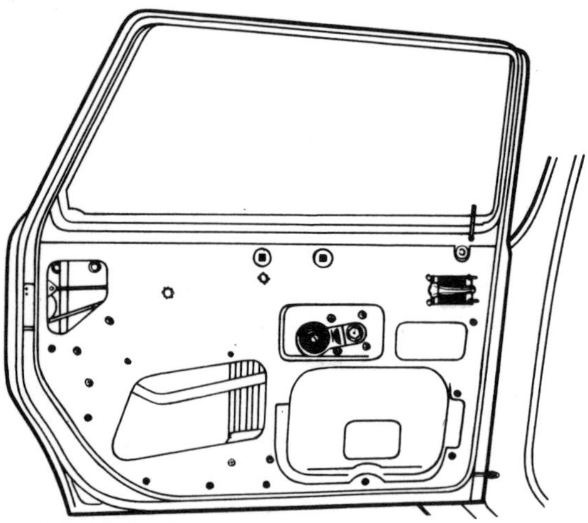

FIG 12:2 Rear door with trim panel removed

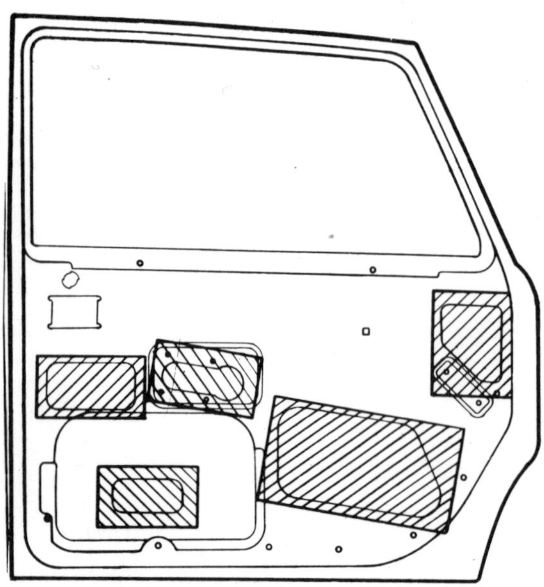

FIG 12:3 Adhesive tape application, rear door

Refitting:

Reverse the removing operations. Ensure all the door locks are greased and the sealing tapes on the doors are secure. If any of the tapes have been disturbed they should be renewed (see **FIGS 12:3** and **12:4**). When fitting the rear trim, locate the liner clips to their cups and snap them into a locking position with sharp taps using the palm of the hand.

Removing door glass:

1 Remove the door trim as described in the last sub-section. Peel off the sealing tape strips that give access to the glass stop.
2 Remove the two crosshead screws that hold the glass stop in position; remove the stop.
3 Wind the window down fully to clear the regulator from the guide channels.
4 Refer to **FIG 12:5** and lift the glass upwards tilting it slightly to clear the top corner.

Refitting:

5 Reverse the removal procedure and renew the disturbed sealing tapes.

Removing regulator:

1 Remove the door trim.
2 Peel off the sealing tapes and hold the glass in the closed position by inserting wedge-shaped pieces of wood between the glass and the door.
3 Take out the seven screws holding the regulator and separate it from the glass channel.
4 Collapse the assembly and withdraw it through the large cut-out in the door.

Refitting:

5 Reverse the removal procedure and renew the disturbed sealing tapes.

Adjusting door locks:

When the exterior door handles are operated there should be a certain amount of free play in the release mechanism before it is activated to allow the door to open. Furthermore, there should be a surplus of travel in the release mechanism immediately after the door has opened. Check and adjust as follows:

1 Close the door fully. Operate the catch noting the initial free play stage and continue exerting pressure until the door opens. At this point check that there is a surplus of movement in the catch.
2 To adjust from inside the door, lengthen or shorten the threaded portion of the link between the door handle and contraction plate.

Removing locks:

1 Remove the door trim as previously described. Close the window and remove the necessary sealing tape.
2 Refer to **FIG 12:6** and release the rods 5 and 6 from the nylon anti-rattle spring clips 12.
3 Release the spring clip from the latch release rod 6 and latch release lever 8, prise the rod from the nylon bush.

4 Unscrew the four screws and detach the interior release catch 3.
5 Release the spring clip from the interior lock control rod 5 and the quadrant 9, prise the rod from the nylon bush.
6 Lower the control rod and free the nylon pivot 2 by trimming it.

Refitting:

7 Reverse the removal procedure.

Removing doors:

1 Remove the pivot pin from the door check-link.
2 Mark the hinge positions and support the door with a jack interspaced by thick cloth.
3 Remove the screws securing the hinges to the door.

Refitting:

4 Follow the removal operations in reverse using a jack to support the door. The door alignment is adjusted by moving the hinges, the holes of which are elongated to provide adjustment in all directions. The striker plate is also adjustable to align the door if there is any up or down movement of the door on closing.

12:4 The bonnet

Removing:

1 Lift the bonnet and support with stay. On the Kimberley models disconnect the wiring from the engine compartment lamp.
2 As a precuation against damage to the rear corners place some cloth around the edges.
3 Mark the hinge positions, obtain the help of a second operator to support and steady the lid and remove the bolts, plain and spring washers.
4 Remove the bonnet and, if necessary, remove the screws securing the stay to the bonnet.

Refitting:

5 Reverse the removal procedure and adjust the alignment at the hinges.

Lock and safety catch:

Removing:

1 Release the control cable at the trunnion.
2 Remove the two set screws with spring and flat washers and note that there is a caged nut on the lefthand side.
3 Release the return spring and detach the lock and locating cup assemblies. A screwdriver slot is provided in the end of the bonnet lock-pin, release the lock nut and unscrew the pin to remove the assembly.

Safety catch:

4 Three screws with locking and plain washers secure the safety catch to the bonnet panel.

Refitting:

5 Reverse the removal procedures.

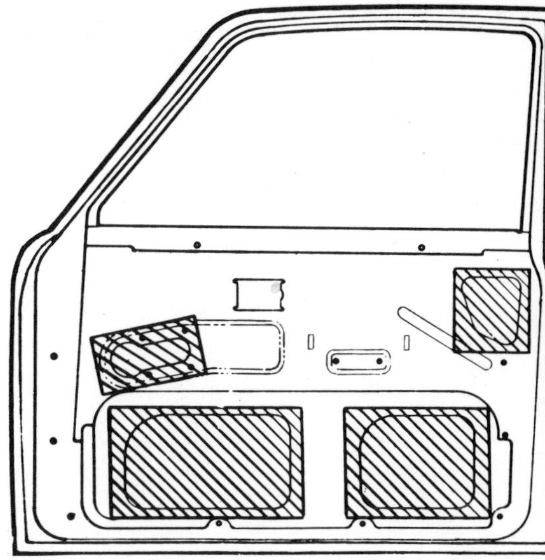

FIG 12:4 Adhesive tape application, front door

12:5 The trunk lid

Removing:

Protect the paint work at the top edges of the lid during removal and obtain the help of a second operator to steady and support the lid.

1 Lift the lid and mark the position of the hinge brackets on the lid.
2 Remove the setscrews securing the hinges to the lid panel. Detach the panel from the hinges.
3 If it is necessary to remove the hinges take out the four setscrews securing them to the parcel shelf panel.

Refitting:

4 Refit in the reverse order of removal. Adjust the alignment at the hinges and striker catch.

Trunk lid lock:

Removing (FIG 12:7):

1 Remove the three setscrews securing the lock assembly to the lid and compress the locking legs of the spring clip to release the lock holder from the lid.
2 The striker catch is secured by three setscrews. If it is necessary to remove it, first mark its position.

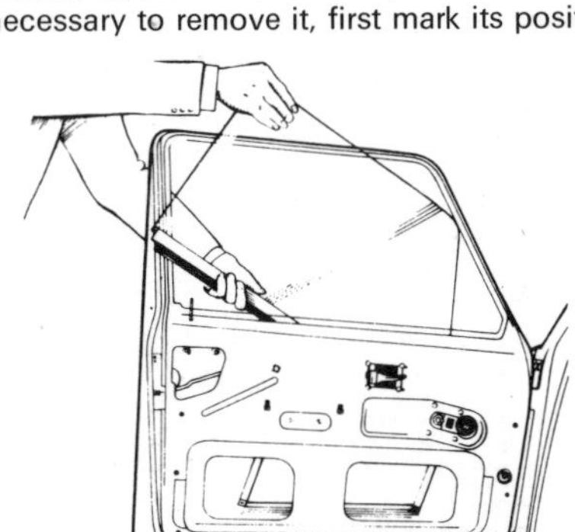

FIG 12:5 Removing the front door glass

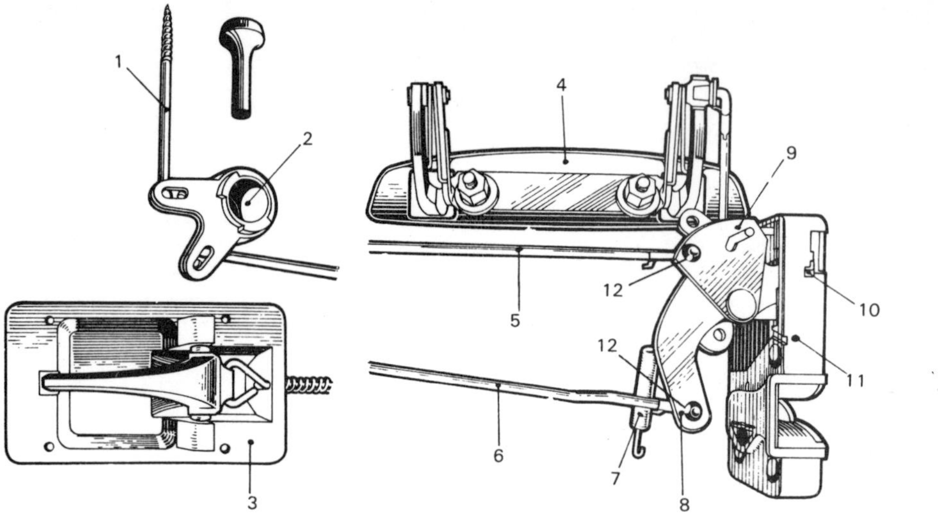

FIG 12:6 Door lock mechanism

Key to Fig 12:6 1 Internal lock control 2 Pivot 3 Internal control 4 External control 5 Lock control rod 6 Latch release rod 7 Spring 8 Latch release lever 9 Locking quadrant 10 Safety catch 11 Lock 12 Nylon clips

Dismantling:

3 Loosen off the locknut on the spindle 8 and withdraw the operating cam 7, spacer panel 6, return spring 5 and lock 1 from the holder 2.

Reassembling:

4 Lubricate the lock and assembly. Insert the lock 1 into the holder 2 and engage the slots. Engage the short leg of the spring 5 into the holder 2 and the long leg into the spacer panel 6.
5 Fit the operating cam 7 into the spacer panel 6 with the tip of the cam opposite to the extended portion of the holder 2 (see illustration).
6 Fit the spindle and tighten locknut.

Refitting:

7 Refit in the reverse order of removal.

12:6 The glove box

Removing:

1 Take out eight PK screws that secure the box to the facia.
2 Take out two PK screws that secure the glove box lid catch and two PK screws that secure the box to the stays.
3 Pull the glove box rearwards to remove.

Refitting:

4 Reverse the removal procedure.

12:7 The facia panel

1 Disconnect the battery earth terminal.
2 Take out the glove box (**Section 12:6**).
3 Remove the instrument panel (**Chapter 11, Section 11:7**).
4 Remove the fresh air vents and ducts (**Section 12:11**).
5 Withdraw two screws from the speaker grille.
6 Pull off the two heater knobs, remove two screws from the heater control panel and withdraw the centre panel.
7 Take out the ashtray and cigar lighter and unscrew ten $\frac{3}{8}$ inch AF speednuts from under the upper crash pad. Lift off the pad.
8 Remove the steering column shroud and the column bolts, spacer and bracket (**Chapter 9, Section 9:3**).
9 Unscrew eight $\frac{3}{8}$ inch AF speednuts from inside the lower crash pad. Remove the pad.

Refitting:

10 Reverse the removal procedure noting that the speed nuts should not be tightened until the crash pads are aligned together and as closely fitted as possible.

12:8 The front grille

The front grille is retained by six cross head screws at the front of the grille. Note that the four side screws are shorter than the two top screws.

12:9 The seats

Removing:

Front bucket type:

1 Slide the seat fully forwards and withdraw the runner rear screws.
2 Slide the seat fully rearwards and withdraw the runner front screws.
3 Lift and tilt forwards to remove the seats through the door.

Front bench type:

1 Remove as described for the front type but obtain the help of a second operator.

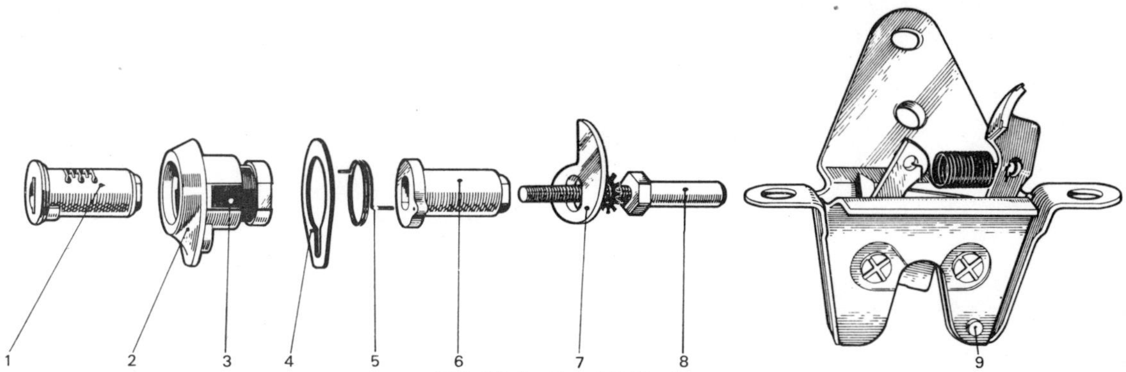

FIG 12:7 Trunk lid lock

Key to Fig 12:7 1 Lock 2 Lock holder 3 Retaining clip 4 Sealer ring 5 Return spring 6 Spacer barrel 7 Operating cam 8 Locking spindle 9 Lock assembly

Rear seats:

1 Lift the seat from the base pan.
2 Withdraw a screw from each lower edge of the squabs and slide the squab upwards to release the clips at the top.

Refitting:

Reverse the removal procedure for all types.

12:10 Renewing windscreen and backlight

Removing windscreen:

Prise wiper arms off spindles. Lift up the end of the finishing strip and pull it from the channel in the windscreen surround. Working inside the car, press the glass outwards at a top corner and gradually ease it out of the rubber. Pull rubber off body flange.

If glass has broken, make quite sure that all particles are removed from heater and demist ducts and tubes. Disconnect demist ducts and use compressed air. Remove particles from rubber surround and check it for cuts or deterioration. Renew if necessary.

Refitting windscreen (FIG 12:8):

Clean old sealer from body flange and check flange for damage. Fit sealing rubber to flange (see 3). Wet channel rubber with a weak solution of soap and water. Working outside the car, place the lower edge of the glass into the channel and use tool 18G.468 or a blunt flat ended tool to peel the rubber lip carefully over the glass (see 1). The tool is like a shallow 'M' with a long leg that fits into the handle.

Inject glazing compound (Dunlop DP.421/2G) into channels between glass and flange (see 2). Use tool 18GA468F to fit the finisher strip 4. The eye of the tool runs in the groove and the roller presses the strip into place. Rock the tool when rounding the corners. Clean off surplus sealer.

Removing and refitting rear screen:

Use the same methods as described for the front windscreen, but remember the supply and earthing cables to the heating element is fitted. Connect these when inserting the lower edge of the glass during refitting.

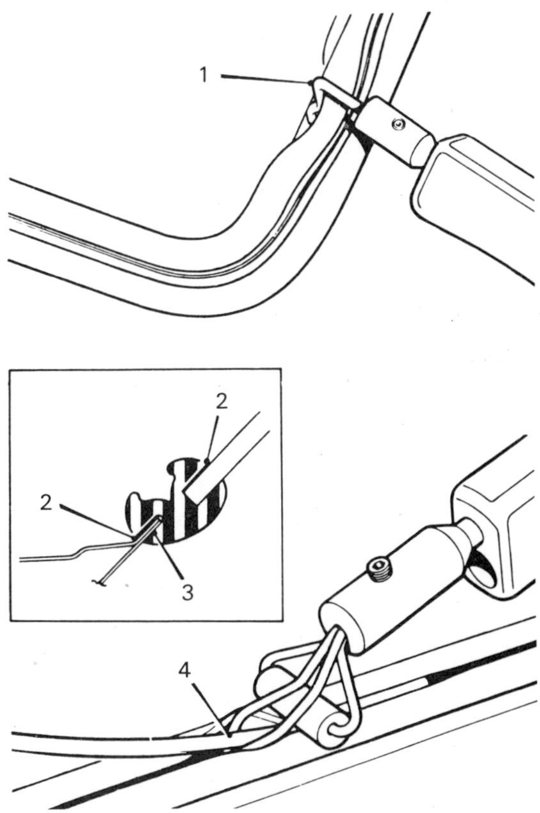

FIG 12:8 Fitting the windscreen and seal strip

Key to Fig 12:8 1 Peeling lip over glass 2 Glazing compound injection points 3 Body flange 4 Finisher strip

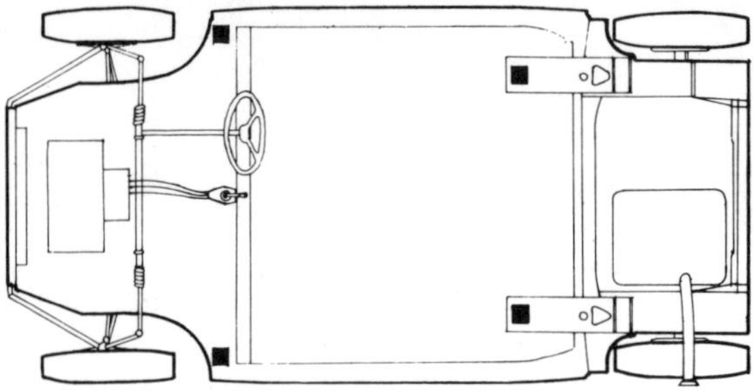

FIG 12:9 Vehicle jacking and support points

12:11 The heating and ventilating system

The interior ventilation is the 'through-flow' type with exhaust vents situated in the rear quarter panels. Even with all windows closed, air will not accumulate in the interior.

Removing swivel air-ducts:

Lefthand side:

1 Remove the glove box (**Section 12:6**).

2 Unscrew two $\frac{3}{8}$ inch AF speednuts and one cross-head screw.

3 Release the hose clip and detach the air-duct from the hose and facia.

Righthand side:

1 Remove the instrument panel (**Chapter 11, Section 11:7**).

2 Complete operations 2 and 3, lefthand side.

Refitting:

3 Reverse the removal procedure. Do not tighten the speednuts too tightly and adjust the glove box latch after completion.

Removing heater:

1 Disconnect the battery.

2 Drain the cooling system and disconnect the heater pipes at the bulk head. To ensure all water is drained from the matrix apply air pressure to the disconnected top pipe.

3 Disconnect the electrical wiring and remove the air and temperature controls.

4 Remove four nuts and plain and spring washers that secure the assembly to the bulkhead.

5 Tip the assembly rearwards and withdraw it.

Refitting:

6 Refit in the reverse order of removal noting the following:

Make sure excessive air is expelled from the matrix.

Adjust the air and temperature controls to give full travel.

Ensure the heater duct drain pipes are hanging clear of the heater pipes.

12:12 Vehicle jacking positions

It is important that the vehicle is raised and supported only at the locations shown in **FIG 12:9**. If a single post jack is used, interspace with a suitable pad to increase the contact area.

When jacking or supporting the front of the vehicle the pad should contact the floor area reinforcement immediately behind the front mudguard, valance flange.

When jacking or supporting the rear of the vehicle the pad should contact the front end of the Hydrolastic displacer shield.

APPENDIX

NOTES

TECHNICAL DATA

Inch sizes are given first followed by metric sizes in brackets

Engine:	
Type, Tasman	Manual 2200, Automatic 2201
Kimberley	Manual 2202, Automatic 2203
Capacity	135.94 cy in (2227 cu cm)
Bore	3.00 (76.2)
Stroke	3.20 (81.28)
Compression ratio (h.c.)	8.6 to 1
Firing order	1, 5, 3, 6, 2, 4
Idling speed, manual	600 rev/min
automatic	550 rev/min in 'P'
Fast idle speed	1000 rev/min
Crankshaft:	
Type	7 main bearings
Main journal diameter	2.2503 to 2.2510 (57.16 to 57.18)
Crankpin journal diameter	1.8757 to 1.8764 (47.65 to 47.66)
Undersizes (main and crankpin)	.010, .020, .030 and .040 (.25, .51, .76 and 1.02)
End float	.002 to .003 (.05 to .07)
End float adjustment	Selective thrust washers on each side of No. 3 main bearing
Main bearings:	
Type	Thin wall, steel-backed halves
Length	.811 to .821 (203.47 to 203.73)
Diametrical clearance	.002 to .0035 (.05 to .076)
Connecting rods:	
Type	Horizontally split big-ends, plain small-ends
Length between centres	5.828 to 5.832 (148.02 to 148.12)
End float on crankpin	.006 to .010 (.15 to .25)
Small-end diameter	.811 to .8115 (20.59 to 20.61)
Bearings	Thin wall, steel-backed halves
Diametrical clearance of bearings	.0015 to .003 (.038 to .076)
Pistons:	
Type	Aluminium, solid skirt, slotted
Clearance in cylinder:	
Top (below oil control groove)	.0018 to .0024 (.045 to .061)
Bottom of skirt	.0006 to .0013 (.010 to .030)
Rings	2 compression, 1 oil control
Gudgeon pin bore	.8128 to .8130 (20.64 to 29.65)
Oversizes	.010 and .020 (.254 and .508)
Piston rings:	
Type:	
Top	Molybdenum filled, torsional
Second	Multoseal
Oil control	Two chrome-faced rings with expander
Width:	
Compression	.0775 to .0780 (1.96 to 1.98)
Ring to groove clearance (compression)	.0015 to .0035 (.03 to .08)
Fitted gap:	
Compression	.008 to .016 (.20 to .40)
Oil control	.015 to .045 (.38 to 1.14)

Gudgeon pin:	
Type	Interference fit in connecting rod
Diameter	.8123 to .8125 (20.63 to 20.64)
Fit in piston	Hand push-fit at 20°C (68°F)
Fit in small-end (interference)	.0009 to .0015 (.022 to .038)
Camshaft:	
Type	Four-bearing, chain driven, overhead
Bearings	Direct in aluminium carrier
Journal diameter:	
Front	1.9370 to 1.9375 (49.190 to 49.20)
Second	1.9683 to 1.9688 (49.99 to 50.01)
Third	1.9995 to 2.00 (50.79 to 50.80)
Fourth	2.0308 to 2.0313 (51.56 to 51.59)
Diametrical clearance	.001 to .002 (.025 to .05)
End float	.002 to .007 (.05 to .17)
Thrust taken	On locating plate at front end
End float adjustment	Renewal of plate
Valve timing marks	Alignment marks on camshaft sprocket, carrier and flywheel
Drive	Chain and sprockets from crankshaft
Chain	.375 (9.52) pitch X 108 pitches
Tappets:	
Type	Bucket, with internal shims for valve adjustment
Outside diameter	1.186 to 1.187 (30.12 to 30.16)
Valves:	
Seat angle	45½ deg. (head 45 deg.)
Head diameter:	
Inlet	1.5 (38.1)
Exhaust	1.216 to 1.220 (30.88 to 31.04)
Stem diameter (both)	.3115 to .3120 (7.91 to 7.93)
Stem clearance (both)	.0015 (.038)
Lift (both)	.36 (.91)
Running clearance (adjust only if less than .012 (.31):	
Inlet	.016 to .018 (.41 to .46)
Exhaust	.020 to .022 (.51 to .56)
Clearance for timing purposes only (both)	.021 (.53)
Valve springs:	
Free length	1.797 (45.70)
Fitted length	1.38 (35.05)
Load at fitted length	52 lb (23.6 kg)
Valve timing:	
Inlet	Opens 9 deg. 4′ BTDC, closes 52 deg. 56′ ABDC (see following setting)
Exhaust	Opens 48 deg. 56′ BBDC, closes 13 deg. 4′ ATDC (with clearance set at .021 (.53)
Timing marks	Notch on crankshaft pulley, marks on front cover
Lubrication system:	
Type	Wet sump, pressure feed
Oil pump	Concentric, serviced as a unit
Oil filter	Fullflow, paper element
Pressure:	
Running	60 lb/sq in (4.2 kg/sq cm)
Idling	15 to 60 lb/sq in (1.1 to 4.2 kg/sq cm)

FUEL SYSTEM

Carburetters:	
Make and type:	
Kimberley	Twin SU, HS6
Tasman	Single SU HS6
Piston springs	Red
Jet size	.100 (2.54)
Needles (standard):	
Kimberley	TP
Tasman	BAS or AYB
Fuel pump:	
Make and type	Goss mechanical
Air cleaner:	
Type:	
Kimberley	Two paper elements in metal cover
Tasman	Single paper element in polypropylene cover

IGNITION SYSTEM

Sparking plugs:	
Make and type	Champion N-9Y
Gap	.025 (.65)
Coil:	
Type	Lucas ALH 12 oil filled
Distributor:	
Make and type	Lucas 29.D6
Rotation of rotor	Anticlockwise (from above)
Dwell angle	35 deg. ±1deg.
Contacts points gap	.014 to .016 (.35 to .40)
Capacitor (condenser) capacity	.18 to .25 mF
Ignition timing:	
Stroboscopic at 1000 rev/min with vacuum disconnected	5 deg. BTDC at 500 rev/min

COOLING SYSTEM

Type	Pressurized with thermostat. Pump and thermostatically controlled electric fan
Thermostat opens:	
Starts opening	82°C (179°F)
Fully open	94°C (201°F)
Pressure cap	Releases at 13 lb/sq in (.90 kg/sq cm)
Driving belt	Tensioned to $\frac{1}{2}$ inch (13 mm) deflection in middle of longest run

CLUTCH

Make and type	Borg and Beck, narrow diaphragm
Clutch plate:	
Diameter	8.75 (222)
Damper springs	Six (progressive take-up)
Release bearing	Ball journal
Master cylinder bore	.625 (15.87)
Slave cylinder bore	.875 (22.2)
Fluid	See 'Brake fluid'

SYNCHROMESH TRANSMISSION

Type	Four forward speeds and reverse Synchromesh on forward gears	
Ratios:	*Gearbox*	*Overall*
Top	1.00 to 1	4.187 to 1
Third	1.38 to 1	5.794 to 1
Second	2.06 to 1	8.627 to 1
First	3.29 to 1	13.78 to 1
Reverse	3.07 to 1	12.87 to 1
End float:		
Idler gear	.003 to .008 (.08 to .20)	
1st- and 3rd-speed gears	.006 to .008 (.15 to .20)	
2nd-speed gear	.005 to .008 (.13 to .20)	
Laygear	.002 to .007 (.05 to .18)	

AUTOMATIC TRANSMISSION

Make and type	Borg-Warner, model 35	
Primary drive:		
Type	Chain and sprockets (helical)	
Ratios:	*Gearbox*	*Overall (1 to 1)*
First	2.39 to 1	9.42 to 1
Second	1.45 to 1	5.71 to 1
Top	1.0 to 1	3.95 to 1
Reverse	2.09 to 1	8.23 to 1
Final drive	3.83 to 1 (18/69)	

FINAL DRIVE

Type	Integral with gearbox. Helical gears and differential
Ratios:	
Synchromesh gearbox	4.87 to 1 (16/67)
Automatic transmission	3.83 to 1 (18/69)
Differential bearings	Preload .003 to .005 (.08 to .13)
Drive shafts	Unequal length, solid, Hardy spicer with constant velocity joints

STEERING

Alignment:	
Front wheel toe-in	$\frac{1}{8}$ (3.2)
Angle of inner wheel with outer wheel at 20 deg.	$21\frac{1}{2}$ deg. $\pm$1 deg.
Manual steering:	
Type	Rack and pinion
Steering wheel turns	3.8 (lock to lock)
Pinion bearing preload	.001 to .003 (.03 to .08)
Damper movement	.001 to .006 (.03 to .15)

SUSPENSION

Trim height (unladen)	$14\frac{7}{8}\pm\frac{1}{4}$ (378$\pm$6) at hub centre to wheel arch
Pressure (unladen)	215 lb/sq in
Front:	
Type	Independent, unequal arms, trailing tie rods, Hydrolastic displacers
Swivel hub inclination (unladen)	12 deg. $\pm\frac{3}{4}$ deg.
Camber angle (unladen)	1 deg. $\pm$1 deg. positive
Castor angle	$1\frac{1}{2}$ deg. $\pm$1 deg. positive
Wheel bearing end float	Zero to .004 (.10)

Rear:

Type	Independent with trailing arms and Hydrolastic displacers
Wheel alignment (unladen)	Parallel
Camber (unladen)	$\frac{1}{2}$ deg. positive
Wheel bearing end float	Zero to .002 (.05)

BRAKES

Type	PBR dual type
Front	Hydraulic disc. Vacuum servo assisted
Rear	Drum with leading and trailing shoes
Handbrake	Mechanical on rear
Both	With tandem master cylinder, rear brakes line has residual pressure valve
Fluid	BLMC HBF-6
Front:	
Disc diameter	10.50 (266.70)
Pad material	Mintex M33
Minimum pad thickness	$\frac{1}{16}$ (1.6)
Rear:	
Drum diameter	9 (229)
Linings:	
Dimensions, primary	1.50 X 10.00 (38.1 X 254)
secondary	1.50 X 7.75 (38.1 X 197)
Material, primary	Mintex BM-RD
secondary	Mintex BM-RE
Wheel cylinder bore	.75 (19.05) stamped on body
Servo unit:	
Type	PBR hydropower
Master cylinder:	
Bore diameter	.80 (20.32)

ELECTRICAL EQUIPMENT

Battery:	
Make and type	12-volt, 9-plate
Capacity at 20 hr rate	46 Ah
Earthing	Negative terminal
Alternator:	
Type	Email (9 diode)
Output at maximum	40 amp at 14.2-volts
Starter motor:	
Make and type	Lucas M40 with pre-engaged pinion
Light running current	40 amp at 6000 rev/min
Minimum brush length	$\frac{3}{16}$ (4.76)
Brush spring tension	40 ozf (1.18 kgfm)
Wiper motor:	
Make and type	Lucas 12 AUW
Running current (rack disconnected):	
Low speed	1.5 amp
High speed	2 amp
Wiper speed after 60 seconds:	
Low speed	46 to 52 rev/min
High speed	60 to 70 rev/min
Armature end float	.008 to .012 (.20 to .30)
Brush spring tension	5 to 7 ozf (140 to 200 gf)

Minimum brush length	.18 (4.7)
Horns:	
Make and type, Kimberley	Twin Lucas 9H Wind Tone (high and low)
Tasman	Single Lucas 9H Wind Tone (high)
Maximum current compensation	3.5 to 4 amp

TYRES

Size and type, radial	165 X 14 tubeless
crossply	6.95 X 14 tubeless
Pressures (normal):	
Radials:	
Front	28 lb/sq in
Rear	22 lb/sq in (full load 28 lb/sq in)
Crossply:	
Front	26 lb/sq in
Rear	22 lb/sq in (full load 26 lb/sq in)
Wheels:	
Type	55 X 14
Stud PCD	5 inch (127 mm)

CAPACITIES

Fuel tank	$10\frac{1}{4}$ gal ($46\frac{1}{2}$ litres)
Cooling system (with heater)	16 pint (9.1 litre)
Transmission system:	
Casing (manual gearchange)	Refill, with filter change, $19\frac{1}{4}$ pints (10.92 litres)
Filter only	1 pint (.6 litre)
Casing (automatic):	
Refill engine sump	12 pint (6.81 litre)
Engine filter only	1 pint (.6 litre)
Gearbox with torque converter	14.8 pint (8.5 litre)

WEIGHTS AND DIMENSIONS

Weights:	
Dry:	
Synchromesh, Kimberley	2549 lb (1160 kg)
Tasman	2516 lb (1143 kg)
Automatic, Kimberley	2627 lb (1193 kg)
Tasman	2541 lb (1150 kg)
Towing weight, maximum	
Automatic, Kimberley	2663 lb (1207 kg)
Tasman	2628 lb (1193 kg)
Manual, Kimberley	2613 lb (1184 kg)
Tasman	2572 lb (1166 kg)
Dimensions:	
Overall length	174.58 inch (4434 mm) 13 ft 10.55 inch (4.20 m)
Overall width	66.58 inch (1690 mm) 5 ft 6.87 inch (1.70 m)
Overall height unladen	57.25 inch (1154 mm) 4 ft 8.3 inch (1.43 m)
Wheelbase unladen	9 ft $0\frac{1}{8}$ inch (2747 mm)
Ground clearance	6.25 inch (158.74 mm)

TORQUE WRENCH SETTINGS

These are in lb ft, or in kgf m in brackets

Engine:	
Oil filter bolt	20 (2.8)
Cylinder head bolts	60 (8.3)
Lifting bracket bolts	30 (4.1)
Camshaft carrier to cylinder head	20 (2.77)
Camshaft sprocket	35 (4.8)
Camshaft cover	6 (.80)
Thermostat housing to cylinder head	10 (1.4)
Manifold to cylinder head:	
Studs	15 (2.1)
Nuts	20 (2.8)
Adaptor plugs	30 (4.1)
Carburetter studs	6 to 8 (.80 to 1.1)
Water pump:	
Bolts	15 (2.1)
Plug (body)	35 (4.8)
Pulley	10 (1.4)
Front cover:	
Studs	6 (.80)
Nuts	18 (2.5)
Flywheel housing:	
Studs	6 (.80)
Nuts and bolts	18 (2.5)
Crankshaft pulley bolt	60 to 70 (8.3 to 9.7)
Timing cover, chain guide strips and pivot pin	20 (2.8)
Big-end nuts	33±3 (4.6±.30)
Main bearing bolts	70 (9.7)
Flywheel bolts	60 (8.3)
Oil pump bolt	20 (2.8)
Engine mounting locknuts	30 (4.1)
Crankcase lower adaptor (automatic):	
Screws	30 (4.1)
Bolts	20 to 25 (2.6 to 3.4)
Clutch:	
Cover	15 (2.1)
Clutch to pressure plate	35 (4.8)
Thrust plate bolt	10 (1.4)
Slave cylinder bolts	35 (4.8)
Transmission:	
Magnetic drain plug	40 (5.5)
Flywheel housing:	
Studs	6 (.80)
Nuts and bolts	18 (2.5)
Casing to block and crankcase extension:	
$\frac{5}{16}$ bolts	18 (2.5)
$\frac{3}{8}$ bolts	25 (3.4)
Front cover	10 (1.4)
Detent plug:	
Small	20 (2.8)
Large	40 (5.5)
First motion shaft nut	120 (16.6)
Final drive pinion nut	150 (20.7)
Speedometer drive housing	20 (2.8)

Final drive:	
Driven gear to differential cage bolts	55 to 60 (7.6 to 8.3)
Final drive pinion nut	150 (20.7)
Differential cover:	
Studs	6 (.80)
$\frac{5}{16}$ nuts	18 (2.5)
$\frac{3}{8}$ nuts	25 (3.4)
Differential end cover bolts	18 (2.5)
Automatic transmission:	
Converter housing:	
Chain cover to housing	5 to 9 (.7 to 1.2)
Turbine shaft nut	20 to 25 (2.8 to 3.5)
Input shaft nut	15 to 20 (2.1 to 2.8)
Pump assembly to housing	5 to 9 (.69 to 1.2)
Pump adaptor to pump housing:	
Bolts	17 to 22 (2.3 to 3.0)
Screw	1.7 to 2.5 (.23 to .35)
Bearing retainer—input shaft	5 to 9 (.69 to 1.2)
Main casing:	
Speedometer drive housing	8 to 18 (1.1 to 2.5)
Crankcase to main casing	20 (2.8)
Main casing to crankcase	30 (4.1)
Steering:	
Steering wheel nut	50 (6.9)
Coupling flange—Manual	12 to 15 (1.7 to 2.1)
Steering lever to hub nut	85 (11.7)
Ball pin housing	70±5 (9.6±.70)
Ball joint nut	35 (4.8)
Tie rod housing locknut	35 (4.8)
Pinion and damper cover bolts	12 to 15 (1.6 to 2.0)
Suspension	
Front:	
Swivel axle ball joint nuts	45 (6.2)
Lower arm pivot nut	45 (6.2)
Tie rod to lower arm	40 to 50 (5.5 to 6.9)
Housing locknut	35 (4.8)
Upper arm pivot	60 (8.3)
Tie rod to bracket (Nyloc nut)	45 to 50 (6.2 to 6.9)
Hub nut (tighten to next hole)	150 (20.7)
Drive flange to brake disc bolts	40 to 45 (5.5 to 6.2)
Caliper to swivel hub	45 to 50 (5.5 to 6.9)
Shield to hub	20 (2.8)
Ball pin housings	70±5 (9.6±.70)
Suspension bracket to body	60 to 70 (8.3 to 9.6)
Rear:	
Radius arm pivot nut	60 (8.3)
Stub axle nut	40 (5.5)
Hydrolastic housing to body	45 (6.2)
Road wheels:	
Wheel nuts	60 (8.3)
Brakes:	
Caliper to hub	45 to 50 (6.2 to 6.9)
Disc to driving flange	38 to 45 (5.2 to 6.2)
Shield to hub	20 (2.8)
Bleed screws	4 to 6 (.5 to .8)
Adjuster nuts	4 to 6 (.5 to .8)
Pedal pivot nuts	12 (1.7)

Master cylinder	
Cylinder to bulkhead	17 (2.3)
Handbrake:	
Lever to floor bracket	15 (2.1)
Cable sector to floor bracket	30 (4.1)
Electrical:	
Distributor:	
Plate retaining screws	8 (1.1)
Clamp bolt	2.5 (.35)
Alternator:	
Mounting bolts	20 (2.8)
Pulley nut	25 (3.4)
Through-bolts	4.5 (.62)
Starter motor:	
Retaining bolts	30 (4.1)
Through-bolts	8 (1.1)
Solenoid fixing nuts	4.5 (.62)
Solenoid terminal nuts	3 (.41)

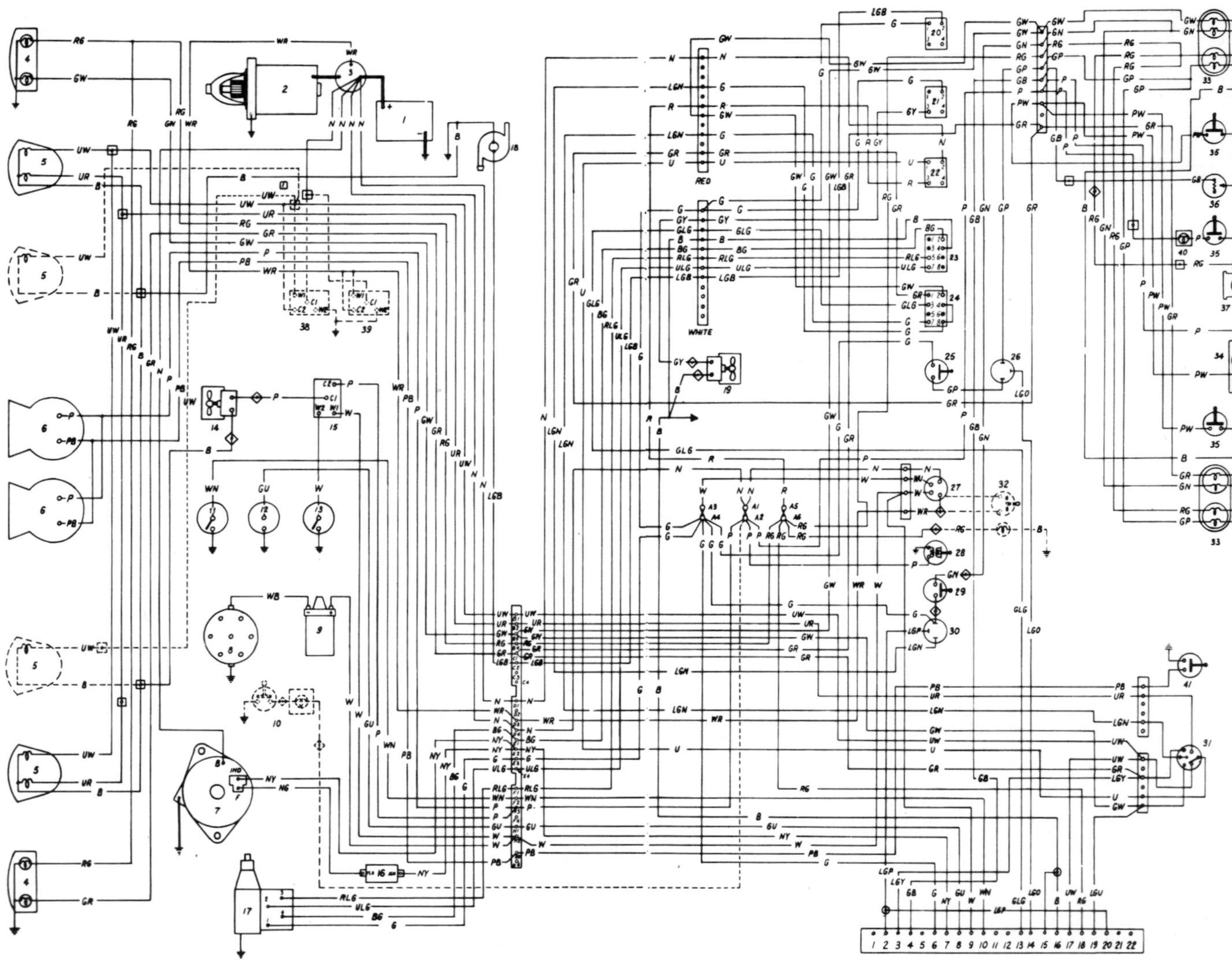

Nº	UNIT
1	BATTERY
2	STARTER
3	STARTER SOLENOID
4	SIDE / FLASHER LAMP
5	HEADLIGHT
6	HORN
7	ALTERNATOR
8	DISTRIBUTOR
9	IGNITION COIL
10	BONNET LIGHT
11	OIL PRESSURE SWITCH
12	TEMPERATURE SWITCH
13	COOLING MOTOR RELAY SW.
14	COOLING MOTOR
15	COOLING MOTOR RELAY
16	ALTERNATOR REGULATOR
17	WIPER MOTOR
18	WINDSCREEN WASHER MOTOR
19	HEATER MOTOR
20	WASHER SWITCH
21	HEATER SWITCH
22	LIGHTING SWITCH
23	WIPER SWITCH
24	HAZARD SWITCH
25	STOPLIGHT SWITCH
26	STOPLIGHT MODULATOR
27	IGNITION STARTER SWITCH
28	CIGARETTE LIGHTER
29	REVERSE LIGHT SWITCH
30	FLASHER/HAZARD UNIT
31	FLASHER, DIP SWITCH
32	INHIBITOR SWITCH
33	STOP TAIL/REVERSE FLASHER LIGHT
34	INTERIOR LIGHT
35	DOOR SWITCHES
36	TANK UNIT – FUEL
37	NUMBER PLATE LAMP
38	RELAY – HEADLIGHTS
39	RELAY–STARTER SOLENOID
40	BOOT LAMP
41	HORN PUSH

COLOUR	KEY
BROWN	N
BLUE	U
RED	R
PURPLE	P
GREEN	G
LIGHT GREEN	LG
WHITE	W
YELLOW	Y
BLACK	B
ORANGE	O
PINK	K
SLATE	S

= CABLE SPLICE

= BULLET RECEPTACLE

= BLADE RECEPTACLE (IN LINE)

FIG 13:1 Wiring diagram for Kimberley and Tasman (early models)

Nº	UNIT
1	BATTURY
2	STARTCR
3	STARTER SOLENOID
4	SIDE / FLASHER LAMP
5	HEADLIGHT
6	HORN
7	ALTERNATOR
8	DISTRIBUTOR
9	IGNITION COIL
10	BONNET LIGHT
11	OIL PRESSURE SWITCH
12	TEMPERATURE SWITCH
13	COOLING MOTOR RELAY SW.
14	COOLING MOTOR
15	COOLING MOTOR RELAY
16	ALTERNATOR REGULATOR
17	WIPER MOTOR
18	WINDSCREEN WASHER MOTOR
19	HEATER MOTOR
20	WASHER SWITCH
21	HEATER SWITCH
22	LIGHTING SWITCH
23	WIPER SWITCH
24	HAZARD SWITCH
25	STOPLIGHT SWITCH
26	STOPLIGHT MODULATOR
27	IGNITION STARTER SWITCH
28	CIGARETTE LIGHTER
29	REVERSE LIGHT SWITCH
30	FLASHER/HAZARD UNIT
31	FLASHER, DIP SWITCH
32	INHIBITOR SWITCH
33	STOP-TAIL-REVERSE-FLASHER LIGHT
34	INTERIOR LIGHT
35	DOOR SWITCHES
36	TANK UNIT – FUEL
37	NUMBER PLATE LAMP
38	RELAY – HEADLIGHTS
39	RELAY-STARTER SOLENOID
40	BOOT LAMP
41	HORN PUSH

COLOUR	KEY
BROWN	N
BLUE	U
RED	R
PURPLE	P
GREEN	G
LIGHT GREEN	LG
WHITE	W
YELLOW	Y
BLACK	B
ORANGE	O
PINK	K
SLATE	S

⊕ = CABLE SPLICE
⊞ = BULLET RECEPTACLE
◇ = BLADE RECEPTACLE (IN LINE)

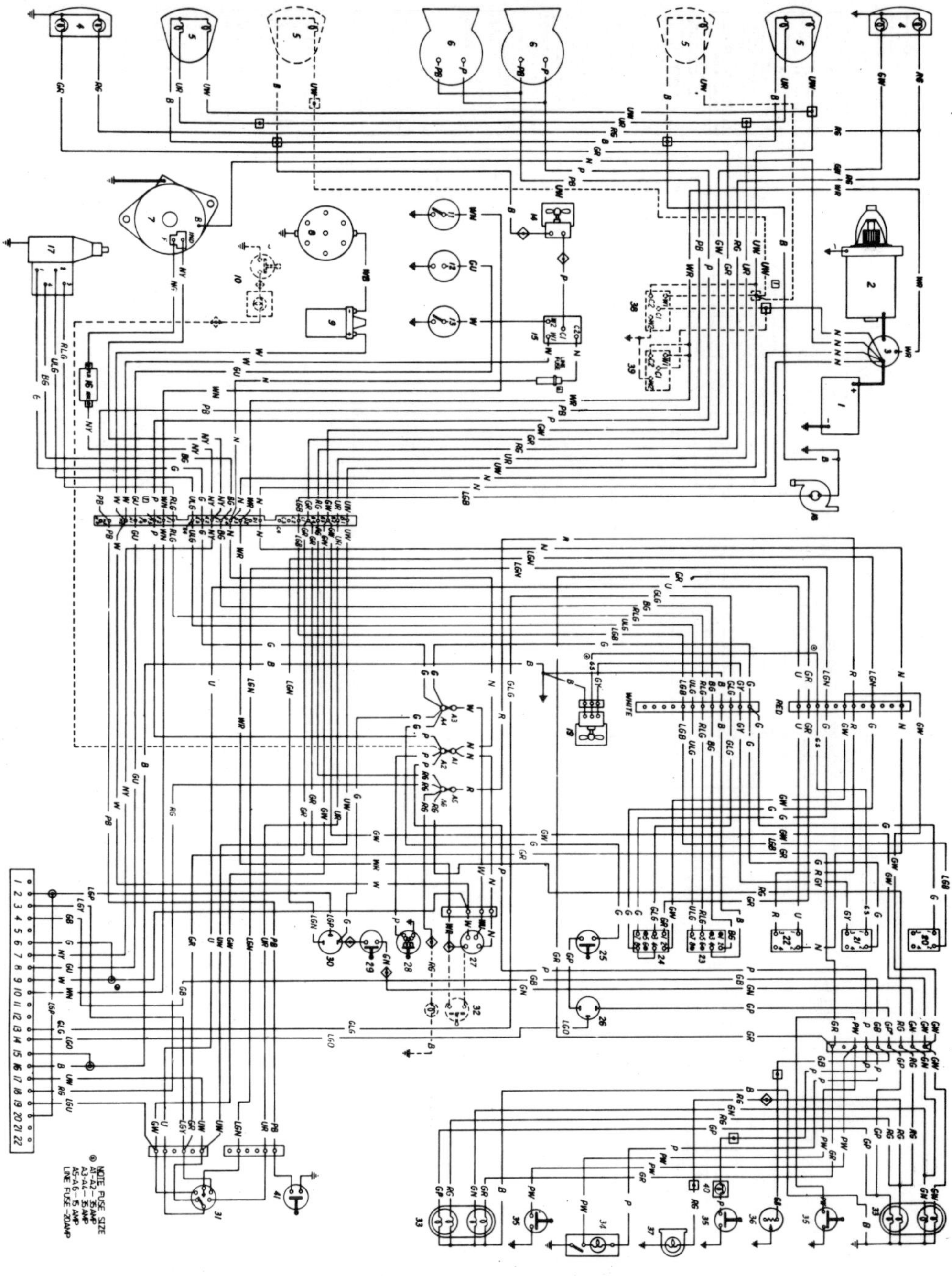

FIG 13:2 Wiring diagram for Kimberley and Tasman (late models)

Inches	Decimals	Millimetres	Inches to Millimetres: Inches	Inches to Millimetres: mm	Millimetres to Inches: mm	Millimetres to Inches: Inches
1/64	.015625	.3969	.001	.0254	.01	.00039
1/32	.03125	.7937	.002	.0508	.02	.00079
3/64	.046875	1.1906	.003	.0762	.03	.00118
1/16	.0625	1.5875	.004	.1016	.04	.00157
5/64	.078125	1.9844	.005	.1270	.05	.00197
3/32	.09375	2.3812	.006	.1524	.06	.00236
7/64	.109375	2.7781	.007	.1778	.07	.00276
1/8	.125	3.1750	.008	.2032	.08	.00315
9/64	.140625	3.5719	.009	.2286	.09	.00354
5/32	.15625	3.9687	.01	.254	.1	.00394
11/64	.171875	4.3656	.02	.508	.2	.00787
3/16	.1875	4.7625	.03	.762	.3	.01181
13/64	.203125	5·1594	.04	1.016	.4	.01575
7/32	.21875	5.5562	.05	1.270	.5	.01969
15/64	.234375	5.9531	.06	1.524	.6	.02362
1/4	.25	6.3500	.07	1.778	.7	.02756
17/64	.265625	6.7469	.08	2.032	.8	.03150
9/32	.28125	7.1437	.09	2.286	.9	.03543
19/64	.296875	7.5406	.1	2.54	1	.03937
5/16	.3125	7.9375	.2	5.08	2	.07874
21/64	.328125	8.3344	.3	7.62	3	.11811
11/32	.34375	8.7312	.4	10.16	4	.15748
23/64	.359375	9.1281	.5	12.70	5	.19685
3/8	.375	9.5250	.6	15.24	6	.23622
25/64	.390625	9.9219	.7	17.78	7	.27559
13/32	.40625	10.3187	.8	20.32	8	.31496
27/64	.421875	10.7156	.9	22.86	9	.35433
7/16	.4375	11.1125	1	25.4	10	.39370
29/64	.453125	11.5094	2	50.8	11	.43307
15/32	.46875	11.9062	3	76.2	12	.47244
31/64	.484375	12.3031	4	101.6	13	.51181
1/2	.5	12.7000	5	127.0	14	.55118
33/64	.515625	13.0969	6	152.4	15	.59055
17/32	.53125	13.4937	7	177.8	16	.62992
35/64	.546875	13.8906	8	203.2	17	.66929
9/16	.5625	14.2875	9	228.6	18	.70866
37/64	.578125	14.6844	10	254.0	19	.74803
19/32	.59375	15.0812	11	279.4	20	.78740
39/64	.609375	15.4781	12	304.8	21	.82677
5/8	.625	15.8750	13	330.2	22	.86614
41/64	.640625	16.2719	14	355.6	23	.90551
21/32	.65625	16.6687	15	381.0	24	.94488
43/64	.671875	17.0656	16	406.4	25	.98425
11/16	.6875	17.4625	17	431.8	26	1.02362
45/64	.703125	17.8594	18	457.2	27	1.06299
23/32	.71875	18.2562	19	482.6	28	1.10236
47/64	.734375	18.6531	20	508.0	29	1.14173
3/4	.75	19.0500	21	533.4	30	1.18110
49/64	.765625	19.4469	22	558.8	31	1.22047
25/32	.78125	19.8437	23	584.2	32	1.25984
51/64	.796875	20.2406	24	609.6	33	1.29921
13/16	.8125	20.6375	25	635.0	34	1.33858
53/64	.828125	21.0344	26	660.4	35	1.37795
27/32	.84375	21.4312	27	685.8	36	1.41732
55/64	.859375	21.8281	28	711.2	37	1.4567
7/8	.875	22.2250	29	736.6	38	1.4961
57/64	.890625	22.6219	30	762.0	39	1.5354
29/32	.90625	23.0187	31	787.4	40	1.5748
59/64	.921875	23.4156	32	812.8	41	1.6142
15/16	.9375	23.8125	33	838.2	42	1.6535
61/64	.953125	24.2094	34	863.6	43	1.6929
31/32	.96875	24.6062	35	889.0	44	1.7323
63/64	.984375	25.0031	36	914.4	45	1.7717

UNITS	Pints to Litres	Gallons to Litres	Litres to Pints	Litres to Gallons	Miles to Kilometres	Kilometres to Miles	Lbs. per sq. In. to Kg. per sq. Cm.	Kg. per sq. Cm. to Lbs. per sq. In.
1	.57	4.55	1.76	.22	1.61	.62	.07	14.22
2	1.14	9.09	3.52	.44	3.22	1.24	.14	28.50
3	1.70	13.64	5.28	.66	4.83	1.86	.21	42.67
4	2.27	18.18	7.04	.88	6.44	2.49	.28	56.89
5	2.84	22.73	8.80	1.10	8.05	3.11	.35	71.12
6	3.41	27.28	10.56	1.32	9.66	3.73	.42	85.34
7	3.98	31.82	12.32	1.54	11.27	4.35	.49	99.56
8	4.55	36.37	14.08	1.76	12.88	4.97	.56	113.79
9		40.91	15.84	1.98	14.48	5.59	.63	128.00
10		45.46	17.60	2.20	16.09	6.21	.70	142.23
20				4.40	32.19	12.43	1.41	284.47
30				6.60	48.28	18.64	2.11	426.70
40				8.80	64.37	24.85		
50					80.47	31.07		
60					96.56	37.28		
70					112.65	43.50		
80					128.75	49.71		
90					144.84	55.92		
100					160.93	62.14		

UNITS	Lb ft to kgm	Kgm to lb ft	UNITS	Lb ft to kgm	Kgm to lb ft
1	.138	7.233	7	.967	50.631
2	.276	14.466	8	1.106	57.864
3	.414	21.699	9	1.244	65.097
4	.553	28.932	10	1.382	72.330
5	.691	36.165	20	2.765	144.660
6	.829	43.398	30	4.147	216.990

HINTS ON MAINTENANCE AND OVERHAUL

There are few things more rewarding than the restoration of a vehicle's original peak of efficiency and smooth performance.

The following notes are intended to help the owner to reach that state of perfection. Providing that he possesses the basic manual skills he should have no difficulty in performing most of the operations detailed in this manual. It must be stressed, however, that where recommended in the manual, highly-skilled operations ought to be entrusted to experts, who have the necessary equipment, to carry out the work satisfactorily.

Quality of workmanship:

The hazardous driving conditions on the roads to-day demand that vehicles should be as nearly perfect, mechanically, as possible. It is therefore most important that amateur work be carried out with care, bearing in mind the often inadequate working conditions, and also the inferior tools which may have to be used. It is easy to counsel perfection in all things, and we recognize that it may be setting an impossibly high standard. We do, however, suggest that every care should be taken to ensure that a vehicle is as safe to take on the road as it is humanly possible to make it.

Safe working conditions:

Even though a vehicle may be stationary, it is still potentially dangerous if certain sensible precautions are not taken when working on it while it is supported on jacks or blocks. It is indeed preferable not to use jacks alone, but to supplement them with carefully placed blocks, so that there will be plenty of support if the car rolls off the jacks during a strenuous manoeuvre. Axle stands are an excellent way of providing a rigid base which is not readily disturbed. Piles of bricks are a dangerous substitute. Be careful not to get under heavy loads on lifting tackle, the load could fall. It is preferable not to work alone when lifting an engine, or when working underneath a vehicle which is supported well off the ground. To be trapped, particularly under the vehicle, may have unpleasant results if help is not quickly forthcoming. Make some provision, however humble, to deal with fires. Always disconnect a battery if there is a likelihood of electrical shorts. These may start a fire if there is leaking fuel about. This applies particularly to leads which can carry a heavy current, like those in the starter circuit. While on the subject of electricity, we must also stress the danger of using equipment which is run off the mains and which has no earth or has faulty wiring or connections. So many workshops have damp floors, and electrical shocks are of such a nature that it is sometimes impossible to let go of a live lead or piece of equipment due to the muscular spasms which take place.

Work demanding special care:

This involves the servicing of braking, steering and suspension systems. On the road, failure of the braking system may be disastrous. Make quite sure that there can be no possibility of failure through the bursting of rusty brake pipes or rotten hoses, nor to a sudden loss of pressure due to defective seals or valves.

Problems:

The chief problems which may face an operator are:

1 External dirt.
2 Difficulty in undoing tight fixings
3 Dismantling unfamiliar mechanisms.
4 Deciding in what respect parts are defective.
5 Confusion about the correct order for reassembly.
6 Adjusting running clearances.
7 Road testing.
8 Final tuning.

Practical suggestion to solve the problems:

1 Preliminary cleaning of large parts—engines, transmissions, steering, suspensions, etc.,—should be carried out before removal from the car. Where road dirt and mud alone are present, wash clean with a high-pressure water jet, brushing to remove stubborn adhesions, and allow to drain and dry. Where oil or grease is also present, wash down with a proprietary compound (Gunk, Teepol etc.,) applying with a stiff brush—an old paint brush is suitable—into all crevices. Cover the distributor and ignition coils with a polythene bag and then apply a strong water jet to clear the loosened deposits. Allow to drain and dry. The assemblies will then be sufficiently clean to remove and transfer to the bench for the next stage.

On the bench, further cleaning can be carried out, first wiping the parts as free as possible from grease with old newspaper. Avoid using rag or cotton waste which can leave clogging fibres behind. Any remaining grease can be removed with a brush dipped in paraffin. If necessary, traces of paraffin can be removed by carbon tetrachloride. Avoid using paraffin or petrol in large quantities for cleaning in enclosed areas, such as garages, on account of the high fire risk.

When all exteriors have been cleaned, and not before, dismantling can be commenced. This ensures that dirt will not enter into interiors and orifices revealed by dismantling. In the next phases, where components have to be cleaned, use carbon tetrachloride in preference to petrol and keep the containers covered except when in use. After the components have been cleaned, plug small holes with tapered hard wood plugs cut to size and blank off larger orifices with grease-proof paper and masking tape. Do not use soft wood plugs or matchsticks as they may break.

2 It is not advisable to hammer on the end of a screw thread, but if it must be done, first screw on a nut to protect the thread, and use a lead hammer. This applies particularly to the removal of tapered cotters. Nuts and bolts seem to 'grow' together, especially in exhaust systems. If penetrating oil does not work, try the judicious application of heat, but be careful of starting a fire. Asbestos sheet or cloth is useful to isolate heat.

Tight bushes or pieces of tail-pipe rusted into a silencer can be removed by splitting them with an open-ended hacksaw. Tight screws can sometimes be started by a tap from a hammer on the end of a suitable screwdriver. Many tight fittings will yield to the judicious use of a hammer, but it must be a soft-faced hammer if damage is to be avoided, use a heavy block on the opposite side to absorb shock. Any parts of the steering system which have been damaged should be renewed, as attempts to repair them may lead to cracking and subsequent failure, and steering ball joints should be disconnected using a recommended tool to prevent damage.

3 If often happens that an owner is baffled when trying to dismantle an unfamiliar piece of equipment. So many modern devices are pressed together or assembled by spinning-over flanges, that they must be sawn apart. The intention is that the whole assembly must be renewed. However, parts which appear to be in one piece to the naked eye, may reveal close-fitting joint lines when inspected with a magnifying glass, and, this may provide the necessary clue to dismantling. Left-handed screw threads are used where rotational forces would tend to unscrew a right-handed screw thread.

Be very careful when dismantling mechanisms which may come apart suddenly. Work in an enclosed space where the parts will be contained, and drape a piece of cloth over the device if springs are likely to fly in all directions. Mark everything which might be reassembled in the wrong position, scratched symbols may be used on unstressed parts, or a sequence of tiny dots from a centre punch can be useful. Stressed parts should never be scratched or centre-popped as this may lead to cracking under working conditions. Store parts which look alike in the correct order for reassembly. Never rely upon memory to assist in the assembly of complicated mechanisms, especially when they will be dismantled for a long time, but make notes, and drawings to supplement the diagrams in the manual, and put labels on detached wires. Rust stains may indicate unlubricated wear. This can sometimes be seen round the outside edge of a bearing cup in a universal joint. Look for bright rubbing marks on parts which normally should not make heavy contact. These might prove that something is bent or running out of truth. For example, there might be bright marks on one side of a piston, at the top near the ring grooves, and others at the bottom of the skirt on the other side. This could well be the clue to a bent connecting rod. Suspected cracks can be proved by heating the component in a light oil to approximately 100°C, removing, drying off, and dusting with french chalk, if a crack is present the oil retained in the crack will stain the french chalk.

4 In determining wear, and the degree, against the permissible limits set in the manual, accurate measurement can only be achieved by the use of a micrometer. In many cases, the wear is given to the fourth place of decimals; that is in ten-thousandths of an inch. This can be read by the vernier scale on the barrel of a good micrometer. Bore diameters are more difficult to determine. If, however, the matching shaft is accurately measured, the degree of play in the bore can be felt as a guide to its suitability. In other cases, the shank of a twist drill of known diameter is a handy check.

Many methods have been devised for determining the clearance between bearing surfaces. To-day the best and simplest is by the use of Plastigage, obtainable from most garages. A thin plastic thread is laid between the two surfaces and the bearing is tightened, flattening the thread. On removal, the width of the thread is compared with a scale supplied with the thread and the clearance is read off directly. Sometimes joint faces leak persistently, even after gasket renewal. The fault will then be traceable to distortion, dirt or burrs. Studs which are screwed into soft metal frequently raise burrs at the point of entry. A quick cure for this is to chamfer the edge of the hole in the part which fits over the stud.

5 **Always check a replacement part with the original one before it is fitted.**

If parts are not marked, and the order for reassembly is not known, a little detective work will help. Look for marks which are due to wear to see if they can be mated. Joint faces may not be identical due to manufacturing errors, and parts which overlap may be stained, giving a clue to the correct position. Most fixings leave identifying marks especially if they were painted over on assembly. It is then easier to decide whether a nut, for instance, has a plain, a spring, or a shakeproof washer under it. All running surfaces become 'bedded' together after long spells of work and tiny imperfections on one part will be found to have left corresponding marks on the other. This is particularly true of shafts and bearings and even a score on a cylinder wall will show on the piston.

6 Checking end float or rocker clearances by feeler gauge may not always give accurate results because of wear. For instance, the rocker tip which bears on a valve stem may be deeply pitted, in which case the feeler will simply be bridging a depression. Thrust washers may also wear depressions in opposing faces to make accurate measurement difficult. End float is then easier to check by using a dial gauge. It is common practice to adjust end play in bearing assemblies, like front hubs with taper rollers, by doing up the axle nut until the hub becomes stiff to turn and then backing it off a little. Do not use this method with ballbearing hubs as the assembly is often preloaded by tightening the axle nut to its fullest extent. If the splitpin hole will not line up, file the base of the nut a little.

Steering assemblies often wear in the straight-ahead position. If any part is adjusted, make sure that it remains free when moved from lock to lock. Do not be surprised if an assembly like a steering gearbox, which is known to be carefully adjusted outside the car, becomes stiff when it is bolted in place. This will be due to distortion of the case by the pull of the mounting bolts, particularly if the mounting points are not all touching together. This problem may be met in other equipment and is cured by careful attention to the alignment of mounting points.

When a spanner is stamped with a size and A/F it means that the dimension is the width between the jaws and has no connection with ANF, which is the designation for the American National Fine thread. Coarse threads like Whitworth are rarely used on cars to-day except for studs which screw into soft aluminium or cast iron. For this reason it might be found that the top end of a cylinder head stud has a fine thread and the lower end a coarse thread to screw into the cylinder block. If the car has mainly UNF threads then it is likely that any coarse threads will be UNC, which are not the same as Whitworth. Small sizes have the same number of threads in Whitworth and UNC, but in the $\frac{1}{2}$ inch size for example, there are twelve threads to the inch in the former and thirteen in the latter.

7 After a major overhaul, particularly if a great deal of work has been done on the braking, steering and suspension systems, it is advisable to approach the problem of testing with care. If the braking system has been overhauled, apply heavy pressure to the brake pedal and get a second operator to check every possible source of leakage. The brakes may work extremely well, but a leak could cause complete failure after a few miles.

Do not fit the hub caps until every wheel nut has been checked for tightness, and make sure the tyre pressures are correct. Check the levels of coolant, lubricants and hydraulic fluids. Being satisfied that all is well, take the car on the road and test the brakes at once. Check the steering and the action of the handbrake. Do all this at moderate speeds on quiet roads, and make sure there is no other vehicle behind you when you try a rapid stop.

Finally, remember that many parts settle down after a time, so check for tightness of all fixings after the car has been on the road for a hundred miles or so.

8 It is useless to tune an engine which has not reached its normal running temperature. In the same way, the tune of an engine which is stiff after a rebore will be different when the engine is again running free. Remember too, that rocker clearances on pushrod operated valve gear will change when the cylinder head nuts are tightened after an initial period of running with a new head gasket.

Trouble may not always be due to what seems the obvious cause. Ignition, carburation and mechanical condition are interdependent and spitting back through the carburetter, which might be attributed to a weak mixture, can be caused by a sticking inlet valve.

For one final hint on tuning, never adjust more than one thing at a time or it will be impossible to tell which adjustment produced the desired result.

NOTES

GLOSSARY OF TERMS

Allen key	Cranked wrench of hexagonal section for use with socket head screws.
Alternator	Electrical generator producing alternating current. Rectified to direct current for battery charging.
Ambient temperature	Surrounding atmospheric temperature.
Annulus	Used in engineering to indicate the outer ring gear of an epicyclic gear train.
Armature	The shaft carrying the windings, which rotates in the magnetic field of a generator or starter motor. That part of a solenoid or relay which is activated by the magnetic field.
Axial	In line with, or pertaining to, an axis.
Backlash	Play in meshing gears.
Balance lever	A bar where force applied at the centre is equally divided between connections at the ends.
Banjo axle	Axle casing with large diameter housing for the crownwheel and differential.
Bendix pinion	A self-engaging and self-disengaging drive on a starter motor shaft.
Bevel pinion	A conical shaped gearwheel, designed to mesh with a similar gear with an axis usually at 90 deg. to its own.
bhp	Brake horse power, measured on a dynamometer.
bmep	Brake mean effective pressure. Average pressure on a piston during the working stroke.
Brake cylinder	Cylinder with hydraulically operated piston(s) acting on brake shoes or pad(s).
Brake regulator	Control valve fitted in hydraulic braking system which limits brake pressure to rear brakes during heavy braking to prevent rear wheel locking.
Camber	Angle at which a wheel is tilted from the vertical.
Capacitor	Modern term for an electrical condenser. Part of distributor assembly, connected across contact breaker points, acts as an interference suppressor.
Castellated	Top face of a nut, slotted across the flats, to take a locking splitpin.
Castor	Angle at which the kingpin or swivel pin is tilted when viewed from the side.
cc	Cubic centimetres. Engine capacity is arrived at by multiplying the area of the bore in sq cm by the stroke in cm by the number of cylinders.
Clevis	U-shaped forked connector used with a clevis pin, usually at handbrake connections.
Collet	A type of collar, usually split and located in a groove in a shaft, and held in place by a retainer. The arrangement used to retain the spring(s) on a valve stem in most cases.
Commutator	Rotating segmented current distributor between armature windings and brushes in generator or motor.
Compression	The ratio, or quantitative relation, of the total volume (piston at bottom of stroke) to the unswept volume (piston at top of stroke) in an engine cylinder.
Condenser	See capacitor.
Core plug	Plug for blanking off a manufacturing hole in a casting.
Crownwheel	Large bevel gear in rear axle, driven by a bevel pinion attached to the propeller shaft. Sometimes called a 'ring gear'.
'C'-spanner	Like a 'C' with a handle. For use on screwed collars without flats, but with slots or holes.
Damper	Modern term for shock-absorber, used in vehicle suspension systems to damp out spring oscillations.
Depression	The lowering of atmospheric pressure as in the inlet manifold and carburetter.
Dowel	Close tolerance pin, peg, tube, or bolt, which accurately locates mating parts.
Drag link	Rod connecting steering box drop arm (pitman arm) to nearest front wheel steering arm in certain types of steering systems.
Dry liner	Thinwall tube pressed into cylinder bore
Dry sump	Lubrication system where all oil is scavenged from the sump, and returned to a separate tank.
Dynamo	See Generator.
Electrode	Terminal, part of an electrical component, such as the points or 'Electrodes' of a sparking plug.
Electrolyte	In lead-acid car batteries a solution of sulphuric acid and distilled water.
End float	The axial movement between associated parts, end play.
EP	Extreme pressure. In lubricants, special grades for heavily loaded bearing surfaces, such as gear teeth in a gearbox, or crownwheel and pinion in a rear axle.

Fade	Of brakes. Reduced efficiency due to overheating.
Field coils	Windings on the polepieces of motors and generators.
Fillets	Narrow finishing strips usually applied to interior bodywork.
First motion shaft	Input shaft from clutch to gearbox.
Fullflow filter	Filters in which all the oil is pumped to the engine. If the element becomes clogged, a bypass valve operates to pass unfiltered oil to the engine.
FWD	Front wheel drive.
Gear pump	Two meshing gears in a close fitting casing. Oil is carried from the inlet round the outside of both gears in the spaces between the gear teeth and casing to the outlet, the meshing gear teeth prevent oil passing back to the inlet, and the oil is forced through the outlet port.
Generator	Modern term for 'Dynamo' When rotated produces electrical current.
Grommet	A ring of protective or sealing material. Can be used to protect pipes or leads passing through bulkheads.
Grubscrew	Fully threaded headless screw with screwdriver slot. Used for locking, or alignment purposes.
Gudgeon pin	Shaft which connects a piston to its connecting rod. Sometimes called 'wrist pin', or 'piston pin'.
Halfshaft	One of a pair transmitting drive from the differential.
Helical	In spiral form. The teeth of helical gears are cut at a spiral angle to the side faces of the gearwheel.
Hot spot	Hot area that assists vapourisation of fuel on its way to cylinders. Often provided by close contact between inlet and exhaust manifolds.
HT	High Tension. Applied to electrical current produced by the ignition coil for the sparking plugs.
Hydrometer	A device for checking specific gravity of liquids. Used to check specific gravity of electrolyte.
Hypoid bevel gears	A form of bevel gear used in the rear axle drive gears. The bevel pinion meshes below the centre line of the crownwheel, giving a lower propeller shaft line.
Idler	A device for passing on movement. A free running gear between driving and driven gears. A lever transmitting track rod movement to a side rod in steering gear.
Impeller	A centrifugal pumping element. Used in water pumps to stimulate flow.
Journals	Those parts of a shaft that are in contact with the bearings.
Kingpin	The main vertical pin which carries the front wheel spindle, and permits steering movement. May be called 'steering pin' or 'swivel pin'.
Layshaft	The shaft which carries the laygear in the gearbox. The laygear is driven by the first motion shaft and drives the third motion shaft according to the gear selected. Sometimes called the 'countershaft' or 'second motion shaft.'
lb ft	A measure of twist or torque. A pull of 10 lb at a radius of 1 ft is a torque of 10 lb ft.
lb/sq in	Pounds per square inch.
Little-end	The small, or piston end of a connecting rod. Sometimes called the 'small-end'.
LT	Low Tension. The current output from the battery.
Mandrel	Accurately manufactured bar or rod used for test or centring purposes.
Manifold	A pipe, duct, or chamber, with several branches.
Needle rollers	Bearing rollers with a length many times their diameter.
Oil bath	Reservoir which lubricates parts by immersion. In air filters, a separate oil supply for wetting a wire mesh element to hold the dust.
Oil wetted	In air filters, a wire mesh element lightly oiled to trap and hold airborne dust.
Overlap	Period during which inlet and exhaust valves are open together.
Panhard rod	Bar connected between fixed point on chassis and another on axle to control sideways movement.
Pawl	Pivoted catch which engages in the teeth of a ratchet to permit movement in one direction only.
Peg spanner	Tool with pegs, or pins, to engage in holes or slots in the part to be turned.
Pendant pedals	Pedals with levers that are pivoted at the top end.
Phillips screwdriver	A cross-point screwdriver for use with the cross-slotted heads of Phillips screws.
Pinion	A small gear, usually in relation to another gear.
Piston-type damper	Shock absorber in which damping is controlled by a piston working in a closed oil-filled cylinder.
Preloading	Preset static pressure on ball or roller bearings not due to working loads.
Radial	Radiating from a centre, like the spokes of a wheel.

Radius rod Pivoted arm confining movement of a part to an arc of fixed radius.

Ratchet Toothed wheel or rack which can move in one direction only, movement in the other being prevented by a pawl.

Ring gear A gear tooth ring attached to outer periphery of flywheel. Starter pinion engages with it during starting.

Runout Amount by which rotating part is out of true.

Semi-floating axle Outer end of rear axle halfshaft is carried on bearing inside axle casing. Wheel hub is secured to end of shaft.

Servo A hydraulic or pneumatic system for assisting, or, augmenting a physical effort. See 'Vacuum Servo'.

Setscrew One which is threaded for the full length of the shank.

Shackle A coupling link, used in the form of two parallel pins connected by side plates to secure the end of the master suspension spring and absorb the effects of deflection.

Shell bearing Thinwalled steel shell lined with antifriction metal. Usually semi-circular and used in pairs for main and big-end bearings.

Shock absorber See 'Damper'.

Silentbloc Rubber bush bonded to inner and outer metal sleeves.

Socket-head screw Screw with hexagonal socket for an Allen key.

Solenoid A coil of wire creating a magnetic field when electric current passes through it. Used with a soft iron core to operate contacts or a mechanical device.

Spur gear A gear with teeth cut axially across the periphery.

Stub axle Short axle fixed at one end only.

Tachometer An instrument for accurate measurement of rotating speed. Usually indicates in revolutions per minute.

TDC Top Dead Centre. The highest point reached by a piston in a cylinder, with the crank and connecting rod in line.

Thermostat Automatic device for regulating temperature. Used in vehicle coolant systems to open a valve which restricts circulation at low temperature.

Third motion shaft Output shaft of gearbox.

Threequarter floating axle Outer end of rear axle halfshaft flanged and bolted to wheel hub, which runs on bearing mounted on outside of axle casing. Vehicle weight is not carried by the axle shaft.

Thrust bearing or washer Used to reduce friction in rotating parts subject to axial loads.

Torque Turning or twisting effort. See 'lb ft'.

Track rod The bar(s) across the vehicle which connect the steering arms and maintain the front wheels in their correct alignment.

UJ Universal joint. A coupling between shafts which permits angular movement.

UNF Unified National Fine screw thread.

Vacuum servo Device used in brake system, using difference between atmospheric pressure and inlet manifold depression to operate a piston which acts to augment brake pressure as required. See 'Servo'.

Venturi A restriction or 'choke' in a tube, as in a carburetter, used to increase velocity to obtain a reduction in pressure.

Vernier A sliding scale for obtaining fractional readings of the graduations of an adjacent scale.

Welch plug A domed thin metal disc which is partially flattened to lock in a recess. Used to plug core holes in castings.

Wet liner Removable cylinder barrel, sealed against coolant leakage, where the coolant is in direct contact with the outer surface.

Wet sump A reservoir attached to the crankcase to hold the lubricating oil.

NOTES

INDEX

NOTES

Alfa Romeo Giulia 1600, 1750 1962 on
Aston Martin 1921-58
Auto Union Audi 70, 80, Super 90, 1966 on
Audi 100 1969 on
Austin, Morris etc. 1100 Mk. 1 1962-67
Austin, Morris etc. 1100 Mk. 2, 3, 1300 Mk. 1, 2, 3 America 1968 on
Austin A30, A35, A40 Farina
Austin A55 Mk. 2, A60 1958-69
Austin A99, A110 1959-68
Austin J4 1960 on
Austin Maxi 1969 on
Austin, Morris 1800 1964 on
Austin, Morris 2200 1972 on
Austin, Morris 1300, 1500 Nomad 1969 on

BMC 3 (Austin A50, A55 Mk. 1, Morris Oxford 2, 3 1954-59)
Austin Healey 100/6, 3000 1956-68
Austin Healey, MG Sprite, Midget 1958 on
Bedford Beagle HA Vans 1964 on
BMW 1600 1966 on
BMW 1800 1964 on
BMW 2000, 2002 1966 on
Chevrolet Corvair 1960-69
Chevrolet Corvette V8 1957-65
Chevrolet Corvette V8 1965 on
Chevrolette Vega 2300 1970 on
Chrysler Valiant V8 1965 on
Chrysler Valiant Straight Six 1966-70
Citroen DS 19, ID 19 1955-66
Citroen ID 19, DS 19, 20, 21 1966 on
Daf 31, 32, 33, 44, 55 1961 on
Datsun 1200 1970 on
Datsun 1300, 1400, 1600 1968 on
Datsun 240C 1971 on
Datsun 240Z Sport 1970 on
De Dion Bouton 1899-1907
Fiat 124 1966 on
Fiat 124 Sport 1966 on
Fiat 125 1967 on
Fiat 128 1969 on
Fiat 500 1957 on
Fiat 600, 600D 1955-69
Fiat 850 1964 on
Fiat 1100 1957-69
Fiat 1300, 1500 1961-67

Ford Anglia Prefect 100E 1953-62
Ford Anglia 105E, Prefect 107E 1959-67
Ford Capri 1300, 1600 OHV 1968 on
Ford Capri 1300, 1600, 2000 OHC 1972 on
Ford Capri 2000, 3000 1969 on
Ford Classic, Capri 1961-64
Ford Consul, Zephyr, Zodiac, 1, 2 1950-62
Ford Corsair Straight Four 1963-65
Ford Corsair V4 1965-68
Ford Corsair V4 2000 1969-70
Ford Cortina 1962-66
Ford Cortina 1967-68
Ford Cortina 1969-70
Ford Cortina Mk. 3 1970 on
Ford Escort 1967 on
Ford Falcon 6 1964-70
Ford Falcon XK, XL 1960-63
Ford Falcon 6 XR/XA 1966 on
Ford Falcon V8 (U.S.A.) 1965-71
Ford Falcon V8 (Aust.) 1966 on
Ford Pinto 1970 on
Ford Maverick 1969 on
Ford Mustang V8 1965-71
Ford Thames 10, 12, 15 cwt 1957-65
Ford Transit 1965 on
Ford Zephyr Zodiac Mk. 3 1962-66
Ford Zephyr Zodiac V4, V6, Mk. 4 1966-72
Ford Consul, Granada 1972
Hillman Avenger 1970 on
Hillman Hunter 1966 on
Hillman Imp 1963-68
Hillman Imp 1969 on
Hillman Minx 1 to 5 1956-65
Hillman Minx 1965-67
Hillman Minx 1966-70
Hillman Super Minx 1961-65
Holden V8 1968 on
Holden Straight Six 1948-66
Holden Straight Six 1966 on
Holden Torana 4 Series HB 1967-69
Jaguar XK120, 140, 150, Mk. 7, 8, 9 1948-61
Jaguar 2.4, 3.4, 3.8 Mk. 1, 2 1955-69
Jaguar 'E' Type 1961 on
Jaguar 'S' Type 420 1963-68

Jaguar XJ6 1968 on
Jowett Javelin Jupiter 1947-53
Landrover 1, 2 1948-61
Landrover 2, 2a, 3 1959 on
Mazda 616 1970 on
Mazda 1200, 1300 1969 on
Mazda 1500, 1800 1967 on
Mercedes-Benz 190b, 190c, 200 1959-68
Mercedes-Benz 220 1959-65
Mercedes-Benz 220/8 1968 on
Mercedes-Benz 230 1963-68
Mercedes-Benz 250 1965-67
Mercedes-Benz 250 1968 on
Mercedes-Benz 280 1968 on
MG TA to TF 1936-55
MGA MGB 1955-68
MGB 1969 on
Mini 1959 on
Mini Cooper 1961 on
Morgan 1936-69
Morris Marina 1971 on
Morris (Aust) Marina 1972 on
Morris Minor 2, 1000 1952-71
Morris Oxford 5, 6 1959-71
NSU 1000 1963 on
NSU Prinz 1 to 4 1957 on
Opel Ascona, Manta 1970 on
Opel GT 1900 1968 on
Opel Kadett, Olympia 993cc 1078cc 1962 on
Opel Kadett, Olympia 1492, 1698, 1897cc 1967 on
Opel Rekord C 1966 on
Peugeot 204 1965 on
Peugeot 304 1970 on
Peugeot 404 1960 on
Peugeot 504 1968-70
Porsche 356A, B, C 1957-65
Porsche 911 1964-69
Porsche 912 1965-69
Porsche 914 S 1969 on
Reliant Regal 1952 on
Renault R4, R4L, 4 1961 on
Renault 6 1968 on
Renault 8, 10, 1100 1962 on
Renault 12, 1969 on
Renault R16 1965 on
Renault Dauphine Floride 1957-67
Renault Caravelle 1962-68
Rover 60 to 110 1953-64
Rover 2000 1963 on
Rover 3 Litre 1958-67
Rover 3500, 3500S 1968 on
Saab 95, 96, Sport 1960-68
Saab 99 1969 on
Saab V4 1966 on

Simca 1000 1961 on
Simca 1100 1967 on
Simca 1300, 1301, 1500, 1501 1963 on
Skoda One (440, 445, 450) 1955-70
Sunbeam Rapier Alpine 1955-65
Toyota Corolla 1100 1967 on
Toyota Corona 1500 Mk. 1 1965-70
Toyota Corona 1900 Mk. 2 1969 on
Triumph TR2, TR3, TR3A 1952-62
Triumph TR4, TR4A 1961-67
Triumph TR5, TR250, TR6 1967 on
Triumph 1300, 1500 1965 on
Triumph 2000 Mk. 1, 2.5 PI Mk. 1 1963-69
Triumph 2000 Mk. 2, 2.5 PI Mk. 2 1969 on
Triumph Dolomite 1972 on
Triumph Herald 1959-68
Triumph Herald 1969-71
Triumph Spitfire, Vitesse 1962-68
Triumph Spitfire Mk. 3, 4 1969 on
Triumph GT6, Vitesse 2 Litre 1969 on
Triumph Toledo 1970 on
Vauxhall Velox, Cresta 1957-72
Vauxhall Victor 1, 2, FB 1957-64
Vauxhall Victor 101 1964-67
Vauxhall Victor FD 1600, 2000 1967 on
Vauxhall Victor 3300, Ventora 1968 on
Vauxhall Victor FE Ventora 1972 on
Vauxhall Viva HA 1963-66
Vauxhall Viva HB 1966-70
Vauxhall Viva, HC Firenza 1971 on
Volkswagen Beetle 1954-67
Volkswagen Beetle 1968 on
Volkswagen 1500 1961-66
Volkswagen 1600 Fastback 1965 on
Volkswagen Transporter 1954-67
Volkswagen Transporter 1968 on
Volkswagen 411 1968 on
Volvo 120 1961-70
Volvo 140 1966 on
Volvo 160 series 1968 on
Volvo 1800 1960 on

NOTES